Molina scores big in this stimulating, thorough, and rigorous text on housing in America. Molina is careful to not simplify the consequences of institutional discrimination through time and across space, but instead highlights the aggregation of systemic inequalities ranging from raced housing policies and debates around home ownership to cases of institutional violence aimed at the poor and homeless. Further, in giving attention to the significance of place and policies at the intersection of race, class, and gender, the author provides a micro-level analysis of the consequences of housing trends, urban sprawl, gentrification projects in the city, and the continual suburbanization of the American landscape. The author's inclusion of case studies will prove to be a valuable tool for students and scholars of urban sociology, social problems, and inequalities in America.

– Gwendolyn Purifoye, *Assistant Professor of Sociology,*
Kent State University at Stark

Housing America offers a valuable social analysis of the role of housing in the United States as both human shelter and investment commodity. A thorough, multidimensional approach to the topic considers housing affordability, our history of housing discrimination, homelessness, homeownership, and residential planning and development. An array of case studies and illustrative graphics augment the accessible, engaging writing. Important teaching resources in each chapter—such as discussion questions, vocabulary terms, and role-playing exercises—make this an essential text for urban studies, urban planning, and housing policy courses.

– Deborah L. Myerson, *AICP, Instructor at Indiana University, Urban Planning*
Consultant, and author of How Did They Do It? Discovering New Opportunities
for Affordable Housing

Molina provides a timely and very important policy analysis of the housing crisis. Her work is an impressive underpinning to Desmond's acclaimed study of residential evictions.

– Lloyd Klein, *Adjunct Associate Professor at City University of New York,*
Hostos Community College

With a deep appreciation and understanding of the political economy of housing, competing theories and debates, the role of race, and the challenges of producing affordable housing, Professor Molina offers a thoughtful, clear, and concise presentation of the key housing issues facing the U.S. Compelling vignettes, case studies, questions for discussion, and stimulating exercises will help educate a new generation of housing advocates, policy makers, and concerned citizens.

– Rachel G. Bratt, *Professor Emerita, Department of Urban and Environmental*
Policy and Planning, Tufts University and Senior Research Fellow, Joint Center
for Housing Studies, Harvard University

Housing America

In an effort to explain why housing remains among the United States' most enduring social problems, *Housing America* explores five of the U.S.'s most fundamental, recurrent issues in housing its population: affordability of housing, homelessness, segregation and discrimination in the housing market, homeownership and home financing, and planning. It describes these issues in detail, why they should be considered problems, the history and fundamental social debates surrounding them, and the past, current, and possible policy solutions to address them. While this book focuses on the major problems we face as a society in housing our population, it is also about the choices we make about what is valued in our society in our attempts to solve them. *Housing America* is appropriate for courses in urban studies, urban planning, and housing policy.

Emily Tumpson Molina is Assistant Professor of Sociology at Brooklyn College, City University of New York, where she teaches courses in urban sociology, quantitative methods, and social problems. Her research interests include housing, urban studies, race and racism, quantitative and geographic methods, and social policy. Her recent work on the foreclosure crisis has appeared in the *Journal of Urban Affairs, City & Community*, and *Housing Policy Debate*.

The Metropolis and Modern Life
A Routledge Series
Edited by Anthony Orum
Loyola University Chicago
and
Zachary P. Neal
Michigan State University

The Metropolis and Modern Life
A Routledge Series
Edited by Anthony Orum
Loyola University Chicago
and
Zachary P. Neal
Michigan State University

This series brings original perspectives on key topics in urban research to today's students in a series of short accessible texts, guided readers, and practical handbooks. Each volume examines how long-standing urban phenomena continue to be relevant in an increasingly urban and global world, and in doing so, connects the best new scholarship with the wider concerns of students seeking to understand life in the twenty-first-century metropolis.

Books in the Series:

Common Ground?
Reading and Reflections on Public Space
Edited by Anthony Orum and Zachary P. Neal

The Gentrification Debates
Edited by Japonica Brown-Saracino

The Power of Urban Ethnic Places
Cultural Heritage and Community Life
Jan Lin

Forthcoming:

Comparative Urban Studies
Hilary Silver

Housing America
Issues and Debates
Emily Tumpson Molina

Urban Tourism and Urban Change
Cities in a Global Economy
Costas Spirou

The Connected City
Zachary Neal

The World's Cities
Edited by A.J. Jacobs

Ethnography and the City
Edited by Richard Ocejo

Housing America
Issues and Debates

Emily Tumpson Molina

Routledge
Taylor & Francis Group

NEW YORK AND LONDON

First published 2017
by Routledge
711 Third Avenue, New York, NY 10017

and by Routledge
2 Park Square, Milton Park, Abingdon, Oxon, OX14 4RN

Routledge is an imprint of the Taylor & Francis Group, an informa business

Library of Congress Cataloging in Publication Data
Names: Molina, Emily Tumpson, author.
Title: Housing America : issues and debates / Emily Tumpson Molina.
Description: 1 Edition. | New York, NY : Routledge, 2017.
Identifiers: LCCN 2016040346 | ISBN 9781138820883 (hardcover : alk. paper) |
ISBN 9781138820890 (pbk. : alk. paper) | ISBN 9781315743646 (ebook)
Subjects: LCSH: Housing–United States.
Classification: LCC HD7293 .M635 2017 | DDC 333.33/80973–dc23
LC record available at https://lccn.loc.gov/2016040346

ISBN: 978-1-138-82088-3 (hbk)
ISBN: 978-1-138-82089-0 (pbk)
ISBN: 978-1-315-74364-6 (ebk)

Typeset in Minion
by Wearset Ltd, Boldon, Tyne and Wear

Contents

Figures

Tables

Acknowledgments

This book would not have been completed without the help and encouragement of many people. Thank you, first, to my mentors in the Sociology PhD Program at the University of California, Santa Barbara. Maria Charles, Nikki Jones, George Lipsitz, and Melvin Oliver nurtured my passion for investigating an array of housing issues while imparting the necessary skills to do so.

Many thanks also to all of my terrific colleagues in the Department of Sociology at Brooklyn College, CUNY, especially Tammy Lewis, Ken Gould, Carolina Bank Muñoz, and Naomi Braine, for valuing this project and encouraging me to pursue it. Special thanks to Tammy Lewis and Ken Gould for their valuable insights on Chapters 3 and 6, and to Ken Gould for providing all the photos for the book.

Thanks to CUNY's Faculty Fellowship Publication Program, which provided me with course release to work on this project and access to the wonderful mentorship of Steve Steinberg and valuable feedback from Lawrence Johnson, Kafui Attoh, Melissa Borja, Seth Offenbach, and Susanna Rosenbaum.

Thank you to Steve Rutter for initially encouraging me to write this book, and to Margaret Moore and Samantha Barbaro at Routledge for seeing it through. I am so grateful for the thoughtful feedback from the series editors, Anthony Orum and Zachary Neal, and anonymous reviewers. Their comments greatly improved the book.

My biggest thanks go to my family. My mother, Carla Tumpson, has never wavered in her support of my work, encouraging me to pursue my goals no matter how unfamiliar they were to her. My deepest gratitude goes to Devin Molina for being my chief source of support and best critic. This book is for him and our daughter, Talia.

CHAPTER 1

Introduction

In March of 1937, Gertrude Doyle and her son Walter staged a sit-down strike in their home of twenty-three years in coastal Ocean City, NJ to protest foreclosure proceedings against them. They were evicted on March 19 when their lender repossessed the property with no opportunity to renegotiate the terms of their loan. The Doyles were among the approximately quarter of American households in foreclosure in 1937 as the country debated how to alleviate the economic suffering of its residents while propping up the devastated housing market. Nearly seventy-five years later, nine people were arrested after protesting the foreclosure of the Gudiel family home in La Puente, CA. The Gudiels faced eviction in 2011 after their lender took ownership of their property without renegotiating their loan. The Gudiels were among more than 4 million Americans who lost their homes to foreclosure each year during the Great Recession, as the country again debated how to alleviate the economic suffering of its residents while propping up the housing market.

In the spring of 1971, New York City officials lamented the city's housing crisis as the homeless population soared, and the relatively new strategy of providing public aid to private developers to build enough housing for the city's residents resulted in construction of only 20 to 45 percent of the units the city required. More than forty years later, in 2014, newly minted mayor Bill de Blasio's administration unveiled a ten-year plan to build or preserve 200,000 units of affordable housing after years of public subsidies to real estate developers yielded a fraction of the housing needed for middle and low-income New Yorkers, and the homeless population mounted.

Remove the dates and it is hard to distinguish between the struggles of the Doyles in 1937 and the Gudiels in 2011, or between New York City administrators in 1971 and in 2014. Why do Americans continue to struggle with the same housing problems decade after decade?

This book explores five of the U.S.'s most fundamental recurrent issues in housing its population in an effort to explain why housing remains among the United States' most enduring social problems. It describes five major housing problems the U.S. currently faces: unaffordable housing; homelessness; segregation and discrimination in the housing market; homeownership and home financing; and housing planning, land use, and the environment. It describes these issues in detail, why they should be considered problems, the history and fundamental social debates surrounding them, and the past, current, and possible policy solutions to address them. While this book focuses on the major problems we face as a society in housing our population, it is also about the choices we make about what is valued in our society in our attempts to solve them.

The Housing Problem

Despite its relative affluence, the world's largest economy and third most populated country faces fundamental problems in housing its residents. In 2013, more than a third of Americans paid more than 30 percent of their income on housing, as real incomes have not kept up with housing prices in recent decades (U.S. Census Bureau 2015). In 2015, more than a half a million people were homeless in America on any given night (U.S. Department of Housing and Urban Development 2014). The number of Americans living in segregated high-poverty neighborhoods is the highest ever recorded, and the average white American continues to live in a neighborhood that is 75 percent white (Jargowsky 2015; Logan and Stults 2011). A staggering one in forty-five American households received a foreclosure filing at the height of the recent housing crisis (RealtyTrac 2010). And low-density housing sprawl on large lots of land continues to dominate trends in housing development despite the environmental costs and increased risks of natural disasters.

Are these problems a reflection of Americans' preferences, an outgrowth of our capitalist system, a reflection of other social inequalities, a result of politics and policy, or some combination? This book considers the problems of affordability, homelessness, segregation, homeownership, and housing planning within the context of larger social debates that surround them from a critical perspective at the intersection of sociology, urban studies, geography, urban planning, and public policy. The chapters in this text will introduce you to the extent and history of each problem, the fundamental sociopolitical debates surrounding them, and the past, current, and future policy proposals designed to solve them. It will ask you to delve deeply into each problem, to grapple with the intricacies, to understand the stakes, and to develop well-informed solutions.

The Significance of Housing

Housing is not simply shelter; it structures our social lives. Americans have long recognized that where we live determines much about the shape and quality of our lives: our health; how our time is spent; whom we know; and how we survive. Housing quality and location contribute fundamentally to our health—the toxins we are exposed to through our buildings' materials, for example, our proximity to environmental hazards, or the time we spend commuting. Where we live determines the quality of our education, which in turn affects our employment prospects. It shapes our personal social networks, which largely shape our social lives and economic opportunities. Where we live also affects the degree to which we are exposed to, at the negative end of the spectrum, life stressors like crime, and on the positive, the institutions necessary for living full, healthy lives, such as hospitals, schools, libraries, and parks.

Housing and Other Social Problems

As a result, the housing problems discussed in this book have repercussions that extend far beyond housing. Decent housing is linked to better health and personal safety, employment opportunities, educational quality, and emotional and physical security. Solving the problems of affordability, homelessness, discrimination, home financing, and land use planning would go a long way toward solving related social problems. Significant changes in housing policy could dramatically affect the provision of education and medical care and access to employment in the U.S., and the extent to which Americans are able to live healthy, productive lives.

In debates over the U.S. educational system and policy, for example, housing is often a central concern. After all, where we live in large part determines where we go to school, and segregated neighborhoods beget segregated schools. Any serious inquiry into how to advance educational equity considers how to integrate neighborhoods. Similarly, debates over the impact of environmental hazards like industrial pollution often touch on housing, as segregated neighborhoods contribute in large part to the disproportionate exposure of poor people and people of color to environmental toxins. Thus, while this book focuses specifically on housing problems, the debates and policies presented extend to a vast array of other social problems.

Housing and Social Inequality

The housing market both reflects and constructs social inequalities in the U.S. Racial, class, and gender inequality are deeply embedded in all of the problems discussed in this book. Housing affordability, for example, has a stronger negative impact on African Americans and Latinos in the U.S., as well as single women. Men are more likely to be homeless than women, and people of color are more likely to be homeless than whites in American society. Segregation and discrimination in the housing market provide the foundation for other forms of social inequality—like educational inequality, for example—and can undermine the benefits of homeownership for poor people and people of color. This book aims to encourage us to think carefully not just about how and why housing problems endure, but about how we might alleviate them—particularly because housing is central to social inequality in the United States.

The Big Debates

Housing problems are a reflection of American society's most fundamental political, economic, and social problems. Housing availability, affordability, policy, financing, and planning are persistently difficult problems to address from generation to generation because they are so deeply embedded within the nation's most fundamental struggles over the rights of residents, the functioning of the capitalist system, and the role of government. Many of the debates discussed in this book are specific to particular issues. For example, what is primarily to blame for housing affordability, or what causes residential segregation? But others are echoed again and again from problem to problem, particularly as we address possible solutions in earnest.

Two primary debates recur throughout each chapter of this book: (1) how do we balance the social and economic goals of housing in a capitalist system?; and (2) what is the government's role in the housing market? These fundamental questions have been echoed in debates over housing problems for decades, as well as in the policies we design to solve them.

Housing as Shelter, Housing as Commodity

As noted in the previous section, the social benefits of adequate, affordable housing are immeasurable. Quality housing underpins quality of life and access to resources. Americans have long recognized that the right to a decent home is central to the "American way of life" and to the nation's prosperity. But housing is not a guaranteed right, and nearly every attempt to provide adequate housing to all Americans has been hopelessly limited or undercut.

In the U.S., housing is a commodity rather than a guaranteed right. Housing is bought and sold in the marketplace, and we rely on the private sector to provide housing for our population. The private housing market—made up of construction, real estate, and other industries—is an economic powerhouse in our society, providing a range of jobs, pumping billions of dollars into the American economy, and carrying significant political weight. Furthermore, the vast majority of Americans' household wealth comes from homeownership. Because housing is commodified in the U.S., housing policies perform economic functions. In fact, the social and economic goals of housing are often in fundamental conflict. There is great—possibly irreconcilable—tension between the fundamental human need for shelter and the social goods associated with housing and protecting the housing industry and property values—Americans' most significant form of wealth. This tension is reflected in debates over housing affordability, segregation, housing finance, and the relationship between housing and the environment.

First, the problem of affordable housing is a locus of this tension. There has never been enough low-rent housing to meet demand in the U.S. The private housing market cannot produce enough housing for the poor because it is essentially unprofitable (Garboden and Newman 2012; Schwartz 2015). This is why New York City, for example, has struggled with an affordable housing crisis for more than forty years.

Almost no one disagrees that safe, adequate, and affordable housing could go a long way toward alleviating the attendant problems of poverty. But the fundamental commodification of housing—that it must generate a profit, or accrue wealth—undermines its public provision. Early arguments over public housing characterized it as "creeping socialism," expressing fears that public housing would compete with private housing developers. Public housing survived only because it was linked to slum clearance of central cities in a scheme meant to increase the land value of urban America. Profitability is central to affordable housing plans. Our primary low-income housing policies, for example, are tax breaks to developers of low-income housing and rent subsidies to those who manage it in the private market—policies designed to prop up the housing industry. Similarly, we encourage home-ownership because it stimulates the construction and real estate industries.

Debates over housing segregation also contend with the tension between the social and economic functions of housing. While racial segregation has abated somewhat in the past thirty years, it remains strong, and economic segregation has risen. The percentage of poor families living in high-poverty neighborhoods doubled nationwide between 1970 and 2009 (Bischoff and Reardon 2013). The concentration of the poor into particular neighborhoods concentrates related social problems, such as crime, and limits access to social mobility. Poverty deconcentration, a central U.S. housing policy discussed in Chapter 3, is designed to help the poor live in more working-class and middle-class communities. But resistance to racial and economic integration is led primarily by property owners who are afraid low-income housing will lower their property values, even as that assumption is challenged by evidence (Massey *et al.* 2013).

Perhaps most clearly, the balance between the social and economic goals of housing is reflected in debates about the relationship between housing and the environment. The protection of property values has complicated and in some cases thwarted environmental and disaster policy. Housing sprawl, for example—the development of new housing on the far outskirts of American cities and in rural areas—is associated with a host of negative environmental impacts, including pollution from traffic and increased exposure to natural disasters such as wildfires and hurricanes. But policymakers often decide to encourage housing growth rather than limit it, precisely for the economic benefits, even if the cost of sprawl—in both dollar terms and in human suffering—is exorbitant in the long run.

Thus, the tensions between the economic and social aims of housing in a capitalist system color nearly every debate over housing discussed in this text. This tension is not unrelated to the second major recurring theme: the role of government in the housing market.

Government and the Housing Market

A second major debate that recurs throughout this book considers the government's role in the housing market. While we continue to debate the shape of housing policy, two major trends have characterized government intervention in the housing market in the past four decades: the neoliberal turn—the political shift toward funding market-based solutions to social problems; and the devolution of housing policy—the reliance on local governments to set and enforce housing policy.

The Neoliberal Turn

The contemporary shift to neoliberalism underlies nearly all of our current policy approaches to the housing problems discussed in this book. Neoliberalism is a system of thought and a set of policies that considers the primary function of government to be supporting and enhancing the capitalist marketplace. Neoliberal policies and approaches include those that support government deregulation of business and industry, free trade, fiscal austerity, and the like. The neoliberal turn in the U.S. substantially shifted social service provision from the public to the private sector, as its proponents considered social goods to be best provided by the capitalist marketplace.

The neoliberal turn shifted our approach toward all of the housing problems discussed in this book, but especially toward affordable housing and homeownership. The federal government directly built and managed low-income housing in the postwar period because it was so unprofitable that the private market could not meet demand. But beginning in the 1960s, the federal government shifted away from the direct provision of low-income housing in the form of public housing to subsidizing the private housing market, so that meeting the demand for affordable housing became profitable. Ultimately, we put great faith in the private sector and in the underlying efficiency of the housing market to provide this essential human need and social good to our most vulnerable households. As we will see, this strategy has not necessarily functioned as expected, as the woes of New York City's leaders in 1971 and again in 2014 illustrate.

The neoliberal turn also fundamentally changed the market for homebuyers and how we finance homeownership. The vast majority of ordinary Americans are able to purchase homes only by taking on debt in the form of mortgages. In contrast to past eras, in which local banks issued mortgages and serviced payments for the life of loans, today's banks, private mortgage companies, and other private entities lend to homebuyers and then package these loans together and sell them to global investors as financial products called mortgage-backed securities, not unlike stocks and bonds. This process, called securitization, was made possible by large-scale deregulation of the financial industry in the 1980s—a critical component of the neoliberal turn. Today, when one makes a mortgage payment, one is essentially paying a return to an investor, fully integrating American homeownership into global financial markets.

This new system of mortgage lending has injected the demands of investors into the system of housing finance, complicating the functioning of local housing markets. The recent foreclosure crisis, for example, resulted largely from the demand for mortgage-backed securities—the pools of mortgages that investors can invest in. Because the demand for these investments was so high, mortgage lenders had the perverse incentive to issue increasing numbers of mortgages with harmful terms for homebuyers. Because they simply packaged and sold the loans, there was no incentive to ensure that people could afford their mortgages. Housing prices rose dramatically all over the country as an unprecedented number of American households purchased homes with free-flowing debt. In the meantime, lenders and brokers operated with virtually no oversight, as fraudulent practices—including lying about borrowers' incomes—were incentivized because the sale of mortgages was so lucrative (Immergluck 2009).

The neoliberal turn that spurred the financial industry and integrated the American housing market into the global economy resulted in the highest foreclosure rate in the U.S. since the Great Depression. Millions of Americans lost their homes and bore incredible personal costs. Consider, for example, the Gudiel family introduced at the beginning of this chapter. Rose

Gudiel purchased her $408,000 home using a lender that aggressively marketed loans to working families, some of which didn't even require a down payment. Four years before she purchased the home, it was worth $149,000. The demand from investors for mortgages like Gudiel's incentivized lenders to market them aggressively, despite the financial and personal harm they could do to buyers—particularly in a climate like the U.S. that has very little consumer protection.

Such disasters force us to contend with the downsides of the market-based provision of social goods, a central component of the neoliberal turn in housing policy. Is the market efficiently providing social goods when there is financial incentive to sell homes to people who cannot afford them? Is the market efficiently providing social goods if homes are not affordable to average Americans? Thus, understanding and attempting to solve the housing problems discussed in this book require a deep consideration of neoliberalism, and whether fundamental social goods like housing should be left to the capitalist marketplace.

Devolution of Housing Policy

In addition to neoliberalism, a second trend characterizes government action on housing problems: the devolution of housing policy. Housing policy and programs, like many other social policies and programs, has devolved to the state and local levels of government since the 1970s, as public support for centralized government waned. States and localities are largely responsible for designing and implementing affordability, homelessness, integration, and housing planning programs.

For example, since the 1970s, the federal government has taken the position that localities best understand and can therefore meet their constituents' housing needs. Rather than building and operating public housing, for example, it offers competitive block grants to states and localities that apply for aid for housing programs. Similarly, rather than regulating housing development for environmental reasons, the federal government offers states the option—but not requirement—to do so.

While the shift toward local control of housing planning is well intentioned, it can have serious negative consequences, as this book will show. Relying on localities to apply for and administer affordable housing programs, for example, can aggravate social inequalities within and between local communities. Middle-class and affluent communities can simply elect not to apply for or administer affordable housing programs in efforts to exclude poor households from their communities. Affordable rental housing is thus certain to be concentrated in the poorest communities with the greatest need and fewest resources. Similarly, the federal government's deference to local zoning laws means the federal government has virtually no oversight or influence over zoning laws that enable sprawl or segregation. People can continue to build new housing in hurricane zones, for example, and receive federal aid in the event of a disaster, but there are no federal regulations against building housing in areas prone to natural disaster.

The combination of the neoliberal shift with the devolution of housing policy puts localities in the difficult position of having to balance economic development in a competitive capitalist system with the provision of social goods. Many localities choose not to improve services for the homeless, for example, because they fear it will attract more homeless people, devaluing their community in a competitive market (Burt 2001). Thus, the tension between housing as a human need and as a commodity and the shape of government intervention in the housing market color the debates about every issue presented in this book. These two major themes are not unique to debates over housing in the U.S. They also color debates over health care, education, and other social goods in capitalist democracies.

Outline of the Book

The five issues that anchor this text—affordability, homelessness, segregation and discrimination, homeownership and financing, and planning and environment—intersect in important ways, and their separation is an organizational strategy rather than an accurate reflection of their distinctiveness. Each chapter begins with the current trends related to the issue at hand before moving to its history, the major social debates that frame it, and a critical presentation of the policies that have been and could be used to address it. A case study, terms, discussion questions, and an application conclude each chapter.

Chapter 2 introduces the problem of housing affordability. It describes how we define affordability, why it is considered a problem, and the extent of the problem. It examines the significance of housing affordability in American society, what accounts for the decreasing affordability of housing, including declining wages and rising housing prices, and past, contemporary, and possible policies that impact housing affordability for American households, such as homeowner aid and tax credits for developers of low-income housing. It also examines central challenges in facing the affordability problem. How should government intervene? How should it balance the need for affordable shelter with housing's status as a commodity?

Chapter 3 describes the problem of segregation and discrimination in the housing market. It describes historical and contemporary patterns of racial and economic segregation in housing in America. It considers the major inequalities between social groups in housing quality, availability, cost, and benefits, their significance, and how they have changed over time. It then summarizes how these inequalities have been explained, including race and class-based explanations, and how they might be ameliorated.

Chapter 4 moves to a discussion of homelessness, beginning with the problems we have in defining it and in counting the homeless population in the U.S. It then discusses why the homeless population has increased in certain areas and abated in others. The chapter then considers the causes of homelessness. Is it the product of individual or structural problems? Does the distinction matter? It then addresses whether we have an obligation to address homelessness, and if so, how we might go about doing so.

Chapter 5 introduces homeownership and the problem of housing finance in the U.S. The chapter focuses on why homeownership is so venerated in American society, how the government encourages and supports homeownership, and whether this approach is ultimately beneficial to society. It also describes fundamental changes in the American system of housing finance, and the pitfalls of those changes—including the recent foreclosure crisis.

Chapter 6 discusses how and where we build housing and how we balance the need for housing with its environmental impact. After decades of low-density housing sprawl, particularly in areas at high risk of natural disasters like hurricanes and wildfires, researchers and policymakers continue to debate the consequences of housing development and where to invest in future housing for the American population. What are the significant patterns in American housing development? What is their environmental impact? How do we balance societal needs for housing with environmental costs and concerns? This chapter details the debates and policy possibilities around sustainable housing development.

In all, this book encourages us to think carefully about how and why housing problems endure, and to think creatively about how we might alleviate them. Despite large and small-scale political and economic changes, we continue to struggle with how to meet our population's most basic needs. The housing market is a locus of many of the issues that dominate news headlines: the relatively stagnant U.S. economy; conflicting views of the roles of government and public policy; and the dramatic rise of income inequality in recent decades. Grappling with our most significant housing problems necessitates a reckoning of our fundamental values, and putting them into practice.

References

Bischoff, Kendra and Reardon, Sean F. 2013. "Residential Segregation by Income, 1970–2009." Providence, RI: US2010 Project Report. Retrieved September 5, 2015. www.s4.brown.edu/us2010/Data/Report/report10162013.pdf.

Burt, Martha R., Pearson, Carol L., and Montgomery, Ann Elizabeth. 2005. Strategies for Preventing Homelessness. Washington, DC: Urban Institute. Retrieved May 13, 2016. www.urban.org/research/publication/strategies-preventing-homelessness.

Garboden, Phillip M. E. and Newman, Sandra. 2012. "Is Preserving Small, Low-End Rental Housing Feasible?" Housing Policy Debate 22(4): 507–526.

Immergluck, Daniel. 2009. *Foreclosed: High-Risk Lending, Deregulation, and the Undermining of America's Mortgage Market.* Ithaca, NY: Cornell University Press.

Jargowsky, Paul. 2015. "Architecture of Segregation." New York, NY: The Century Foundation. http://apps.tcf.org/architecture-of-segregation.

Logan, John and Stults, Brian J. 2011. "The Persistence of Segregation in the Metropolis: New Findings from the 2010 Census." Providence, RI: US2010 Project Report. www.s4.brown.edu/us2010/Data/Report/report2.pdf.

Massey, Douglas S., Albright, Len, Casciano, Rebecca, Derickson, Elizabeth, and Kinsey, David N. 2013. *Climbing Mount Laurel: The Struggle for Affordable Housing and Social Mobility in an American Suburb.* Princeton, NJ: Princeton University Press.

RealtyTrac. 2010. "2009 Year End Forelosure Report." Retrieved December 30, 2015. www.realtytrac.com/landing/2009-year-end-foreclosure-report.html.

Schwartz, Alex F. 2015. *Housing Policy in the United States,* third edition. New York, NY: Routledge.

U.S. Census Bureau. 2015. American Housing Survey 2013 National Summary Tables. Retrieved July 15, 2015. www.census.gov/programs-surveys/ahs/data/2013/national-summary-report-and-tables--ahs-2013.html.

U.S. Department of Housing and Urban Development. 2014. "The 2014 Annual Homeless Assessment Report (AHAR) to Congress." Retrieved April 21, 2016. www.hudexchange.info/onecpd/assets/File/2014-AHAR-Part-2.pdf.

p 13-26
p 26 -end

CHAPTER 2

Housing Affordability

anti afforable housing w/ story roots

why so far afield?

overall stats

In August of 2016, residents of the town of Agawam in Western Massachusetts filed a petition with the local city council opposing the possible development of affordable housing on a former farm by a nonprofit. Since 1969, the state of Massachusetts has had a goal of keeping at least 10 percent of communities' housing stock affordable. Currently, only 4 percent of Agawam's housing is affordable. The petition was signed by people living as far away as New Jersey, Oregon, Texas, and Florida. One signatory said, "Agawam has enough low income housing apartment complexes," and another stated, "I don't want to see more government funded housing. It just runes (*sic*) neighborhood. There's enough handouts in the world as it is. People need to start working harder!!!" (Berry 2016).

In 2014 alone, rents rose 7 percent in the U.S. while incomes rose only 1.8 percent (Christie 2014). In July of 2015, only 11 percent of homes were available to median-income families in the San Francisco metropolitan area, and less than a quarter of homes were affordable for the typical household in New York. And the nation's largest cities and economic powerhouses don't hold the monopoly on unaffordable housing—only about half of homes were affordable to the typical household in Laredo, TX in 2015, and inland California communities are the least affordable for their typical residents (National Association of Home Builders 2015).

The gap between incomes and housing prices has been rising steadily for decades as the share of American households financially burdened by housing costs has risen significantly in the past fifty years. In 2013, more than 35 percent of American households paid more than a third of their income in

housing-related costs (U.S. Census Bureau 2015a). While the need for affordable housing grows, it is essentially unprofitable for private developers, neces-
sitating government intervention. But government action on affordable
housing is often met with protest like that in Agawam.

Why has housing become so much less affordable? Why is this considered a
problem? How have we addressed it, and what should we do about it in the
future? This chapter examines the significance of housing affordability in American society, what accounts for the decreasing affordability of housing, and past,
contemporary, and possible policies that impact housing affordability for American households. It also examines the central challenges we face in addressing
the housing affordability problem. How should government intervene? How
should government balance the social and economic goals of housing?

Defining the Affordability Problem

What is housing affordability, and why is it considered a problem in U.S.
society? Housing affordability is determined by both household income and
housing costs. While researchers debate different ways of determining
whether housing is affordable, housing affordability is most commonly meas-
ured by the share of households paying at least 30 percent of their monthly
income on housing costs[1] (Schwartz and Wilson 2007; Tighe and Mueller
2013). Financial institutions, for instance, often use the 30 percent threshold
as a measure of affordability for approving mortgages, insurance, and related
costs for homeowners (Schwartz and Wilson 2007). Households that spend
between 30 percent and 50 percent of their income on housing-related costs
are generally considered moderately burdened, while households that spend
50 percent or more of their income on housing-related costs are severely burdened (Schwartz and Wilson 2007).

In 2013, nearly two-fifths (37 percent) of American households spent 30
percent or more of their monthly income on housing-related costs. Nearly a
fifth (18 percent) of U.S. households spent more than half of their income on
housing-related costs (see Table 2.1 and Figure 2.1). The number of households that are cost burdened has exceeded 30 million since the early 1990s
(Stone 2006).

Housing costs have always been higher for renters, but they have significantly risen for both renters and homeowners in the last thirty years, and
particularly since around 2000. In 1985 about 30 percent of renters and 15
percent of owners were burdened by housing costs, spending 35 percent or
more of their monthly income on housing-related costs. In 2009, nearly half
of renters and a quarter of homeowners spent more than 35 percent of their
income on housing (Figure 2.2).

Housing affordability has decreased in the past fifty years, especially
among certain groups. But why is this a problem? Researchers note that when

Table 2.1 Housing cost burden in the U.S. (%)

	% Income Paid in Housing Costs		
	Less than 30%	*30–49%*	*50%+*
Household Characteristics			
Homeowners	73	15	12
Renters	43	26	30
Black	50	24	26
Latino	49	25	26
Elderly	63	17	20
Poor	14	18	68
Location Characteristics			
Central City	59	23	18
Suburban	64	19	17
Rural	70	16	14
Northeast	59	20	21
Midwest	69	17	15
South	65	18	17
West	57	22	21
All Households	63	19	18

Source: American Housing Survey 2013, Tables C-10-AO, C-10-OO, C-10-RO.

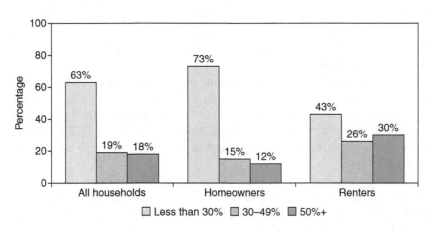

Figure 2.1 Percentage of U.S. households' income paid in housing costs in 2013

Source: U.S. Census Bureau 2015a.

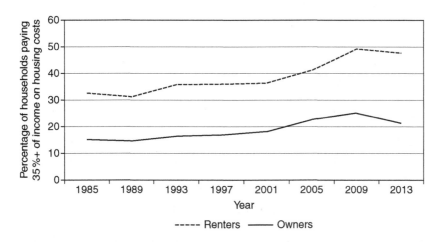

Figure 2.2 Housing cost burden on U.S. households 1985–2013

Source: Eggers and Thackeray 2007; American Housing Survey 2009, 2013.

housing creates squeeze

households spend more of their income on housing, there is less to spend on food, health care, transportation, child care, education-related expenses, and other life-sustaining goods. When households have limited funds for necessities, health, wellbeing, quality of life and productivity often suffer—potentially adding costs to society at large. Increased housing burdens also eat into disposable income that could be spent on other goods and services, thus shrinking the overall economy (Viveiros and Sturtevant 2014). Housing affordability is a problem to the extent that it hinders households' socio-economic potential and limits overall economic growth.

To be sure, while housing costs have risen for all sectors of American society, housing affordability is a much more significant problem for renters and for the poor (Quigley and Raphael 2004; Stone 2006). Renters carry a significant share of the burden: rental affordability has significantly decreased in the past fifty years, especially in the 1970s and 2000s (Joint Center for Housing Studies 2011). Currently, more than half of all renters spend 30 percent or more of their budget on housing, and a third spend more than 50 percent of their income on housing (Figure 2.1). Renters are more than twice as likely to be severely burdened by housing costs (30 percent of renters versus 12 percent of owners). And while for homeowners housing costs have generally declined in the wake of the Great Recession, for renters they have risen (Viveiros and Sturtevant 2014).

Poor households also face extraordinary housing cost burdens. More than 85 percent of poor households spend more than 30 percent of their income on housing; nearly seven in ten spent more than 50 percent of their budget on housing (Figure 2.3). In 2012, nearly 80 percent of extremely low-income

pull are stat from p 15–16 to discuss

share stats but emphasis dissent/?'s

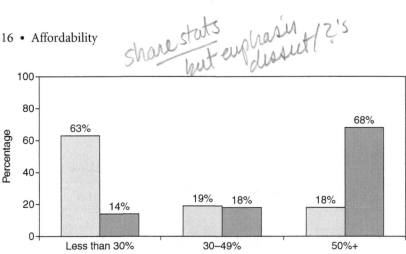

Figure 2.3 Percentage of poor and non-poor households' income paid in housing costs in 2013

Source: American Housing Survey 2013.

low-income households – 57%+ on housing

working households and more than 30 percent of very low-income working households spent more than 50 percent of their income on housing (Viveiros and Sturtevant 2014). Only thirty-nine affordable units are available for every 100 extremely low-income renters (Steffen *et al.* 2015). Only about 25 percent of eligible households receive federal housing assistance, and even households receiving assistance face cost burdens (Joint Center for Housing Studies 2011; Viveiros and Sturtevant 2014). In 2007, the majority (57 percent) of all assisted renter households paid more than 30 percent of their income for housing, and nearly a third paid more than 50 percent (Joint Center for Housing Studies 2011). Indeed, housing cost burdens would be even higher without the limited federal low-income housing assistance currently available and used (Viveiros and Sturtevant 2014).

renters burdened

But affordability challenges don't only impact renters and the lowest-income households. Homeowners and middle-income households also contend with decreasing housing affordability. Between 1999 and 2011, the share of homeowners with severe cost burdens (paying more than 50 percent of their income in housing-related costs) increased by more than 77 percent (4.5 million households); the severe cost burden among renters during this period increased by 65 percent (Schwartz 2015); and in the wake of the Great Recession, a larger share of middle-income homeowners face moderate and severe housing cost burdens compared to similarly situated renters (Schwartz 2015).

Rent burdens in particular have increased the most among lower-middle-income households in the past fifty years (Joint Center for Housing Studies 2011). Nearly 60 percent of lower-middle-income renters pay more than

Δ? ideology of home ownership

30 percent of their income for housing, up from 21 percent in 1960. And nearly a quarter of middle-income renters are cost burdened, compared to 4 percent in 1960 (Joint Center for Housing Studies 2011). More than one-quarter of working low- and moderate-income renters and nearly one-fifth of homeowners are severely burdened (Viveiros and Sturtevant 2014).

Location also plays a role in affordability. Residents of central cities are more heavily burdened by housing costs than those in suburbs and rural areas: 44 percent of central city households are housing cost burdened versus 36 percent of suburban households and 30 percent of rural households (Table 2.1). Because housing cost burdens are impacted by both incomes and housing costs, affordability is a pronounced problem in higher-cost housing markets, as well as in places with limited economic opportunities—and particularly in places where these conditions intersect. Metropolitan regions in California, New York, and Florida lead the nation in housing costs, particularly Miami, New York, Los Angeles, San Diego, and Orlando, while housing tends to be relatively cheaper in the South and Midwestern regions, particularly in places like Pittsburgh, Minneapolis, Oklahoma City, Kansas City, and Buffalo (Figures 2.4 and 2.5; Viveiros and Sturtevant 2014).

However, the top ten most affordable rental markets include places in high-cost markets like Worcester, MA and Washington, DC as well as in low-cost markets like Wichita, KS, El Paso, TX, and Harrisburg, PA. Similarly, both low- and high-cost markets are among the nation's least affordable for rentals: places like Miami, FL, Stockton, CA, McAllen, TX, and Knoxville, TN. And high-cost markets like New York, NY and Honolulu, HI share similar rental cost burdens with Little Rock, AR and Dayton, OH (Joint

[handwritten margin note: need unites but where do they live?]

Figure 2.4 U.S. median home value in dollars—2014

Source: Social Explorer, American Community Survey.

Sum: income, race, location are key factors

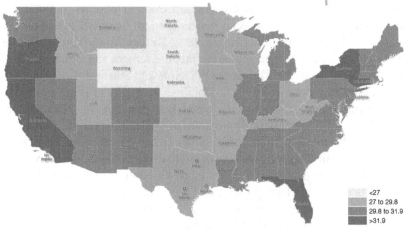

Figure 2.5 U.S. median rent as percentage of household income—2014

Source: Social Explorer, American Community Survey.

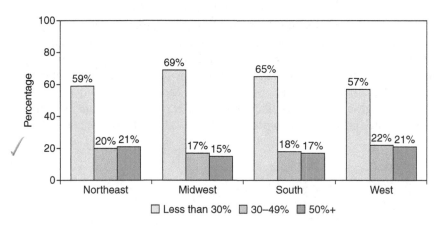

Figure 2.6 Percentage of U.S. households' income paid in housing costs in 2013 by region

Source: U.S. Census Bureau 2015a.

Racial Factors

Center for Housing Studies 2011). Thus, places all over the U.S. struggle with housing affordability (Figure 2.6).

Affordability challenges are also especially marked among Black and Latino households (Stone 2006). Black and Latino households are more burdened by housing costs, with 26 percent of both groups severely burdened by housing costs compared with 18 percent of all households. Larger households and households headed by women and lone elderly individuals also carry particularly large housing cost burdens (Stone 2006). Members of social groups for whom housing is further limited by discrimination—like other nonwhite households, families with children, disabled individuals, and GLBTQ individuals—may also face greater affordability issues (see Chapter 3).

The Roots of Decreasing Affordability *causes*

Why have housing cost burdens risen in the past decades? Social scientists, policymakers, and public officials debate the extent to which household incomes and housing costs impact the rising housing cost burden in American society. *→ Demand + supply side reasons 3 key factors p. 24*

① Wage Stagnation

Housing affordability is partially determined by household incomes. Controlling for inflation, average wages have fallen in the last twenty years (Tilly 2006). The vast majority of American workers have experienced stagnant or declining wages since 1979, largely due to a dramatic shift from an industrial to a service-based economy, the decline of unions, and lax labor policies (Gould 2015). Even widespread economic growth during the 1990s and early 2000s failed to translate into higher wages for most American workers (Tilly 2006). Women's wages still lag behind men's, people of color earn wages far *gender + race* below their white counterparts, and even educated workers' wages have declined (Gould 2015; Tilly 2006). The household incomes of renters, for whom housing unaffordability is most pronounced, has held below 1980 levels since 2001 (Joint Center for Housing Studies 2011). But changes in wages and income do not only impact renters. For homeowners, the increase in housing costs has outpaced average income growth since the 1990s (Brennan and Lipman 2008; Schwartz 2015).

Employment—even full-time employment—does not guarantee affordable housing. As of 2015, a full-time minimum wage worker cannot afford a one-bedroom apartment at the fair market rent[2] in a single U.S. state (Bolton *et al.* 2015). Comparing the minimum income needed to purchase the average home or fair market two-bedroom rental in more than 200 metropolitan areas in the U.S. with the average income of workers in a broad set of occupations, only about a third pay well enough to afford a home purchase or rental, an additional quarter pay well enough to afford a rental, and the remaining 45 percent do not pay well enough to afford either (Schwartz 2015). Thus, stagnant wages among all sectors of U.S. society mean that people must pay a larger share of their incomes for housing than in the past.

Housing Costs *otherside of coin*

But household incomes are not entirely to blame for lack of affordable housing—housing costs have increased dramatically for both renters and owners in the past thirty years. Rents have increased by more than 16 percent in real terms since 1980 (Joint Center for Housing Studies 2011). The increase in rents was responsible for a larger share of the overall decrease in affordability between the 1970s and the 1990s than were stagnant incomes. In the 1990s, nearly all the decline in housing affordability among the poorest renters was due to increasing rents (Quigley and Raphael 2004). Housing sale prices have also increased dramatically since 1970, particularly since 2000 (Figure 2.7). The median home value (adjusted for inflation) in the U.S. was $17,000 in 1970, climbing to $79,100 in 1990 and soaring to $179,900 in 2010.

Some of the increase in housing costs over the past forty years can be attributed to an overall increase in housing quality during this period for both renters and homeowners. For example, nearly all rental units in the U.S. have indoor plumbing, in stark contrast to fifty years ago (Quigley and Raphael 2004). Housing quality and size has particularly improved for the poorest American households over the past half-century. However, housing price increases are greater than can be attributed only to quality increases (Quigley and Raphael 2004).

In general, housing costs are dependent on the quality and quantity of housing in a market, government regulations, and sociocultural factors. Economists argue that the housing market essentially operates by filtering housing through a "quality hierarchy" (Quigley and Raphael 2004). For example, when an affluent household moves into a new housing development, their old home may then be occupied by a new household who cannot

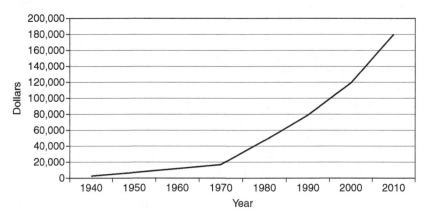

Figure 2.7 U.S. median home value, 1940–2010 (in current dollars)

Source: Flanagan and Wilson 2013.

afford a new development but can afford to buy their first home. The rental they previously occupied then becomes available to a household who cannot afford to buy but can perhaps afford a rental upgrade, leaving behind a rental unit for a household with an even lower income. Generally, new housing is occupied by the most affluent American households, with moderate- and lower-income households occupying older housing in a hierarchy of property values and neighborhood quality.

Thus, the total supply of housing is affected by the construction of new units, the movement of old units through the quality hierarchy, and the removal of old units through abandonment, destruction, or conversion. A larger supply of housing lowers its overall cost, and new housing construction in any part of the market should theoretically increase the supply of housing units. The supply of affordable, especially low-income housing, is affected by housing construction at all quality and price levels (Quigley and Raphael 2004). Most places depend on the "filtering" effect to supply enough affordable housing for low- and moderate-income households. As Malpezzi and Green argue, "to the extent that a city makes it easy for any type of housing to be built, it will also enhance the available stock of low-cost housing" (Malpezzi and Green 1996). Yet the supply of affordable housing remains limited. In 1998, for example, 200,000 renting families in seventeen metropolitan areas could afford to purchase a home, but only 30,000 were available for purchase (Stegman *et al.* 2000).

Why might affordable housing opportunities continue to be limited? Other forces complicate the filtering process and also limit the supply of affordable housing—especially for low-income households. The most significant conditions affecting the supply of affordable housing in the U.S. are diminished public resources for affordable housing and the power of local zoning laws (Mukhija *et al.* 2015). The private market has historically failed to provide enough low-rent housing to meet demand, while public spending on affordable housing has waned and changed form, and local land use policies preclude development of affordable housing. In addition, U.S. tax policy fosters speculation in housing values: housing sale prices are exempt from capital gains taxes, encouraging speculative investment in real estate that can artificially inflate housing prices (Espino 2005).

Limits of the Free Market

The private housing market has never produced enough low-rent housing to meet demand. Nearly all new housing is built for the high end of the market (Figure 2.8; Quigley and Raphael 2004), and little has become affordable through the filtering process. At the same time, higher-income households rent more than 40 percent of the units available to extremely low-income households and 35–40 percent of units available to low-moderate and

Figure 2.8 New luxury housing under construction in New York City, 2016

needs to be incentives

moderate-income households, further limiting the supply of affordable housing (Steffen *et al.* 2015).

Furthermore, there is little incentive to produce affordable housing given that it yields smaller profits than luxury housing for developers. Low rents almost never cover property developers' and owners' construction and maintenance costs (Garboden and Newman 2012; Schwartz 2015). Even housing priced for moderate-income households does not often garner a handsome enough profit for developers to warrant construction. As a result, new construction of affordable housing is limited. At the same time, limited profit margins often don't cover the costs of maintenance of existing affordable units, making it more likely that owners of existing affordable rental housing will choose to divest so thoroughly that the housing becomes uninhabitable, thereby removing affordable units from the market.

Finally, in places undergoing gentrification, older housing units may not depreciate in value and thus yield lower rents through the filtering process—they may, in some cases, command higher rents over time. Landlords may also convert affordable rentals to condominium units or renovate to yield a higher rent, removing units from the affordable rental supply (Kennedy and Leonard 2001). The Joint Center for Housing Studies estimates that nationally nearly one-third of units renting for $400 a month in 1999 had been demolished, vacated, or converted for higher rents by 2009 (Schwartz 2015).

constant cycle + $ for landlord

Public Support for Affordable Housing

Given that the market does not provide enough affordable rental housing to meet demand, federal, state, and local governments offer subsidies to increase the supply. The largest single subsidy for affordable housing is the mortgage interest tax deduction for homeowners (discussed at length in Chapter 5), but public support for affordable rental housing has waned and shifted in the past fifty years. The federal government has reduced the Department of Housing and Urban Development's budget by almost half since 1976 (from $56.4 billion to $29.25 billion, in 2004 dollars), even as the cost of subsidizing homeowner mortgages continues to grow enormously (Dolbeare *et al.* 2002). The number of publicly subsidized low-rent housing units has decreased over time. Nearly one-fifth of public housing units (18 percent) were lost between 1994 and 2012 (Schwartz 2015: 164). Many of these units were redeveloped into mixed-income communities, resulting in a net loss of affordable units. The federal HOPE VI program, designed to redevelop severely distressed public housing into mixed-income housing funded through public-private partnerships, replaced about 45 percent of the low-rent units it demolished between 1993 and 2007 (Schwartz 2015). Thus, the declining supply of low-rent units contributed to rising rents.

HUD ↓50%

20% drop n units

↳ desire to mix low/moderate reduces avail low

Local Land Use Policies

While the supply of affordable rentals is limited, barriers to new affordable housing construction abound. Local zoning restrictions in particular limit the affordable housing supply. Many localities require large lot sizes and

[handwritten margin: policy discrim against poor → individual prop values / self-interest.]

prohibit multifamily construction, limiting housing density in an effort to boost property values. Environmental growth controls can also limit new construction and therefore the affordable housing supply. Cities that limit housing construction—through growth controls, for example—tend to have higher-cost housing (Schill 2005). Places that limit construction through zoning regulations for minimum lot sizes and other density controls are particularly unaffordable (Quigley and Rosenthal 2005). Partly as a result of anti-density policies, much of the national affordable housing stock consists of mobile and manufactured housing, which is more expensive to finance, rarely appreciates in value, and sits on rented land, limiting it as an option for many American households (Schwartz 2015).

[handwritten margin: limit construct = ↑ value]

Overall, the decreasing affordability of housing over the past thirty years can be attributed to both demand-side and supply-side factors. Household incomes continue to stagnate or decline for American workers, making them less able to afford both rents and sales prices. At the same time, housing costs have risen dramatically, and account for a decrease in housing affordability for the poor. A variety of conditions have contributed to the limited supply—and thus higher costs—of low and moderately priced housing: its unprofitability in the open market, the decline of public support for affordable rental housing, and political barriers to new construction of affordable housing.

[handwritten margin: 3 key factors]

Affordable Housing Policy Development in the U.S.

As housing becomes less affordable across all sectors of American society, researchers, stakeholders, and policymakers continue to debate how to address housing affordability. These debates illuminate the historically rooted and ongoing tensions in American housing policy. First, and most fundamentally, experts and policymakers continue to debate whether and to what extent the government should interfere in the housing market. Second, housing affordability is intrinsically tied to the housing, construction, and real estate industries, and the vast majority of U.S. household wealth is tied to homeownership. Affordable housing policies weigh both the social and economic benefits of housing to varying degrees. Other central concerns in affordable housing policy—whether housing should be considered a right, segregation and discrimination, the role of homeownership in U.S. society, and how to balance the need for housing with environmental concerns—are discussed more fully in later chapters.

[handwritten margin: housing – tied to economic success / ideology]

Influencing Wages

[handwritten margin: ① options / regulate wages]

Government can impact housing affordability by influencing wages, housing costs, or both. Given that housing is much less affordable for the working and middle classes than it has ever been, policies might direct toward raising wages. The federal government has only acted to influence wages by setting a minimum wage. However, as of 2015, a full-time worker earning the minimum wage cannot afford a one-bedroom apartment at fair market rent in a single U.S. state (Bolton *et al.* 2015). In the absence of federal action, some local governments have set higher minimum wages in places such as Los Angeles, Lousiville, Chicago, and Albuquerque, among others (National Employment Law Project 2015). While the federal government created a public employment program during the New Deal to great success, the neoliberal turn in U.S. policy has moved focus away from public provision to subsidizing the private sector. Currently all areas of government aim to incentivize the private sector to create jobs. The extent to which these jobs are secure and pay living wages varies greatly.

Unionized employees' wages are historically higher than their non-union counterparts (Long 2013), but between 1973 and 2007 private sector union membership fell from 34 percent to 8 percent for men and from 16 percent to 6 percent for women. The decline is due to a loss of jobs in traditionally unionized industrial and manufacturing sectors and to increased efforts on the part of employers to discourage employee unionization (Western and Rosenfeld 2011). As unions have declined, so has their political power—and thus the enforcement of labor laws. At the same time, job opportunities in the public sector—which tends to pay higher wages, feature less discrimination, and have stronger union participation than jobs in the private sector—have also declined over time in the U.S (Bureau of Labor Statistics 2015a, 2015b; Cooper *et al.* 2012). To the extent that housing affordability rests on strong wages, government at all levels could work to encourage unionization, nourish a strong public sector, and protect, strengthen, and enforce labor laws.

Influencing the Housing Market

Housing affordability, as we know, also depends on housing costs. Government can influence the housing market by constructing housing and regulating mortgage markets, real estate industry practices, taxes on housing sales, and costs and location of housing (Schwartz 2015). Historically, the federal government has intervened in the housing market in varied ways to make homes affordable to both homeowners and renters. Historians refer to this strategy as a "two-tier" housing policy: one strand of housing policy provides aid to homeowners, largely through tax incentives and financing; the other strand provides direct housing subsidies to qualifying low-income households in a variety of forms (Radford 1996). These policies aim to make homeownership more affordable for those who qualify and to ease the rental cost burden of the poorest households. Low-income rental housing policies are the focus of this chapter, while policies that encourage and support homeownership are discussed in Chapter 5.

Gvt shift from ① providing housing to ② incentivized home ownership ↓ ③ state level

Although researchers and policymakers continue to debate whether and how the government should influence the housing market, affordable housing policy in the last seventy years has shifted from government's direct provision of housing to subsidizing the private providers of affordable housing and further incentivizing homeownership. The implementation of policy has also shifted to become less centralized, with state and local governments, agencies, and nonprofits largely responsible for shaping, coordinating, administering—and increasingly funding—housing programs (Schwartz 2015). This policy shift reflects overall political trends toward neoliberalism —that government should function to support private markets—and the overall devolution of housing policy over the past forty years. As Krumholz argues, "Affordable housing policy in the U.S. is driven by interest group politics, popular prejudices, and the business considerations that dominate our political system" (Krumholz 2004).

The Origins of Affordable Housing Policy

Although the first government-constructed housing projects were built during World War I to house wartime workers in places like Philadelphia, PA, Baltimore, MD, New London, CT, and Bath, ME, large-scale federal construction of housing began in earnest during the New Deal under the purview of the Public Works Administration (PWA), beginning in 1933 (Karolak 2000). On the eve of the Great Depression, the private housing market did not provide enough suitable housing for the increasing concentration of workers in American cities, resulting in crowded, dilapidated housing conditions in slums across urban America (Chudacoff *et al.* 2015; Massey and Denton 1993). Despite the need for action in the low-rent housing market, Congress was much more interested in spurring activity in the construction and related industries than in providing low-income housing when it created the nation's first public housing program (Radford 1996; van Hoffman 2000).

The PWA initiated a variety of public works projects that included highways, public buildings, slum clearance, and fifty-eight of the nation's first low-rent housing projects in Philadelphia (the Carl Mackley Houses), New York (the Harlem River Houses), Cleveland (Lakeview Terrace), and other locales (Radford 2000). These new high-quality developments were lauded by architects, planners, and residents. Both low- and moderate-income people flocked to the new developments, impressed by their quality, price, and amenities. The Harlem River Houses, for example, boasted interior parks, a clinic, a child care facility, library, and youth recreation programs (Radford 2000). PWA housing had no income restrictions and attracted a broad range of residents from different socioeconomic backgrounds.

When Congress established a permanent public housing program in 1937 and amended it in 1949, many of these advantages were lost. Facing great

[handwritten margin note at top: "gut builds twin housing story long dreg ✓ #'s"]

opposition from segments of the housing, construction, and real estate industries, which felt threatened by competition in the housing market, Congress mandated new public housing built under the new, permanent United States Housing Authority to be built as cheaply as possible, to be restricted to only the poorest households, and to be formally tied to slum clearance: a unit of slum housing was to be destroyed for every unit of public housing built (van Hoffman 2000). Control over site selection was ceded to local governments. These features limited where public housing could be built, protecting suburban developers from having to compete with publicly funded housing and protecting landlords from having to lower rents to compete with public housing (Radford 2000). *[handwritten: → powerful interest groups backed it.]* *[handwritten margin: new criteria]*

In the wake of World War II, social and economic conditions brought the housing shortage to crisis proportions. Employment opportunities for African Americans continued to draw black workers from the South during the Great Migration of 1940–1970, putting great pressure on the limited and discriminatory low-rent housing market (Massey and Denton 1993). The 1949 Housing Act authorized the construction of an additional 810,000 units of public housing by 1955, a dramatic increase over the 1937 Housing Act. Congress killed proposals in the Housing Act of 1949 to aid the "forgotten third" of American households that earned too much to qualify for public housing but too little to purchase a home, rejecting funding for housing cooperatives, nonprofit housing arrangements, and resident control of public housing. Supported by labor, women's, and veterans' groups, the real estate, building, and banking industries lobbied successfully against housing cooperatives in particular (Biles 2000; van Hoffman 2000).

But even as affordable housing units became harder and harder to come by in the private housing market (Tighe and Mueller 2013), the federal government failed to appropriate enough funding to meet the ambitious 1949 goal for new public housing units, afraid of what some politicians warned was "creeping socialism" (Orlebeke 2000). At the same time, federal urban renewal programs demolished 425,000 low-rent units, replacing them with only 125,000 new units, the majority of which were luxury housing, while new federally funded highways designed to aid suburban homeownership cut through low-rent neighborhoods, destroying at least 330,000 housing units between 1957 and 1968 (Biles 2000; Mohl 2000). Still, only a paltry one-quarter of the public housing units authorized in 1949 were constructed by 1959 (Figure 2.9; Orlebeke 2000). *[handwritten margin: destruct but no replacent.]*

Public housing survived in the immediate postwar era only because it was linked to urban renewal: households displaced from slum clearance and highway construction that aided suburban settlement were among the only households in new public housing (Bauman et al. 2000). But many of the "slums" from which thousands of households—nearly all poor, primarily Black—were displaced, to aid in the redevelopment of downtowns in an *[handwritten margin: slum displacent]*

Figure 2.9 Wyckoff Gardens, Brooklyn, NY, built in 1948

Source: Ken Gould.

effort to increase property values and tax revenues, were found to be any-thing but. One housing expert noted that a hefty 50 percent of so-called slum dwellers lived in fine housing, and that public housing rents were nearly double what they had paid (Biles 2000).

Public housing, gutted, vilified, and chronically underfunded, could never live up to the ideals its supporters touted. Rather than a high-quality, afford-able, mixed-income alternative in a private housing market that never provided adequately for low-rent households, public housing projects became ware-houses for the very poor, largely African Americans displaced from slum clear-ance programs designed to redevelop downtowns. By 1957, virtually all (97 percent) public housing units built in slum clearance areas were inhabited by nonwhite households (Hirsch 2000). As deindustrialization progressed in the wake of World War II and scores of industrial jobs disappeared from urban centers, public housing increasingly served unemployed households and those on public assistance (Biles 2000), a population many outspoken city and sub-urban residents did not want in their backyards. The postwar public housing program—best characterized by Hirsch (2000) as "new construction of densely packed high-rise projects, characterized by the concentration of 'problem' families, the loss of local managerial control over tenant screening, and the removal of 'over-income' households"—resulted in a hopelessly limited and thus largely failed social experiment that nevertheless provided thousands of low-rent units to the nation's poorest and most vulnerable families. In the end, only 1.3 million public housing units were built (Dreier 2006).

The Neoliberal Shift

shift out of cities a/or alternative

Affordable housing policy in the early 1960s began to shift away from public housing to the strategy of subsidized private development of low-income housing. Rather than directly constructing, maintaining, and operating low and moderate-income housing with public funds, the federal government moved toward providing funding in the form of tax incentives, below-market rate financing, and other subsidies to the private sector to spur affordable housing development, part of a larger trend of neoliberalism that shifted the burden of social service provision from the public to the private sector. The 1961 Housing Act enticed developers into the affordable housing business with below-market financing (Orlebeke 2000). The nascent Department of Housing and Urban Development, created in 1965, pursued the privatization of public housing, and the Housing Act of 1968 established a goal of 26 million new housing units, 23 percent of which were for low- and moderate-income families. It aimed to meet this goal by providing subsidies and incentives to developers (Orlebeke 2000). After these programs resulted in widespread fraud on the part of developers, President Richard Nixon declared a moratorium on all federally subsidized housing programs in early 1973, officially breaking with past low-income housing policy.

Just as the New Deal brought about a sea change in American housing policy, the Housing Act of 1974 marked a distinct shift in affordable housing policy. The federal government shifted its focus from direct production of housing to subsidizing rents and housing developments. It also began the process of shifting the responsibility for housing policy and programs to state and local governments.

shift to state rental subsidy

While the shift toward subsidizing the private housing market began in the early 1960s, it was formalized and expanded in 1974 by authorizing funding for the Section 8 New Construction/Substantial Rehabilitation and Existing Housing programs. Both programs authorized the federal government to pay 75 percent (later 70 percent) of low-income households' rents in an effort to entice the private housing market to provide high-quality, affordable housing. In the New Construction/Substantial Rehabilitation program, a so-called "supply-side" program, federal subsidies were attached to housing units designated for low-income renters. Housing subsidies were attached to low-income tenants in the Existing Housing program, a so-called "demand-side program" (Brassil 2010; Schwartz 2015).

Through the New Construction/Substantial Rehabilitation program, developers and landlords could set aside any number of units designated for low-income tenants, and the federal government would pay them 75 percent (later 70 percent) of the fair market rent for the unit, with tenants responsible for the remainder (Schwartz 2015). The program also provided owners of Section 8 housing with access to below-market financing through state housing agencies and generous tax deductions. Units were designated low-income: if one household moved out, another qualifying household could move in, with landlords receiving the guaranteed rental subsidy from the federal government. Despite being terminated by the Reagan administration in 1983 in a far-reaching campaign for fiscal conservatism, the program generated more than 850,000 affordable housing units (Olsen 2003; Schwartz 2015).

The Existing Housing program provided rental subsidies to low-income households (originally households earning up to 80 percent of the area-adjusted median income) to use in the private market wherever they wished, provided the housing unit met basic quality standards. The federal government would then pay households' landlords 75 percent (later 70 percent) of the fair market for the unit, with distinct amounts established for each metropolitan area in the U.S. Tenants were free to move when they wished and take the subsidy with them to use in any qualifying unit. The Reagan administration adopted a variant of this program, the Freestanding Voucher program, which established a maximum allowable rent and allowed tenants to pay more than 30 percent of their income in rent if they wished. The Section 8 Existing Housing and Freestanding Voucher programs existed simultaneously until they were merged in 1998 in the Quality Housing and Work Responsibility Act (Schwartz 2015). The Section 8 Existing Housing program was extraordinarily popular after its inception; by 1980, nearly 600,000 households were using vouchers compared to the 333,000 that were housed in Section 8 New Construction/Substantial Rehabilitation units the same year (Olsen 2003). Housing vouchers are currently one of the primary means of providing affordable housing in the U.S.

Congress authorized a final, less well-known means of spurring development of low-income housing in the private sector in 1986. The Low-Income Housing Tax Credit (LIHTC), not a federal budget item but codified in the Tax Reform Act of 1986, provides generous tax credits to developers who build and operate housing for low-income households. The amount of each tax subsidy is determined on a project-by-project basis, using a complicated formula that takes into account the number of units designated for low-income renters, the development's cost, and the location of the project. The LIHTC is the main source of low-income housing construction in the U.S., accommodating almost twice as many households as public housing. It has helped to fund 2.6 million housing units in more than 40,000 projects for

low-income households (U.S. Department of Housing and Urban Development 2015b).

This policy shift also reflects the historical and ongoing tension between
the social and economic goals of housing policy (Tighe and Mueller 2013).
Promoting homeownership and subsidizing the private low-rent sector has
the added advantage of stimulating the construction and real estate industries. Thus, government has intervened to subsidize rents and homeowner
tax burdens rather than to produce housing or boost stagnating incomes
directly. Both its supply and demand-side programs are designed to incentivize the private sector to provide affordable housing, attempting a tenuous
balance between the social and economic benefits of the housing market.

The Devolution of Housing Policy and Programs

Housing policy and programs—like many other social policies and
programs—devolved to the state and local levels of government through the
1970s, 1980s, and 1990s. Public support for decentralized government—
partly a conservative backlash against federal New Deal, Great Society, and
civil rights legislation—grew throughout the 1970s and contributed to the
elections of Ronald Reagan, George H. W. Bush, and Bill Clinton in the
1980s and 1990s (Dreier 2006).

The 1974 Housing Act initiated the process of providing localities much
more freedom in the allocation of federal funding for affordable housing,
social services, and economic development. Community Development Block
Grants replaced older centralized programs, such as Urban Renewal and
Model Cities. Localities were awarded a percentage of funding ("block
grants") based on the size of their population. While Community Development Block Grants (CDBGs) can be used to fund housing-related programs,
funds for new housing construction are limited to "housing of last resort ...
carried out by a nonprofit or neighborhood organization as part of a neighborhood revitalization, community economic development, or energy conservation project" (Schwartz 2015: 269). The federal government initiated
HOME, an additional block grant program that supports low-income homeownership, in 1990.

Since the 1970s, housing programs are increasingly developed and administered through state and local governments in the face of federal disinvestment and with the idea that localities best understood and could best serve
their constituents' needs. State and local governments have thus played a
much stronger role in making housing affordable since the 1980s (Bratt 1992;
Schwartz 2015). Local control, however, means that some localities can
simply refuse to provide affordable housing (see Chapter 3). It also intimately
ties affordable housing development to local zoning laws. Federal programs
such as CDBG and HOME are administered by state and local entities and

join a whole host of locally developed and run housing programs that vary dramatically across the country (Brassil 2010; Stegman 1999).

Contemporary Affordable Housing Policies and Programs

Two central questions guide affordable housing policy: (1) how should government intervene to provide affordable housing?; and (2) how should government balance the social and economic goals of housing? Currently, greatly influenced by the powerful real estate lobby (Bratt *et al.* 2006), government intervenes to support the private sector and local governments and functions to preserve property values in middle-class and affluent communities. Current policies are shaped by three factors: the inability of the private market to provide enough low-rent housing to meet demand, decreased support for and devolution of housing policy, and the dominance of local land use zoning laws.

To make housing more affordable, federal, state, and local governments provide both direct subsidies and tax incentives and credits (see Figure 2.10). While the former—including public housing and housing vouchers—are more commonly discussed in the public sphere, the latter—including the homeowner mortgage interest deduction and low-income housing tax credit—actually constitute a much larger share of federal housing expenditures each year (Schwartz 2015). Current affordable housing policies and programs that subsidize homeownership include the mortgage interest tax deduction, the property tax deduction, the property sales tax reduction, and some CDBG and HOME-funded programs. Other programs and policies provide affordable rental housing for qualifying households, including housing vouchers, Section 8 projects, public housing, and the low-income

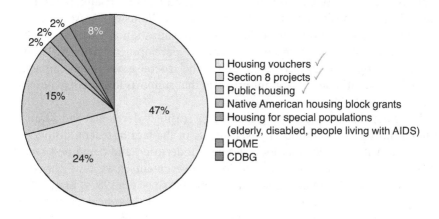

Figure 2.10 Subsidized rental housing, 2014

Source: Schwartz 2015.

housing tax credit. In practice, many of the subsidized homeownership programs are meant to provide "workforce housing," or housing for public serv-
ants like police and teachers who earn too much to qualify for rental
subsidies but too little to afford market rates. In contrast, the rental subsidy
programs are usually known as "affordable housing" for the poor that sometimes includes other services. Some of these programs are funded and administered by the federal government, others by state or local governments, and
still others by nonprofits and/or government-nonprofit partnerships.

Making Homeownership Affordable

By far the largest federal affordable housing subsidies are tax credits and
incentives for homeowners. The federal government provided about four-
and-a-half times as much money in tax deductions for homeowners as it
spent on housing programs in 2012: $220 billion in mortgage interest tax
deductions to homeowners compared to $47.9 billion on direct housing
assistance (Schwartz 2015). Homeowners are also able to deduct property
tax payments from their taxes and a large portion of home sales profits from
capital gains taxes (Schwartz 2015). These tax benefits account for 86
percent of all federal tax expenditures and aided more than 34 million
homeowners in 2012 (Schwartz 2015). Of course, homeownership must be
affordable to households before they can take advantage of this benefit, so it
tends to reward higher-earning households. Indeed, the vast majority of this
benefit goes to households making more than $100,000 per year (Schwartz
2015).

Beyond tax deductions and incentives, the federal government also funds
state-run and locally run programs to encourage homeownership among
low- and middle-income households through the HOME and CDBG programs. The federal government also provides financial backing to state-issued
mortgage revenue bonds that subsidize homeownership for first-time low-
and moderate-income homebuyers (Schwartz 2015). State-issued mortgage
revenue bonds helped fund more than 2.9 million mortgages through 2010
(Schwartz 2015). These policies, as well as debates around the government's
role in promoting homeownership, are discussed at length in Chapter 5.

Affordable Rental Housing

While the federal government funds and administers programs and policies
to encourage homeownership, homeownership still remains unattainable for
many U.S. households—particularly for younger generations saddled with
student loan debt, the working class, and the poorest, most vulnerable households for whom rental housing costs are a severe burden. Thus, affordable
housing policy also extends to rental housing.

One approach to making rental housing more affordable is simply to build more of it. Theoretically, an expanding supply would meet the increased demand for rental housing and provide for households of all income brackets through the filtering process. However, as discussed earlier in the chapter, the housing market generally does not operate this way in high-cost and gentrifying markets where landlords can attain high rents for relatively low-quality properties. In addition, low-income housing construction is cost prohibitive everywhere, so the private market has historically not provided enough (Schwartz 2015).

Given these circumstances, government involvement in the low-rent housing market is all but certain (Schwartz 2015). The federal government funds affordable housing for qualifying households through direct subsidies, such as rental vouchers, Section 8 projects, public housing, and competitive funding for locally developed projects. In addition, it provides indirect subsidies, including the low-income housing tax credit to support affordable housing construction. Federal funds can be allocated for particular groups like the elderly or people with disabilities and can be implemented by government agencies or private and/or nonprofit partners (Schwartz 2015). Although state and local agencies are largely responsible for the distribution of housing subsidies, the vast majority of funding for affordable housing and related programs comes from the federal government (Katz et al. 2003). Currently about seven million households in the U.S. receive federal aid for rental housing (Schwartz 2015).

Due to the neoliberal turn and the troubled history of public housing in the U.S., no new public housing has been built since the mid-1990s, and the vast majority of public housing units were built between 1949 and 1979 (Schwartz 2015). No new Section 8 or other subsidized projects have been constructed since the early 1980s. This is in stark contrast to other nations, such as Singapore and the Netherlands. In Singapore, 80 percent of the population lives in high-quality public housing with a host of amenities, including access to transit and green space (Dewan 2014). More than 50 percent of the population lives in "social housing" in the Netherlands (Austerberry 2013).

In the U.S., the federal government funds the maintenance of existing public housing in an effort to maintain the rapidly dwindling affordable housing stock. Public housing operations account for about 14 percent of federal spending on rental housing (Schwartz 2015: 9). Most localities have very few public housing units: about half of U.S. localities manage fewer than 100 public housing units. Larger cities tend to have more public housing: about 15 percent of the nation's public housing is in New York City, for example (Schwartz 2015). These also tend to be gentrifying places with high housing costs, where the maintenance of current public housing is central to maintaining even a limited affordable housing stock. Given the fraught

Rental = disenfrancment (handwritten annotation)

history of public housing, such a strategy for providing affordable housing is politically unpopular but tenable.

The federal government also provides rental assistance in the form of housing vouchers (originally the Section 8 Existing Housing program and often colloquially known as "Section 8"). Housing choice vouchers pay the difference between 30 percent of tenants' income and the fair market rent of units, determined by the Department of Housing and Urban Development. Housing vouchers account for about a third of federal rental housing assistance (Schwartz 2015: 9).

Housing vouchers have several advantages. Theoretically, they allow qualifying households to live in the qualifying units of their choice, expanding their options beyond where existing public housing and Section 8 projects are located. Subsidizing rents is also cheaper than building new affordable housing. Vouchers can also stabilize weak housing markets, help households who would not otherwise be able to compete in tight housing markets, and provide struggling landlords with stable rental income to maintain their properties, theoretically preventing rental units from deteriorating to the point of abandonment and restricting the supply of low-rent housing (Katz *et al.* 2003).

However, the pool of landlords willing to accept vouchers is limited, with many landlords discriminating against Section 8 tenants (see Chapter 3). As a result, voucher holders tend to live in poorer neighborhoods than other renters, although fewer voucher holders live in very poor neighborhoods compared to their public housing counterparts (Schwartz 2015). In places with tight housing markets, finding a qualifying unit can be extraordinarily difficult, as landlords have little incentive to rent to voucher households. When landlords do rent to voucher households, they are often overcharged in rent (Desmond and Perkins 2016). Finally, voucher holders have largely struggled to enter high-opportunity neighborhoods, partly as a result of discrimination but also because the best neighborhoods restrict multifamily housing.

Another set of rental assistance programs includes those administered as block grants: the federal government provides competitive funding to states and localities based on population size. These include the rental assistance programs that join homeownership programs for low- and moderate-income households through the HOME program, the National Housing Trust Fund, and housing programs initiated and maintained through the Community Development Block Grant program. These programs fund affordable rental development and rehabilitation and vary widely across locales. Without additional subsidies, however, HOME-funded projects usually aid households earning about the median income rather than the poorest households. CDBG projects are able to aid households earning up to 80 percent of the area median income, making these projects also less likely to help the very poor.

CDBG housing programs aided more than 80,000 households in 2014 (U.S. Department of Housing and Urban Development 2015a).

Private and nonprofit developers subsidized through the LIHTC and block grant programs currently provide the vast majority of federally subsidized housing for low-income people (Tighe and Mueller 2013). For-profit developers typically have greater resources than nonprofits to construct affordable housing but are much less likely to take advantage of all available subsidies provided for the poorest households. Nonprofits, on the other hand, have many fewer resources and less reach, despite intentions to provide for the very poor. As a result, little affordable housing is constructed for the lowest-income households, and the units that are developed tend to be in poor communities (Tighe and Mueller 2013).

The last, and largest, housing assistance program is the Low-Income Housing Tax Credit (LIHTC), which subsidizes not qualifying households but investors who construct affordable housing units by paying 70 percent of project development costs (Olsen 2003). The LIHTC accounts for about a third of federal spending on rental housing (Schwartz 2015: 9). The federal government allocates $1.25 per resident for states to disburse to developers of affordable housing in a competitive process. States must give priority to projects that will house the lowest-income households and projects that will remain affordable for the longest periods, and 10 percent of LIHTC tax credits must be given to nonprofit housing developers (O'Regan and Quigley 2000). Still, LIHTC house relatively few very poor households. Less than 30 percent of LIHTC tenants are considered very poor, as opposed to 90 percent of Section 8 project tenants and 81 percent of public housing tenants (Wallace 1995).

The LIHTC is perhaps the best example of the neoliberal shift in housing policy, in that it allows the federal government to stay out of the market directly but to subsidize the private market to provide a public good. It requires no direct appropriations and no political debate; it is simply a tax incentive buried in the federal tax code that few people associate with federal rental subsidies. Developers may also take advantage of other tax credits to provide affordable housing, including the historic rehabilitation tax credit (Schwartz 2015). The LIHTC does have some disadvantages, however. It incentivizes building affordable housing in poor communities by offering larger subsidies there. It subsidizes real estate developers rather than households, and the government has little oversight regarding site selection, tenant selection, and possible fraudulent activities.

While federal affordable housing funding sources are distinct, in practice affordable housing is often developed by both for-profit and nonprofit organizations using a variety of federal funding sources, including HOME, the LIHTC, federally backed but locally issued tax-exempt bonds, and state and local sources (Dreier 2006). The devolution of American housing policy has culminated in a patchwork of affordable housing policies and programs that differ across states and localities, making the scope and impact of affordable housing policy nearly impossible to evaluate.

Alternative Housing Arrangements

Alternative forms of housing, including cooperatives and community land trusts, also aim to make housing more affordable for American households. In cooperatives, households buy "shares" rather than the unit in which they live, which can be an apartment, townhome, or single-family residence. The cooperative retains ownership of all units, and all residents collectively share the equity. Pooling resources allows cooperatives to keep costs down, making them often more affordable to middle- and working-class households than traditional homeownership (National Cooperative Law Center 2015). First developed in Britain and France in the industrial age, co-ops are a relatively rare form of housing tenure, but they exist all over the country and particularly in the New York region. Low-income and limited-equity cooperatives offer some of the highest-quality and most affordable housing in the U.S. and have the added advantage of helping households accrue wealth.

Community land trusts work in a similar way, with resident-led, nonprofit organizations retaining perpetual stewardship over particular areas. Houses, gardens, commercial areas, and other facilities on the land may be maintained and sold, but the land is forever retained for these purposes at an affordable level (Davis 2014; Meehan 2014). There are currently 243 community land trusts in the U.S., with the largest numbers in Washington, California, Florida, New York, and Massachusetts (Meehan 2014).

Despite their overall success, the federal government maintains no specific programs to fund or provide tax incentives to cooperatives and community land trusts, but some qualify and receive funding through the CDBG and HOME block grant programs and/or state and local housing finance programs.

Limitations of Federal Housing Policy

Criticisms of contemporary affordable housing policy abound. First, and most significantly, funding for affordable housing is simply too limited to make a significant impact on struggling households. Currently only about 25 percent of eligible American households receive housing assistance (Bolton *et al.* 2015). The average waiting period for a public housing unit is eleven months; for housing vouchers, it is twenty-eight months. In places with large housing authorities, such as New York City, the wait can be up to eight years (U.S. Department of Housing and Urban Development 1999).

Second, subsidies to landlords to operate low-rent housing sometimes exceed the costs of maintaining public housing, leading to criticisms that affordable housing subsidies are "expensive bribes to lenders and developers," especially as significant numbers opt out of their government contracts over time (Bratt *et al.* 2006; Dreier 2006: 115).

Third, the three largest forms of rental housing assistance—housing choice vouchers, the Low-Income Housing Tax Credit, and public housing—tend to locate qualifying households in relatively poor areas, concentrating poverty in specific districts with limited opportunities for socioeconomic mobility (see Chapter 3).

Fourth, while the federal block grant approach offers much more local freedom to tailor programs to the specific needs of residents, this design also aggravates inequalities among neighboring communities. Middle-class and affluent communities wishing to preserve property values and low density can simply avoid applying for or receiving federal subsidies. In this context, each locality pursues its own economic interests without having to consider the overall impact of these parochial decisions on the provision of affordable housing (Schill 2005; see also Fischel 2001). Affordable rental housing is thus certain to be concentrated in the poorest communities that are overburdened with social services costs. The devolution of housing policy forces housing providers to compete against each other for very limited funding.

Finally, local zoning laws that limit density and new construction to single-family homes and large lots also work to limit the supply of housing, effectively restricting construction of multifamily rental developments and keeping housing costs high. The federal government has virtually no over-sight or influence over local zoning laws that limit affordable housing con-struction (Schwartz 2015). As more and more American households are unable to afford rising housing prices, these shortcomings of housing policy have become more urgent and problematic.

Local Affordable Housing Initiatives

In the absence of more aggressive and centralized federal affordable housing policies and programs, some states and localities have initiated their own. Two of the most common local policies are rent control and inclusionary zoning (IZ), also called inclusionary housing.

Rent Control

Rent regulation laws, also called rent control or rent stabilization, set price limits on rental housing. Both states and municipalities have passed rent control laws from New York State to several municipalities in California. The first rent controls were enacted during the World War I housing shortage to prevent rent gouging by unscrupulous landlords (Gyourko and Linneman 1989). New York has the oldest rent control program, while Boston, Washington, DC, San Francisco, and other municipalities enacted forms of rent regulation in the 1970s to combat spiking inflation and protect elderly tenants on fixed incomes (Arnott 1997). Current rent controls are relatively limited in scope and typically allow rent increases when a tenant moves and exempt new housing units. Many researchers argue that rent controls limit the affordable housing stock by reducing housing quality and discouraging investment, and lead to increased rents for unregulated units (Arnott 1997; Bratt *et al.* 2006). Others argue that they are necessary to maintaining an affordable housing supply in a productive society; without them, tenants are vulnerable to dramatic rent increases and subsequent disruption (Čapek and Gilderbloom 1992). The most densely populated and prosperous places in the U.S. tend to have more rent regulation.

Inclusionary Zoning
Inclusionary zoning either requires or provides incentives to housing developers to reserve a share of new housing for low- or moderate-income households at below-market rates. Localities vary greatly in their means of implementing inclusionary zoning, in the proportion of affordable units they require from developers, the income limits for recipients of affordable units, and the time period that affordable units must remain affordable. Montgomery County, MD was one of the first localities to initiate mandatory inclusionary zoning in 1974, along with a host of communities in Northern California (Mukhija *et al.* 2015). By 2008 approximately 500 local governments in at least twenty-five states established inclusionary zoning programs (Calavita and Mallach 2010). The vast majority of places with inclusionary zoning rules are suburban, and are located in New Jersey, Maryland, Massachusetts, and California (Mukhija *et al.* 2015).

Supporters of inclusionary zoning programs argue that they not only increase the affordable housing stock but can also facilitate economic integration of households in mixed-income communities (Mukhija *et al.* 2015). Montgomery County's inclusionary zoning program produced more than 13,000 new affordable units through 2012, the majority of which were owner-occupied units (Urban Institute 2012), and California's programs produced about 34,000 units through 2003 (Fox and Rose 2003). Evidence of the impact of inclusionary zoning on racial and economic integration is mixed (Kontokosta 2013).

Opponents of inclusionary zoning have two main criticisms. First, they argue IZ requirements impede affordable housing development by imposing costs on developers that they may then pass along to buyers. Research from San Francisco and Boston shows that inclusionary zoning had very little effect on housing prices and increased the affordable housing stock only slightly (Schuetz *et al.* 2011). Other research on California suggests that inclusionary zoning policies may increase the multifamily housing stock, while the price of single-family homes increases and the size of single-family homes decreases (Bento *et al.* 2009). Opponents also hold that IZ programs jeopardize the poor because most affordable units do not go to the most needy households (Mukhija *et al.* 2015). For example, the majority of known IZ programs in California require 10–14 percent of new developments to be set aside for affordable housing (California Coalition for Rural Housing and Nonprofit Housing Association of Northern California 2003), and of those only about a quarter go to the lowest-income households (Nonprofit Housing Association of Northern California 2007).

Overall, research suggests that the most successful inclusionary zoning programs are mandatory, older programs, with density bonuses, small-project exemptions, and low fees that allow developers to "buy out" of the program (Mukhija *et al.* 2015). Without state-level requirements, oversight, and enforcement, inclusionary zoning laws have few teeth and are thus not as successful. Local initiatives are likely to fail without state or federal support (Quigley and Raphael 2004).

Case Study: Mount Laurel, NJ

Twenty miles east of Camden, NJ lies suburban Mount Laurel, NJ. While Camden lost half of its population between 1950 and 2010, the victim of dramatic deindustrialization and white flight (see Chapter 3), Mount Laurel remained economically stable, gaining many of Camden's former residents in the 1960s. By 2010, Camden was more than 90 percent Black and Latino, and nearly 40 percent of its population lived in poverty. On the other hand, Mount Laurel was about 15 percent Black and Latino, and less than 4 percent of the population lived in poverty (U.S. Census Bureau 2015b).

A vibrant community of mostly Black farmworkers resided in Mount Laurel for generations before massive highway construction displaced many families in the 1950s; most moved to segregated, dilapidated housing that local officials continuously campaigned to condemn throughout the 1960s. Facing few options other than moving to nearby declining Camden and Philadelphia, residents organized to try to find a way to stay in their hometown in the face of dramatic displacement. In 1969, frustrated with the prohibitively high cost of housing in their hometown, a group of low-income, mostly minority residents joined with a local developer to build thirty-six units of affordable housing (Massey *et al.* 2013).

Local government blocked construction as it violated the township's zoning laws that favored single-family housing on large lots. Residents and their legal representation challenged the township, arguing that its zoning laws prevented the construction of affordable housing, effectively barring low-income, particularly minority, households from living in Laurel and benefiting from its resources. The New Jersey Supreme Court ruled in their favor in a 1975 landmark decision that required all New Jersey municipalities to produce their "fair share" of affordable housing. A second decision in 1983 reaffirmed the court's initial decision, ordering the township to calculate its fair share of affordable housing units and re-zone quickly to support new construction (Massey *et al.* 2013).

Mount Laurel residents vehemently opposed the construction of afford- *fears* able housing in their suburban hamlet. Many angry residents feared that constructing affordable housing would raise taxes, lower property values, and attract crime. Resident protest was so strong that the local planning board *almost* failed to approve the new affordable development envisioned in 1969 until *30 yrs!* 1997; the development was finally completed in 2000 and christened the Ethel Lawrence Homes (Massey *et al.* 2013).

Today, the 140 units that comprise the Ethel Lawrence Homes are leased to households earning between 10 percent and 80 percent of the area median *mixed* income of $84,632 (U.S. Census Bureau 2015c), a range that mimics the early *income* PWA developments, which avoided concentrating the very poor in public housing. In contrast to other publicly subsidized housing developments that typically set aside 10–14 percent of new units at affordable rates, 100 percent of the Ethel Lawrence Homes are affordable.

Given the Mount Laurel residents' intense resistance to the development and the nation's fraught history of affordable housing policy, residents, researchers, policymakers, and advocates paid special attention to this experiment in suburban affordable housing development. Ten years out, the Ethel Lawrence Homes had no discernible impact on crime rates, taxes, or home values in immediate neighborhoods or Mount Laurel as a whole. A third of neighboring residents did not even realize that the Ethel Lawrence Homes were an affordable housing development, while residents of the development experienced meaningful increases in a host of measures of quality of life (Massey *et al.* 2013).

Despite the two landmark legal decisions requiring New Jersey municipalities to construct their fair share of affordable housing, echoing patterns in countless suburbs in the U.S., half of all residential development in New Jersey since 1986 has occurred on lots at least a half-acre in size (Massey *et al.* 2013). Such exclusionary land use policies limit the supply of housing. Combined with anti-multifamily zoning, these local policies and practices severely constrain the affordable housing market. Political opposition to the fair-share policy is strong, and the future of affordable housing development in New Jersey is uncertain.

Terms

Wage stagnation
Quality hierarchy
Two-tier housing policy
Neoliberalism
Housing vouchers
Low-Income Housing Tax Credit
Rent control
Inclusionary zoning

Discussion Questions

How is housing affordability defined? For whom is it a particular problem?

Why might decreasing housing affordability be considered a social problem?

What accounts for the decreasing affordability of housing in the U.S. over time?

What are some limitations of the "free market" for housing? What is the housing filtering process, and what complicates it?

How has government intervened to provide affordable housing over time? How should it intervene in the future?

How has government balanced the social and economic goals of housing? What should this balance look like in the future?

If you were a resident of Agawam, MA, would you sign the petition described at the beginning of the chapter? Why or why not?

Application

You are an elected leader of one of thirty suburban districts outside a major, thriving city. Your district boasts a high homeownership rate, excellent schools, and virtually no crime. However, housing prices in your district are astronomical, particularly rents. Vacancies have become more common as fewer households can afford to live in your community. You will work with the leaders of the other suburban districts in your area, as well as from the city, to present a plan to your state legislature that aims to make housing more affordable across your metropolitan region.

Draft an affordable housing plan that summarizes the problem and presents a set of policies that aim to solve it, using at least five scholarly research sources. Discuss the resources you will need, and where and from whom you expect to find opposition to your plan.

Notes

1 Other measures include the "shelter poverty" (Stone 2006), median housing cost-to-income ratio, the share of occupied units with monthly costs below 30 percent of median income, and, for rental markets, the "supply gap," which accounts for the fact that many relatively high-income households occupy low-rent housing (Joint Center for Housing Studies 2011).
2 Fair market rents are determined by the U.S. Department of Housing and Urban Development.

References

Arnott, Richard. 1997. "Rent Control." In *The New Palgrave Dictionary of Economics and the Law*, edited by P. Newman. London: Palgrave Macmillan.

Austerberry, Elizabeth. 2013. "Netherlands Follows Britain's Lead on Social Housing." *The Guardian*, June 21, 2013. Retrieved August 20, 2016. www.theguardian.com/ housing-network/2013/jun/21/netherlands-britain-social-housing-provision.

Bauman, John F., Biles, Roger, and Szylvian, Kristin. 2000. *From Tenements to the Taylor Homes: In Search of an Urban Housing Policy in Twentieth-Century America*. University Park, PA: Pennsylvania State University Press.

Bento, Antonio, Lowe, Scott, Knapp, Gerrit-Jan, and Chakraborty, Arnab. 2009. "Housing Market Effects of Inclusionary Zoning." *Cityscape: A Journal of Policy Development and Research* 11(2): 7–26.

Berry, Conor. 2016. "Opposition to Possible Affordable Housing Project in Agawam May Be Exercise in Futility." *MassLive*, August 2, 2016. Retrieved August 15, 2016. www.masslive.com/news/index.ssf/2016/08/growing_opposition_to_possible. html.

Biles, Roger. 2000. "Public Housing and the Postwar Urban Renaissance, 1949–1973." In J. F. Bauman, R. Biles, and K. M. Szylvian, eds, *From Tenements to the Taylor Homes: In Search of an Urban Housing Policy in Twentieth-Century America*, pp. 143–162. University Park, PA: Pennsylvania State University Press.

Bolton, Megan, Bravve, Elina, Miller, Emily, Crowley, Sheila, and Errico, Ellen. 2015. *Out of Reach*. Washington, DC: National Low Income Housing Coalition.

Brassil, Margaret M. 2010. *The Creation of a Federal Partnership: The Role of the States in Affordable Housing*. Albany, NY: State University of New York Press.

Bratt, Rachel G. 1992. "Federal Constraints and Retrenchment in Housing: The Opportunities and Limits of State and Local Governments." *Journal of Law and Politics* 8(4): 651–701.

Bratt, Rachel G., Stone, Michael E., and Hartman, Chester. 2006. *A Right to Housing: Foundation for a New Social Agenda*. Philadelphia, PA: Temple University Press.

Brennan, Maya, and Lipman, Barbara J. 2008. *Stretched Thin: The Impact of Rising Housing Expenses on America's Homeowners and Renters*. Washington, DC: The Center for Housing Policy.

Bureau of Labor Statistics. 2015a. "Union Membership Rate in Private Industry Was 6.6 Percent in 2014; Public Sector 35.7 Percent." *The Economics Daily*. Washington, DC: Department of Labor.

Bureau of Labor Statistics. 2015b. *Employer Costs For Employee Compensation— March 2015*. Washington, DC: U.S. Department of Labor.

Calavita, Nico and Mallach, Alan. 2010. *Inclusionary Housing in International Perspective: Affordable Housing, Social Inclusion, and Land Value Recapture.* Cambridge, MA: Lincoln Institute of Land Policy.

California Coalition for Rural Housing and Nonprofit Housing Association of Northern California. 2003. *Inclusionary Housing in California: 30 Years of Innovation.* Sacramento, CA: CCRH and NPH.

Čapek, Stella and Gilderbloom, John I. 1992. *Community Versus Commodity: Tenants and the American City.* Albany, NY: SUNY Press.

Christie, Les. 2014. "Rents Are Soaring—And So Are Evictions." *CNN Money,* October 29, 2014. Retrieved August 15, 2016. http://money.cnn.com/2014/10/29/real_estate/evicted/.

Chudacoff, Howard P., Smith, Judith E., and Baldwin, Peter C. 2015 [1981]. *The Evolution of American Urban Society.* Upper Saddle River, NJ: Pearson.

Cooper, David, Gable, Mary, and Austin, Algernon. 2012. "The Public-Sector Jobs Crisis: Women and African Americans Hit Hardest by Job Losses in State and Local Governments." Economic Policy Institute Issue Brief #339 (May 2). Washington, DC: Economic Policy Institute.

Davis, John. 2014. "Origins and Evolution of the Community Land Trust in the United States." In J. Davis, ed., *The Community Land Trust Reader.* Cambridge, MA: Lincoln Institute of Land Policy.

Desmond, Matthew and Perkins, Kristin L. 2016. "Are Landlords Overcharging Housing Voucher Households?" *City & Community* 15(2): 137–162.

Dewan, Shaila. 2014. "Rent Too High? Move to Singapore." *New York Times Magazine,* April 29, 2014. Retrieved August 20, 2016. www.nytimes.com/2014/05/04/magazine/rent-too-damn-high-move-to-singapore.html?_r=0.

Dolbeare, Cushing N., Basloe Saraf, Irene, and Crowley, Sheila. 2002. *Changing Priorities: The Federal Budget and Housing Assistance 1976–2007.* Washington, DC: National Low Income Housing Coalition.

Dreier, Peter. 2006. "Federal Housing Subsidies: Who Benefits and Why?" In R. G. Bratt, M. E. Stone, and C. Hartman, eds, *A Right to Housing: Foundation for a New Social Agenda,* pp. 105–108. Philadelphia: Temple University Press.

Eggers, Frederick J. and Alexander Thackeray. 2007. *32 Years of Housing Data.* Washington, DC: U.S. Department of Housing and Urban Development Office of Policy Development and Research. Retrieved December 1, 2016. www.huduser.org/datasets/ahs/AHS_taskC.pdf.

Espino, N. Ariel. 2005. "Inequality, Segregation, and Housing Markets: The U.S. Case." In D. P. Varady, ed., *Desegregating the City: Ghettos, Enclaves, and Inequality,* pp. 145–157. Albany: State University of New York Press.

Fischel, William. 2001. *The Homevoter Hypothesis: How Home Values Influence Local Government Taxation, School Finance, and Land-Use Policies.* Cambridge, MA: Harvard University Press.

Flanagan, Christine and Wilson, Ellen. 2013. *Home Value and Homeownership Rates: Recession and Post-Recession Comparisons from 2007–2009 to 2010–2012.* American Community Survey Briefs. Washington, DC: U.S. Census Bureau.

Fox, Radhika and Rose, Kalima. 2003. *Expanding Housing Opportunity in Washington, DC: The Case for Inclusionary Zoning.* Oakland, CA: PolicyLink.

Garboden, Phillip M. E. and Newman, Sandra. 2012. "Is Preserving Small, Low-End Rental Housing Feasible?" *Housing Policy Debate* 22(4): 507–526.

Gould, Elisa. 2015. "2014 Continues a 35-Year Trend of Broad-Based Wage Stagnation." Economic Policy Institute Issue Brief #393 (February 19). Washington, DC: Economic Policy Institute.

Gyourko, Joseph and Linneman, Peter. 1989. "Equity and Efficiency Aspects of Rent Control: An Empirical Study of New York City." *Journal of Urban Economics* 26: 54–74.

Hirsch, Arnold R. 2000. "Choosing Segregation: Federal Housing Policy between *Shelley* and *Brown*." In J. F. Bauman, R. Biles, and K. M. Szylvian, eds, *From Tenements to the Taylor Homes: In Search of an Urban Housing Policy in Twentieth-Century America*, pp. 206–225. University Park, PA: Pennsylvania State University Press.

Joint Center for Housing Studies. 2011. *The State of the Nation's Housing 2011*. Cambridge, MA: Harvard University Press.

Karolak, Eric J. 2000. "'No Idea of Doing Anything Wonderful': The Labor-Crisis Origins of National Housing Policy and the Reconstruction of the Working-Class Community, 1917–1919." In J. F. Bauman, R. Biles, and K. M. Szylvian, eds, *From Tenements to the Taylor Homes: In Search of an Urban Housing Policy in Twentieth-Century America*, pp. 60–80. University Park, PA: Pennsylvania State University Press.

Katz, Bruce, Austin Turner, Margery, Destorel Brown, Karen, Cunningham, Mary, and Sawyer, Noah. 2003. *Rethinking Local Affordable Housing Strategies: Lessons from 70 Years of Policy and Practice*. Washington, DC: Brookings Institution and Urban Institute.

Kennedy, Maureen and Leonard, Paul. 2001. *Dealing with Neighborhood Change: A Primer on Gentrification and Policy Choices*. Washington, DC: Brookings Institution Center on Metropolitan and Urban Policy.

Kontokosta, Constantine E. 2013. "Mixed-Income Housing and Neighborhood Integration: Evidence from Inclusionary Zoning Programs." *Journal of Urban Affairs* 36(4): 716–741.

Krumholz, Norman. 2004. *The Reluctant Hand: Privatization of Public Housing in the U.S.* Chicago, IL: City Futures.

Long, George. 2013. "Differences between Union and Nonunion Compensation, 2001–2011." *Monthly Labor Review*, April. Washington, DC: Bureau of Labor Statistics.

Malpezzi, Stephen and Green, Richard K. 1996. "What Has Happened to the Bottom of the U.S. Housing Market?" *Urban Studies* 33(10): 1807–1820.

Massey, Douglas S. and Denton, Nancy A. 1993. *American Apartheid: Segregation and the Making of the Underclass*. Cambridge, MA: Harvard University Press.

Massey, Douglas S., Albright, Len, Casciano, Rebecca, Derickson, Elizabeth, and Kinsey, David N. 2013. *Climbing Mount Laurel: The Struggle for Affordable Housing and Social Mobility in an American Suburb*. Princeton, NJ: Princeton University Press.

Meehan, James. 2014. "Reinventing Real Estate: The Community Land Trust as a Social Invention in Affordable Housing." *Journal of Applied Social Science* 8(2): 113–133.

Mohl, Raymond. 2000. "Planned Destruction: The Interstates and Central City Housing." In J. F. Bauman, R. Biles, and K. M. Szylvian, eds, *From Tenements to the Taylor Homes: In Search of an Urban Housing Policy in Twentieth-Century America*, pp. 226–242. University Park, PA: Pennsylvania State University Press.

Mukhija, Vinit, Das, Ashok, Regus, Lara, and Slovin Tsay, Sara. 2015. "The Tradeoffs of Inclusionary Zoning: What Do We Know and What Do We Need to Know?" *Planning Practice & Research* 30(2): 225–235.

National Association of Home Builders. 2015. *Housing Opportunity Index: 2nd Quarter 2015*. Washington, DC: National Housing Center. Retrieved on September 1, 2015. www.nahb.org/en/research/housing-economics/housing-indexes/housing-opportunity-index.aspx.

National Cooperative Law Center. 2015. "The Characteristics of Housing Cooperatives." Retrieved August 8, 2015. http://nationalcooperativelawcenter.com/what-is-a-housing-cooperative/the-characteristics-of-housing-cooperatives/.

National Employment Law Project. 2015. *City Minimum Wage Laws: Recent Trends and Economic Evidence*. Retrieved September 1, 2015. www.nelp.org/content/uploads/City-Minimum-Wage-Laws-Recent-Trends-Economic-Evidence.pdf.

Nonprofit Housing Association of Northern California. 2007. *Affordable by Choice: Trends in California Inclusionary Housing Programs*. San Francisco, CA: NPH.

Olsen, Edgar O. 2003. "Housing Programs for Low-Income Households." In R. A. Moffitt, ed., *Means-Tested Transfer Programs in the United States*. Chicago, IL: University of Chicago Press.

O'Regan, Katherine M. and Quigley, John M. 2000. "Federal Policy and the Rise of Nonprofit Housing Developers." *Journal of Housing Research* 11(2): 297–317.

Orlebeke, Charles J. 2000. "The Evolution of Low-Income Housing Policy, 1949 to 1999." *Housing Policy Debate* 11(2): 489–520.

Quigley, John M. and Raphael, Steven. 2004. "Is Housing Unaffordable? Why Isn't It More Affordable?" *Journal of Economic Perspectives* 18(1): 191–214.

Quigley, John M. and Rosenthal, Larry A. 2005. "The Effects of Land Use Regulation on the Price of Housing: What Do We Know? What Can We Learn?" *Cityscape* 8(1): 69–138.

Radford, Gail. 1996. *Modern Housing for America: Policy Struggles in the New Deal Era*. Chicago, IL: University of Chicago Press.

Radford, Gail. 2000. "The Federal Government and Housing during the Great Depression." In J. F. Bauman, R. Biles, and K. M. Szylvian, eds, *From Tenements to the Taylor Homes: In Search of an Urban Housing Policy in Twentieth-Century America*, pp. 102–120. University Park, PA: Pennsylvania State University Press.

Savage, Howard A. 2009. *Who Could Afford to Buy a Home in 2004?* Census Housing Reports H21/09-1, Washington, DC.

Schill, Michael H. 2005. "Regulations and Housing Development: What We Know." *Cityscape: A Journal of Policy Development and Research* 8(1): 5–19.

Schuetz, Jenny, Meltzer, Rachel, and Been, Vicki. 2011. "Silver Bullet or Trojan Horse? The Effects of Inclusionary Zoning on Local Housing Markets in the United States." *Urban Studies* 48(2): 297–329.

Schwartz, Alex F. 2015. *Housing Policy in the United States*, third edition. New York, NY: Routledge.

Schwartz, Mary and Wilson, Ellen. 2007. *Who Can Afford to Live in a Home? A Look at Data from the 2006 American Community Survey.* Washington, DC: U.S. Census Bureau.

Steffen, Barry L., Carter, George R., Martin, Marge, Pelletiere, Danilo, Vandenbroucke, David A., and Yao, Yunn-Gann David. 2015. *Worst Case Housing Needs 2015 Report to Congress.* Washington, DC: U.S. Department of Housing and Urban Development.

Stegman, Michael A. 1999. *State and Local Housing Programs: A Rich Tapestry.* Washington, DC: Urban Land Institute.

Stegman, Michael A., Quercia, Roberto G., and McCarthy, George W. 2000. "Housing America's Working Families." *New Century Housing* 1(1). The Center for Housing Policy: 1–48.

Stone, Michael E. 2006. "Housing Affordability: One-Third of a Nation Shelter-Poor." In R. G. Bratt, M. E. Stone, and C. Hartman, eds, *A Right to Housing: Foundation for a New Social Agenda*, pp. 38–60. Philadelphia, PA: Temple University Press.

Tighe, J. Rosie and Mueller, Elizabeth. 2013. *The Affordable Housing Reader.* New York, NY: Routledge.

Tilly, Chris. 2006. "The Economic Environment of Housing: Income Inequality and Insecurity." In R. G. Bratt, M. E. Stone, and C. Hartman, eds, *A Right to Housing: Foundation for a New Social Agenda*, pp. 20–37. Philadelphia, PA: Temple University Press.

Urban Institute. 2012. "Expanding Housing Opportunities through Inclusionary Zoning: Lessons from Two Counties." Washington, DC: U.S. Department of Housing and Urban Development.

U.S. Census Bureau. 2015a. "American Housing Survey 2013 National Summary Tables." Retrieved July 15, 2015. www.census.gov/programs-surveys/ahs/data/2013/national-summary-report-and-tables--ahs-2013.html.

U.S. Census Bureau. 2015b. "DP-1 – Profile of General Population and Housing Characteristics: 2010 for Mount Laurel Township, Burlington County, New Jersey." Retrieved August 6, 2015. http://factfinder.census.gov/faces/tableservices/jsf/pages/productview.xhtml?src=bkmk.

U.S. Census Bureau. 2015c. "DP03 Selected Economic Characteristics from the 2006–2010 American Community Survey 5-Year Estimates for Mount Laurel Township, Burlington County, New Jersey." Retrieved August 6, 2007. http://factfinder.census.gov/faces/tableservices/jsf/pages/productview.xhtml?src=bkmk.

U.S. Department of Housing and Urban Development. 1999. *Waiting in Vain: An Update on America's Rental Crisis.* Washington, DC: HUD.

U.S. Department of Housing and Urban Development. 2009. "American Housing Survey 2013 National Summary Tables": 2009. Washington, DC: U.S. Department of Housing and Urban Development Office of Policy Development and Research. Retrieved December 1, 2016. www.census.gov/prod/2011pubs/h150-09.pdf.

U.S. Department of Housing and Urban Development. 2015a. *CDBG Accomplishment Report FY 2005–2014.* Washington, DC: HUD.

U.S. Department of Housing and Urban Development. 2015b. "Low Income Housing Tax Credit Database." Retrieved August 5, 2015. www.huduser.org/portal/datasets/lihtc.html#data.

U.S. Median Home Value in Dollars, 2014. Social Explorer, www.socialexplorer.
com/395aadcc17/view (based on data from 2014 American Community Survey;
accessed December 1, 2016).

van Hoffman, Alexander. 2000. "A Study in Contradictions: The Origins and Legacy
of the Housing Act of 1949." *Housing Policy Debate* 11(2): 299–326.

Viveiros, Janet and Sturtevant, Lisa. 2014. *Housing Landscape 2014*. Washington, DC:
National Housing Conference.

Wallace, James E. 1995. "Financing Affordable Housing in the United States."
Housing Policy Debate 6: 785–814.

Western, Bruce and Rosenfeld, Jake. 2011. "Unions, Norms, and the Rise in U.S.
Wage Inequality." *American Sociological Review* 76(4): 513–537.

challenges faced when economic minority

CHAPTER 3

Housing Segregation and Discrimination

Fair Housing Act,
Segrega.

The summer of 2015 marked nearly fifty years since the passage of the landmark Fair Housing Act, which outlawed discrimination in housing sales and
rentals based on race, color, religion, sex, or national origin. That summer
the U.S. Department of Housing and Urban Development (HUD)
announced a final rule that requires any locality accepting HUD funds to
show evidence of "affirmatively furthering fair housing." This lesser-known
part of the Fair Housing Act—for "meaningful actions to be taken to over-
come the legacy of segregation, unequal treatment, and historic lack of access
to opportunity in housing"—had gone generally unenforced since the law's
passage (U.S. Department of Housing and Urban Development 2015a). Why,
in 2015, did the federal government take such a strong stand on housing
segregation, a half-century after housing discrimination was outlawed?

As recently as 2010, the average white American continues to live in a
neighborhood that is 75 percent white (Logan and Stults 2011). Moreover,
the number of Americans living in high-poverty neighborhoods is the highest
ever recorded, having increased dramatically since 2000 (Jargowsky 2015).
This chapter explains why these patterns continue, and why they are considered a problem in American society. It describes historical and contemporary patterns of racial and economic housing segregation in American
cities and regions. What are the major inequalities between social groups in
housing quality, availability, cost, and benefits in American society? How
have they changed over time? Why are they significant? How have these
inequalities been explained, and how might they be ameliorated? This
chapter considers various explanations for these trends and examines the

core questions

policies and practices that contribute to them. It also critically reviews policies that have attempted to address these problems.

Contemporary Residential Segregation

Examining the scope, dynamics, causes, and consequences of discrimination and segregation in the housing market is central to understanding both contemporary housing issues and the dynamics of contemporary social inequalities. Persistent segregation in the housing market ensures that the personal and social benefits of adequate, safe, and affordable housing are not distributed equally to U.S. households. Racial residential segregation and the segregation of the poor in the vast majority of American cities and regions result in a host of negative social consequences. Segregation affects the ability of individuals to build wealth and maintain good health. It decreases access to educational opportunities, job prospects, and conventional financial services, and it increases concentrated poverty and the risk of incarceration (Carr and Kutty 2008; Hartman and Squires 2010; Massey and Denton 1993). Thus, inequalities generated or reinforced through the housing market result in a vast array of negative individual and social consequences.

Racial Segregation

While there are certainly exceptional places, racialized groups continue to live in highly segregated areas in the vast majority of American metropolises. Generally, white and Asian Americans live in overwhelmingly white neighborhoods, while Black and Hispanic/Latino households tend to live in considerably less white communities. In 2010, the typical white American lived in a neighborhood that was 77 percent white, 8 percent Black, 10 percent Hispanic/Latino, and 4 percent Asian. In contrast, the typical Black American lived in a neighborhood that was 56 percent white, 24 percent Black, 14 percent Hispanic/Latino, and 4 percent Asian. The typical Hispanic/Latino American lived in a neighborhood that was 62 percent white, 13 percent Black, 20 percent Latino, and 4 percent Asian, while the typical Asian American lived in a neighborhood that was 70 percent white, 10 percent Black, 12 percent Hispanic/Latino, and 7 percent Asian (see Figure 3.1).

These trends have only marginally improved over time. The segregation of Black Americans, in particular, has declined nationwide in the past thirty years: Black households live in less segregated communities in 2010 than they did in 1980, in general (see Figure 3.2). A typical measure of residential segregation is the dissimilarity index, which measures the percentage of people of a racial/ethnic group in a place that would need to move to achieve integration. Dissimilarity indices show that white/Black segregation decreased by about 14 percent from 1990 to 2010, as did Black/Latino segregation

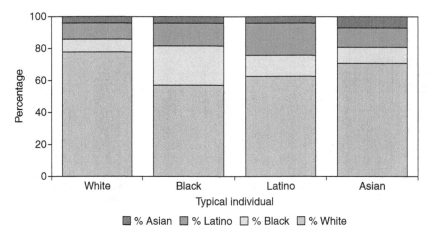

Figure 3.1 Average neighborhood racial composition in the U.S. by race/ethnicity

Source: Brown University, U.S. 2010 American Communities Project.

(–15 percent), and Black/Asian segregation (–15.6 percent). Segregation of Asian Americans has stayed roughly constant, with the exception of Black/Asian segregation. White/Latino segregation has also stayed relatively constant over the past thirty years, increasing slightly in recent years.

Importantly, these trends do not simply reflect racialized groups' class status. Affluent minority households remain largely segregated from affluent white households (Iceland and Wilkes 2006; Jargowsky 2014). And poor Black and Latino households live in neighborhoods with considerably higher poverty rates than do poor whites (Squires and Kubrin 2006). The worst urban conditions in which whites reside are considerably better than the average conditions of Black communities (Sampson and Wilson 1995).

Economic Segregation

As well as being segregated by race, Americans are also segregated by class—education, occupation, and income—both within and between regions. Some metropolises attract a larger share of the wealthy and highly educated, particularly those with booming knowledge and finance-based economies such as the San Francisco Bay Area. Others remain largely populated by the middle and working classes. But stark class segregation remains within all cities and regions.

While racial residential segregation has largely remained steady or declined slightly over the last thirty years, economic segregation has worsened. As of 2013, 14.5 percent of Americans live in poverty, and income inequality has increased dramatically over the past thirty years (DeNavas-Walt and Proctor

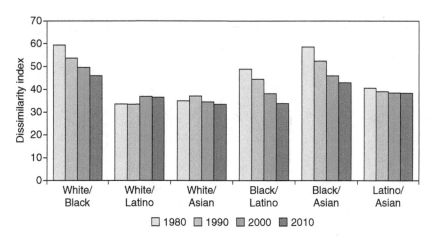

Figure 3.2 Residential segregation of racial/ethnic groups 1980–2010

Source: Brown University, U.S. 2010 American Communities Project.

2014). The striking rise in income inequality is spatially represented in the geography of American housing. During the last thirty years, the segregation of the wealthy and the poor rose in 90 percent of America's thirty largest metropolitan areas (Taylor and Fry 2012). The poor have become increasingly concentrated in poor neighborhoods: the percentage of poor families in poor neighborhoods doubled nationwide between 1970 and 2009 (Bischoff and Reardon 2013). Concentrated poverty also grew fastest between 2000 and 2009 in neighborhoods with more multifamily housing, rentals, older housing, higher housing-cost burden, and larger Black and Latino populations (Pendall *et al.* 2014).

The poor are most severely segregated in the Midwestern and Northeast regions of the U.S., particularly in cities like Milwaukee, Hartford, Philadelphia, Cleveland, Detroit, New York, Buffalo, Denver, Baltimore, and Memphis, where deindustrialization has impacted employment and infrastructure severely and gentrification has not taken hold (Florida and Mellender 2015). Many of the cities with the highest levels of poverty segregation are college towns, but income segregation tends to be more severe in larger, denser metropolises and in regions with larger Black populations (Florida and Mellender 2015).

People are also segregated by education and occupation. People with low levels of education tend to be more segregated in larger, denser regions and in places with higher housing costs, but less segregated in places with more blue-collar jobs. Occupational segregation is most severe in regions that are larger, denser, wealthier, more expensive, politically liberal, and racially diverse. It is also particularly severe in places with strong knowledge economies and strong public transit systems. For example, members of the affluent "creative class" tend to live near central business districts, public transit hubs, universities and other educational institutions, and coastlines and waterfronts. Places with more blue-collar employment opportunities and larger working classes tend to be less economically segregated in general (Florida *et al.* 2014). Large metropolises with the highest levels of overall economic segregation include Austin, Columbus, San Antonio, Houston, Los Angeles, New York, Dallas, Philadelphia, Chicago, and Memphis.

Housing segregation in the U.S. reflects enduring racial and class inequalities and discrimination. The extent to which discrimination against other groups—families with children, people with disabilities, the LGBTQ community—results in segregation is less researched and less well understood (for important examples, see Turner *et al.* 2005; Friedman *et al.* 2013).

Consequences of Residential Segregation

These patterns—the result of a combination of individual preferences, public policies, and patterned practices of developers, home sellers, buyers, lenders, real estate professionals, and landlords—have serious social consequences. Residential segregation constrains opportunities for upward socioeconomic mobility for residents of predominantly Black and Latino neighborhoods, while enhancing opportunities for whites (Ellen *et al.* 2016). Discrimination and constrained choice in the housing market contribute to and perpetuate other social inequalities around wealth, education, health, crime, and employment.

Historically, housing has been a cornerstone of opportunity in the United States, providing important means of upward mobility by enabling households to build wealth in the form of home equity. Persistent patterns of residential segregation and housing and lending discrimination, however, have hindered homeownership and thwarted its benefits for people of color, as is discussed at length later in this chapter. Homeownership rates remain highest for whites, at nearly 70 percent nationwide, while the homeownership rates of Blacks, Latinos, and all other racial minorities trail them at 43 percent, 46 percent, and 55 percent, respectively (U.S. Census Bureau 2014). Black and Latino Americans in particular are less likely to get mortgages and favorable interest rates, and their homes do not appreciate at the same rates as those of whites (Flippen 2001; Krivo and Kaufman 2004; Ross and Yinger 2002). Homes owned by Blacks and Latinos are worth less on average, even as these groups tend to have a much larger share of their household wealth in their homes (Alba and Logan 1993; Charles 2006; Ellen 2000; Flippen 2004; Krivo and Kaufman 2004; Oliver and Shapiro 2006). This disparity exists across all ranges of income and property value (Flippen 2004). Furthermore, Black and Latino homeowners often live in lower-income, more dangerous neighborhoods with worse schools than the neighborhoods of their white counterparts, regardless of income and education (Logan 2002; Oliver and Shapiro 2006; Pattillo 2007; Pattillo-McCoy 1999). Black homeowners are actually penalized for homeownership: they reside in neighborhoods that are poorer and more segregated than their renting counterparts (Charles 2003).

Because wealth status is largely inherited, racially unequal property values produced through housing segregation persist from generation to generation. Home equity can be used as a "transformative asset" (Shapiro 2004) or inherited wealth that can be used to provide households tools of upward mobility beyond their own achievements. Those assets can be exchanged for other life-sustaining resources, such as college educations, down payments for children's first homes, and health care. Thus, racial and class inequalities in the housing market contribute to unequal wealth and assets that are passed down through generations. African Americans of all class statuses have historically had particularly limited access to opportunities for wealth building through inheritance and investment opportunities (particularly in small businesses), so these patterns are especially deleterious (Oliver and Shapiro 2006).

 Housing segregation also limits other life-sustaining opportunities, such as health care, education, and employment. Neighborhood segregation affects health status because it disproportionately exposes residents to violent crime, poor public services, and "food deserts," and contributes to disparate treatment in health care settings and disparities in levels of care provided by hospitals and clinics (Acevedo-Garcia et al. 2008; Williams and Collins 1995). The American system of housing segregation also ensures that people of color and poor people will bear the brunt of industrial pollution and other environmental hazards (Bullard 1990). Indeed, neighborhood racial composition is the single most salient factor in predicting the location of waste facilities. By the late 1980s, a staggering 60 percent of African Americans and Latinos lived in communities with toxic waste sites (United Church of Christ 1987). In the early 1980s, while African Americans made up 20 percent of the Southeast U.S., 75 percent of commercial landfills in the southeast U.S. were in predominantly Black neighborhoods (U.S. General Accounting Office 1983).

Housing segregation also reinforces inequity in educational opportunities. The system of relying on property taxes to fund public education ensures educational inequity that is directly tied to inequalities in home values in segregated neighborhoods (Squires and Kubrin 2006). Furthermore, because schools are generally zoned, their demographic composition mirrors that of the surrounding neighborhood: segregated neighborhoods beget segregated schools. Residential segregation also influences employment opportunities. In recent history, employment opportunities were concentrated in suburban communities, making it difficult for poor central city residents who relied heavily on public transportation to access them. Furthermore, discrimination based on neighborhood residence results in barring many poor, particularly Black urban residents from well-paying jobs (Wilson 1996).

Racial and class segregation in housing also increases exposure to social harms. In predominantly Black and Latino neighborhoods, bank branches are less common than check-cashing outlets, pawnshops, and other high-cost financial institutions. As a result, residents of segregated Black and Latino neighborhoods pay higher fees and have fewer opportunities for investment of income (Squires and Kubrin 2006). Furthermore, residents of low-income and predominantly Black and Latino neighborhoods are disproportionately exposed to violent crime and the criminal justice system, including higher rates of incarceration for the same or similar crimes committed in more affluent communities. Mauer (2010) illustrates how police departments have both under- and over-policed segregated neighborhoods, most recently culminating in controversial programs like "stop, question, and frisk" in predominantly poor and Black neighborhoods in New York and Chicago. In addition, re-entry programs for previously incarcerated individuals are also limited in their ability to prevent recidivism because the segregated neighborhoods many former prisoners return to have few job prospects, under-served educational institutions, few resources for those with substance abuse and mental health issues, and high levels of violence and criminal activity (Miller 2014).

Thus, racial and class segregation in housing has significant social consequences and contribute to a whole host of seemingly unrelated social inequalities. These patterns have deep historical roots in past social policies and practices.

The History of Residential Segregation in the U.S.

Residential segregation has not always existed in its present form, but it is heavily influenced by past patterns. Housing segregation as we know it emerged primarily in the post-World War II period, but its foundations were laid well before then. Because cities were smaller, to facilitate walking during the colonial and industrial periods of the eighteenth and nineteenth centuries, households lived close to one another. Zoning did not yet exist; residential, industrial, and commercial areas were in close proximity, often existing within yards of each other (Chudacoff et al. 2015 [1981]). In many cities, some neighborhoods were relatively mixed in terms of race and ethnicity: many white families and families of color lived within close proximity of each other (Borchert 1980). However, this "integration" was anything but; in Washington DC, for example, many neighborhoods had nearly equal proportions of white and Black residents, but white residents lived almost exclusively on the exterior of blocks while Black households resided in interior alleyways (Borchert 1980).

Immigration during the industrial period of the late 1800s and early 1900s changed the social geography of American cities, particularly in the East and Midwest. Largely barred from native-born white communities, immigrants formed ethnic enclaves with shared national origin, languages, and customs. Racist ideas about the Irish, Italians, Poles, Jews, and other ethnic groups were popular during this era, and the reaction against such groups was so vehement that immigrant policy was eventually altered to prevent many of those groups from immigrating to the U.S. Immigrants faced a severely limited housing market, and overcrowded tenements lined the streets of ethnic enclaves in cities nationwide (Chudacoff *et al.* 2015 [1981]).

Zoning emerged in American cities in the late nineteenth century and was common in most metropolises by 1920, designating certain districts for industrial, commercial, and residential activities. Single-family and multi-family residences were zoned in separate spaces, effectively barring economic and racial integration. Restrictive covenants—written and oral agreements among whites to sell or rent only to other whites—also increasingly constrained racial and ethnic groups to particular neighborhoods, becoming illegal only in 1948.

The New Deal ushered in a new set of housing policies and practices that would forever change the shape of the American metropolis. The Great Depression devastated the American housing market and employment opportunities for Americans. The federal government responded with a "two-tier" housing policy: a set of policies designed to benefit the working and middle classes and another set to benefit the poor (Radford 1996). Each of these strands of policy worked both to institutionalize existing patterns of racial and economic segregation and to create new ones.

In an effort to support the housing and building industries and to provide economic aid to the working and middle classes, the federal government instituted the Home Owners Loan Corporation (HOLC) and Federal Housing Administration (FHA) to insure newly developed thirty-year, low-cost, self-amortizing mortgage loans to ordinary working Americans and to set industry standards for mortgage lending. The HOLC and FHA, responsible for insuring millions of home mortgages in the New Deal and postwar periods, helped to swell the American middle class by encouraging home-ownership. The system operated, however, by funneling money and credit into new suburban white neighborhoods at the detriment of older, urban, integrated, and predominantly Black neighborhoods.

The federal government viewed predominantly nonwhite neighborhoods, diverse neighborhoods, older neighborhoods, and neighborhoods that integrated single-family and multifamily housing stock as inherently unstable and risky. The federal government denied mortgage insurance—thus setting industry standards for mortgages more generally—to these communities, as well as to projects designed to house racial minorities in rental housing and to upgrading old structures, a tactic called redlining (Jackson 1985).

New Deal housing programs institutionalized viewing racial differences through a lens of property values, on the basis that people of color, old housing, and rental housing threatened property values. As a result, white neighborhoods, particularly newly developed suburban communities outside city limits, benefited from generous financial backing by the federal government, while older, more racially and economically diverse urban communities struggled to garner investment. The real estate and lending industries followed the federal government's lead, considering redlined neighborhoods too risky for credit, directly contributing to an intense domino effect of disinvestment in redlined neighborhoods. *sum:* ①

At the same time that one arm of the federal government worked to underwrite the growth of (white) suburbia, another arm worked to construct ② and manage housing for America's poor. The nation's first public housing projects were constructed during the New Deal era, and decisions regarding their geographic placement and residential policies created unprecedented new patterns of residential segregation. The massive migration of both African Americans from the South and immigrants to the nation's cities prior to and during the New Deal era contributed to a chronic housing shortage in neighborhoods where they settled. The private housing market failed to provide low-income housing to meet increasing demand, and the housing stock that did exist was poorly maintained. Thus, through the newly established United States Housing Authority (USHA) in 1937, the federal government began to construct, finance, and manage public housing for the poor.

Initially, public housing was designed to facilitate upward social mobility. *intent* Relatively high income limits were adopted to avoid concentrating the very poor together, so that households of varying incomes within the set of qualifying incomes would be housed next to one another. Housing projects were located near jobs to facilitate employment of residents. They were also designed to house the thousands of people (primarily African Americans) displaced by burgeoning publicly funded urban renewal projects—the redevelopment of existing slums on valuable inner-city land for business uses. *unintended*

However, public housing policy resulted in more entrenched patterns of *consequence* residential segregation. Restrictions built into the Housing Act of 1937 severely limited the possibilities of local public housing programs, dictating how localities could build public housing and for whom. And the federal government left the implementation of public housing policy to local municipalities, who could refuse to construct public housing, maintain residential segregation, and use discriminatory tenant selection policies. In cities such as Detroit and Chicago, city officials responded to pressure from local civic organizations, real estate professionals, and homeowners by encouraging and approving plans to concentrate public housing projects inside city limits—especially in disadvantaged communities—rather than in burgeoning suburban communities (Hirsch 1983; Jackson 1985). New public housing was also concentrated on vacant, outlying land to keep costs down, resulting in new islands of poverty in outlying urban areas far from the central city districts where many residents had ties to former neighborhoods and to their jobs. Finally, and most importantly, federal guidelines explicitly called for white housing projects and Black housing projects, with projects located according to existing neighborhood racial composition. This combination— of building on existing slums, and of creating new pockets of segregated housing projects—resulted in a massive concentration of Black people in existing Black enclaves and on outlying, isolated land, as well as the maintenance of racial boundaries within neighborhoods.

New public housing construction also spurred further migration of the middle and working classes of means from urban communities to the suburbs. Suburban land was cheaper, housing newer, and loans widely available. Households with the means left cities in droves for the idyllic suburban dream, leaving the poor and people of color increasingly isolated in the urban core. Whites in particular hoped to leave behind the crowded cities that housed large numbers of racial and ethnic minorities, a trend known as white flight.

By 1970, after two decades of urban renewal and white flight, public housing projects in most large cities had become Black reservations, highly segregated from the rest of society and characterized by extreme social isolation. The replacement of low-density slums with high-density towers of poor families also reduced the class diversity of the ghetto and brought about a geographic concentration of poverty that was previously unimaginable. This new segregation of Blacks—in economic as well as social terms—was the direct result of an unprecedented collaboration between local and national government (Massey and Denton 1993: 57).

New suburban communities largely barred Black households, leaving working and middle-class African Americans confined to older urban communities, often near public housing, and to a limited selection of new suburbs. Within these markets they faced new mechanisms of discrimination. Real estate professionals engaged in racial steering, whereby white households are shown only homes in white neighborhoods and nonwhite buyers are directed to nonwhite neighborhoods. This practice was meant to protect property values in white communities and served to limit the housing market available to people of color. Real estate professionals also engaged in blockbusting, a tactic that played into white fears about neighborhood racial composition and property values. Real estate agents identified blocks that white households were vacating and sold those homes to a few Black families. They then aroused fear in the remaining white households, arguing convincingly that if they did not sell, their homes would be worth much less. Whites sold at a discount, and agents then dramatically raised the prices for new Black homebuyers. This practice led to more entrenched fears about race and property values and inflated housing costs for racial and ethnic minorities.

A small group of exceptional real estate developers and builders saw racial and ethnic minorities as an untapped market and sold suburban homes to middle-class and affluent minorities. African Americans bought homes in Ronek Park, Roosevelt, Freeport, Hempstead, and other parts of Long Island, NY, for example (Baxandall and Ewen 2000). As African Americans accessed the suburban dream, white households fled these suburban communities in droves in the fear that their suburban investments would be worth nothing with neighbors of color, thereby maintaining the color line. *Blacks came + whites left*

The segregative consequences of federal housing policies, white flight, racial steering, and blockbusting were made more severe with the simultaneous large-scale shifts in the American economy. In the post-World War II period, the American economy began a long and gradual process of deindustrialization: the transformation of the American economy from a manufacturing to a service-based economy. This shift led to the flight of stable, relatively well-paying jobs from inner cities to other regions of the country with corporate-friendly tax structures and union laws and to other countries, leaving many urban residents without opportunities for gainful employment. Pittsburgh, for example, lost 24 percent of its jobs and 37 percent of its population between 1940 and 1980 (Sugrue 1993). In addition, the failure of urban schools to prepare inner-city children sufficiently for work in the postindustrial economy contributed to their inability to find meaningful, well-paying work (Wilson 1978; 1987; 1996).

The disappearance of manufacturing jobs severely affected the working classes, but researchers show that the group most negatively impacted by deindustrialization was Black men. Deindustrialization began at the precise time at which massive numbers of African Americans left the Jim Crow-era south for manufacturing opportunities in cities (Sugrue 1993; Wilson 1996). A combination of persistent employment discrimination, technological advancement, and general urban economic decline contributed to vastly limited employment opportunities for Black men. These conditions led to large-scale deproletarianization: the process by which large numbers of poor people became nearly completely unattached from the formal labor market, and a class of persistently poor people emerged in America. Prior to deindustrialization, individuals and households were more apt to cycle in and out of poverty over a lifetime. Deindustrialization created a class of persistently poor (Sugrue 1993).

It was not until large-scale deindustrialization impacted American cities and regions in this post-World War II period that the urban poor as a class became more concentrated and segregated within particular urban neighborhoods (Sugrue 1993). By the late 1960s, those who could afford to had left

American cities in droves, lured by the dream of suburbia and leaving behind the increasingly concentrated poor in their stead. The loss of industry and population contributed to fiscal crises of metropolises nationwide, as cities struggled to provide services to an increasingly needy population.

Despite the passage of a slew of civil rights legislation that outlawed discriminatory practices like redlining and racial steering, including the Fair Housing Act, the Home Mortgage Disclosure Act, and the Community Reinvestment Act, American cities remained highly segregated throughout the 1980s, and urban neighborhoods suffered from severe disinvestment and neglect. In addition, as the Black middle class benefited from civil rights laws, they increasingly self-segregated—to the extent that they could in a limited housing market—from the Black poor, adding another dimension to the history of racial and economic segregation in the American metropolis (Wilson 1987).

Debating the Causes of Residential Segregation

Current patterns of racial and economic residential segregation have been partially inherited from and influenced by the past, but are not simply a relic of history. Why does residential segregation remain, despite the passage of civil rights laws outlawing discrimination in housing and lending? How is it maintained and reproduced? Researchers in the last thirty years have debated the factors responsible for contemporary patterns of residential segregation. One argument is that residential segregation is primarily the geographic expression of economic or class inequality and reflective of individual residential choices constrained only by income and wealth. Another school of thought posits that housing segregation is the product of distinct and ongoing patterns of racial discrimination.

Spatial Assimilation Theory *choice/income*

Spatial assimilation theory emphasizes the influence of class on residential outcomes. It posits that residential segregation is the result of socioeconomic inequality: people live where they can afford, and income and wealth inequality translate into economic segregation. Similarly, racial/ethnic segregation results from the different economic positions that racial/ethnic groups hold (Charles 2003). From this perspective, immigrants often first occupy enclaves—spatially and culturally distinct spaces—but as households improve their socioeconomic standing, they then move to more integrated, higher-status communities. Similarly, the residential segregation of African Americans is largely the result of employment discrimination. Job prospects are more limited for African Americans than for whites, translating into lower incomes and higher poverty rates. Their housing choices are thus constrained by their relative class status.

Evidence suggests that spatial assimilation occurs among Asian Americans and Latinos, although the extent varies considerably across cities and regions (Alba and Logan 1993; Pais *et al.* 2012). Asians and Latinos are less segregated from whites than Blacks, and upward socioeconomic mobility tends to translate into better-quality and less-segregated neighborhoods (Logan and Alba 1993; Woldoff and Ovadia 2009). Middle-class African Americans, however, live in more segregated communities than their white counterparts (Alba *et al.* 2000), and Black middle-class communities are far more likely to border poor neighborhoods than white middle-class neighborhoods (Adelman 2005; Pattillo-McCoy 1999).

Place Stratification Theory = *Racism*

The other major strand of theory that attempts to account for residential segregation is place stratification theory, which highlights the roles of racism and discrimination in the housing market. This perspective maintains that racist attitudes of individual homebuyers and discrimination on the part of real estate industry professionals limit the residential options of racialized groups.

Some researchers argue that individual prejudices primarily account for residential segregation. In general, whites prefer predominantly white neighborhoods while African Americans prefer 50:50 integration, neighborhoods in which they are the slight majority, or racially mixed communities (Emerson *et al.* 2001; Farley and Frey 1994; Farley *et al.* 1997; Charles 2000, 2003, 2006; Krysan and Farley 2002). A more recent study of Houston suggests that only whites seem to consider race in neighborhood choice: other racial and ethnic groups have no significant preferences (Lewis *et al.* 2011). White demand for neighborhoods wanes with increasing minority populations, even in middle- and upper-class neighborhoods with relatively low crime rates (Charles 2006; see also Ellen 2000).

While some whites clearly object to having Black neighbors, according to Ellen, some white households do not. Instead, "race matters … as a signal of neighborhood quality" (Ellen 2000: 48). Residential segregation is a function of race-based neighborhood stereotyping, where "white avoidance of racially mixed neighborhoods is rooted primarily in certain negative race-based stereotypes that whites hold about the fundamental quality of such neighborhoods—and not on any categorical unwillingness to live among Black households" (Ellen 2000: 35). In other words, Black neighbors and neighborhoods are associated with decreased neighborhood quality, including poorer schools and higher crime rates.

Other research shows that discrimination occurs beyond individuals making residential choices, documenting racial discrimination in the mortgage, insurance, and real estate sectors, primarily through housing audits

(Ross and Yinger 2002; Squires 1994; Squires and O'Connor 2001). Paired testing studies that compare otherwise identical applicants show that Black and Latino home seekers are shown fewer units, given less help navigating financing options, and steered to neighborhoods with large Black and Latino populations (Turner *et al.* 2013). Black and Latino home seekers learn about 25 percent fewer units than their white counterparts with comparable characteristics. Whites are also more likely to receive follow-up calls and special rental incentives like a month's free rent and reduced security deposits, while racial/ethnic minorities are more likely to wait longer to hear from brokers and have their housing needs overlooked but their incomes overemphasized (Turner *et al.* 2013). Black home seekers are steered to predominantly Black neighborhoods 40 percent of the time and Latinos 28 percent of the time, and whites are more likely to hear negative things about integrated neighborhoods. While racial steering is technically illegal, it is often practiced in marketing: units in Black neighborhoods are not advertised as often or as widely (Turner *et al.* 2013).

Parallel practices also prevail in the mortgage-lending industry. Controlling for credit and risk, Blacks and Latinos are more likely than comparable whites to be denied a conventional home loan (Ross and Yinger 2002). Blacks and Latinos are more likely to receive subprime loans—higher-cost loans and loans with characteristics that increase default risk—than their similarly positioned white counterparts, even after taking into account credit scores (Avery *et al.* 2006, 2007; Barr *et al.* 2011; Bocian *et al.* 2011; Calem *et al.* 2004). Recent evidence shows rampant racial discrimination in mortgage lending leading up to the recent housing crisis (Massey *et al.* 2016).

Other discriminatory tactics abound in the housing market. It is legal to discriminate based on source of income, for example, except where localities have strengthened laws against it. It is also legal to discriminate against the formerly incarcerated. Furthermore, exclusionary zoning—guidelines for minimum lot sizes and maximum density requirements—allow localities to prohibit the construction of multifamily buildings, effectively segregating many renters from homeowners (Pendall 2000). Density zoning is among—if not the—most significant structural barrier to racial and economic integration in the U.S. (Massey *et al.* 2013; Rothwell 2011; Rothwell and Massey 2009, 2010). Private homeowner associations also contribute to greater racial residential segregation (Meltzer 2013). Discrimination built into federal low-income housing policy also contributes to residential segregation. The Low-Income Housing Tax Credit—the primary means by which low-income housing is developed in the U.S.—incentivizes building low-income housing in poor neighborhoods and is highly concentrated in struggling communities (Oakley 2008; Schwartz 2015).

Most scholars agree that spatial assimilation—the process by which increasing social status translates into higher-quality neighborhoods—best explains the residential patterns of Asians and to some extent Latinos, while place stratification—the process by which racism and discrimination hinders residential mobility—best explains the residential patterns of African Americans and some Latinos (see, for example, Alba and Logan 1993).

Policy Responses to Residential Segregation

A set of policies developed in the last forty years attempts to address segregation and discrimination in both housing policy and in the private housing market. In general, policies aimed at easing residential segregation are designed to support the private housing market and fall into four basic strands: those that attempt to disperse the poor from high-poverty neighborhoods into less poor communities (deconcentration policies); those that attempt to make high-poverty or highly segregated communities more attractive to a wider variety of potential residents (revitalization policies); those that encourage affluent communities with more amenities to include a fair share of affordable housing in their districts (fair share policies); and those that further fair housing law (fair housing policies). Programs in each of these categories have had varying degrees of success.

Deconcentration Policies

Federal low-income housing policy has emphasized poverty deconcentration since the 1970s. The infamous high-rise, superblock public housing projects like Pruitt-Igoe in St Louis and Cabrini-Green in Chicago became synonymous with a whole host of social problems like crime, drug use, teenage pregnancy, and other so-called social dysfunctions. From the 1970s, deconcentrating the poor—and to a much smaller extent, racial minorities—became the focus of housing policy, supported by the idea that neighborhood contexts impact residents' life chances.

Deconcentration programs took two forms: scattering low-income housing sites; and scattering low-income households across metropolitan areas to facilitate better social integration. The first set of programs centered on scattering federally subsidized low-income housing across metropolitan areas rather than concentrating low-income housing in a few neighborhoods as had been done in the past. Scatter-site housing faced great neighborhood opposition in communities all over the country and remained relatively limited in scope.

The second set of programs falls under the general umbrella of mobility programs. Rental vouchers (sometimes called Section 8 vouchers) are the primary means of deconcentrating those who qualify for low-income housing subsidies. In theory, they allow low-income households to choose where they want to live, with the federal government subsidizing a portion of their rent.

Rather than being confined to neighborhoods where public housing is located, as in the past, rental vouchers enable the dispersal of poor households in metropolitan areas. Vouchers theoretically enable poor households to access the amenities of safer, less distressed communities than those typically surrounding public housing.

Qualifying incomes for housing vouchers have ranged widely over time; currently, households with incomes in the fortieth percentile or below in each metropolitan area—50 percent in high-cost markets—qualify for rental voucher assistance. Households pay 30 percent of their income toward the rent of their home, and the federal government covers the difference between their contribution and the fair market rent of the unit. Fair market rents vary dramatically across the U.S. In San Antonio-New Braunfels, TX, vouchers will cover rents up to $870 a month for a two-bedroom apartment; in San Francisco, CA, vouchers will cover rents up to $1,795.

In some respects, vouchers have been more successful than public housing. Households do have more residential choices: voucher recipients reside in 88 percent of the nation's neighborhoods, whereas public housing is located in only 8 percent of American neighborhoods (McClure *et al.* 2012). Compared to public housing residents, voucher recipients generally live in neighborhoods with less poverty and slightly less racial segregation (Schwartz 2015). Despite offering more residential choice, evidence suggests that vouchers have been less successful by other important measures. They have not been particularly successful at ameliorating racial segregation. Most voucher holders reside in predominantly nonwhite neighborhoods and places with high poverty rates (Schwartz 2015). If vouchers offer households the chance to occupy any neighborhood of their choice, why would this be the case?

There are at least two reasons. Landlords and units must qualify for the voucher program—that is, they must not charge more than the federally mandated fair market rent for each metropolitan area, and they must agree to inspections that ensure the quality of the housing. Because it is a voluntary program for landlords, many choose not to take vouchers, limiting the supply of available housing for voucher recipients. Landlords have very little incentive to take housing vouchers in tight housing markets, for example, when they can successfully charge rents higher than the fair market value.

Another limiting factor is that voucher recipients can only rent from fair market rent units, effectively confining them to neighborhoods with relatively low rents, especially in metropolitan areas with tight housing markets. Very low-income households (earning less than 30 percent of the area's median income) must receive at least 75 percent of housing vouchers. The average annual income of voucher holders was $12,800 in 2013, compared to the U.S. median income of $51,939. In practice, then, the voucher program often concentrates the poorest of the poor in relatively few neighborhoods.

To help address these shortcomings of housing vouchers and facilitate economic and racial integration of low-income households, other mobility programs combine housing vouchers with services such as counseling and landlord recruitment, though these are generally fairly limited in scope. Two local programs in Minneapolis and Chicago are the result of housing discrimination lawsuits brought against the respective public housing agencies for concentrating public housing in predominantly African American and poor communities.

Spurred by a 1976 court decision, Chicago's Gautreaux Program provided housing vouchers and individual housing counseling to 7,100 African Americans who qualified for public housing to find rental accommodation in predominantly white communities, particularly in the Chicago suburbs, through 1998 (Rosenbaum 1995). A similar lawsuit prompted the creation of the Special Mobility Program, a similar mobility program in Minneapolis (Goetz 2003). Modeled after the Gautreaux Program and established in 1992, the federal Moving to Opportunity program provided a combination of housing vouchers and counseling to place households that qualified for public housing in neighborhoods with low poverty rates in Baltimore, Chicago, Los Angeles, New York, and Boston. Importantly, however, the Moving to Opportunity program differed from Gautreaux in that it did not aim to facilitate racial—only economic—segregation and included no requirements that participants find housing in suburban communities.

These mobility programs have had mixed success. They have unquestionably helped households move to neighborhoods with lower poverty rates, and the Gautreaux and Special Mobility programs enabled housing voucher families to access white-majority communities with higher median incomes (Schwartz 2015). However, Moving to Opportunity, the largest and most comprehensive of the mobility programs, shows very mixed results. On one hand, program participants reported feeling safer, much happier with their housing, and enjoying generally higher levels of wellbeing than voucher recipients who did not take part in the program. On the other hand, Moving to Opportunity participants show no significant improvements in employment, education, or income, and generally moved to predominantly Black neighborhoods (Briggs *et al.* 2010; Sanbonmatsu *et al.* 2011; Schwartz 2015).

Revitalization Policies

A second set of federal policies designed in part to remedy residential segregation attempts to revitalize distressed communities in order to attract higher-income households, theoretically resulting in better economic—and to some extent racial—integration. The best-known mixed-income development program is HOPE VI, a program that demolishes existing public housing, replacing it with low-density, mixed-use, mixed-income developments managed by private sector partners. Created in 1992, the program has awarded more than $6 billion to local housing authorities that demolished at least 150,000 public housing units between 1993 and 2005 (Castells 2010). Former residents are given vouchers for use in the private housing market, and are sometimes given priority for the low-income units once the project is rebuilt. Overall, however, about one in five former public housing residents returns to redeveloped mixed-income housing. The vast majority of former residents move to other racially segregated, poor communities (Clampet-Lundquist 2004; Goetz 2013; Kleit and Manzo 2006).

goal

These patterns have led some researchers to question whether HOPE VI has enabled the gentrification of urban communities while displacing the majority of the poor who rely on subsidized housing (Fraser *et al.* 2012). Only about 11 percent of former public housing residents return to HOPE VI developments, and only 30 percent receive vouchers to relocate in the private housing market. The vast majority end up in other public housing projects or lose housing assistance altogether (National Housing Law Project *et al.* 2002). While many of the former public housing residents who receive vouchers relocate to slightly less poor, safer neighborhoods, these places are as racially segregated as public housing (Oakley *et al.* 2013b). Questions remain about the overall impact mixed-income redevelopment has on the quality of life of poor households. Without dramatic changes in other social policies, the effect of fashioning mixed-income communities might simply result in gentrification, rather than the broader goals of social uplift that underlie deconcentration and revitalization programs (Bridge *et al.* 2011; Fraser *et al.* 2012; Oakley *et al.* 2013a).

Furthermore, there is a distinctly racial component to HOPE VI: the cities that have pursued demolishing and redeveloping public housing tend to have disproportionate numbers of Black residents in public housing (Goetz 2013). This is a troubling trend given the history of displacement countless Black communities faced in urban America under the original urban renewal and public housing programs (Fullilove 2004).

Without broader actions in the private market to meet the requirements of the Fair Housing Act, market-based initiatives like HOPE VI are at best limited in their impact on segregation and at worst reinforce and strengthen patterns of segregation.

Fair Share Policies

A third set of policies that address residential segregation compels typically middle-class and affluent localities to contribute their "fair share" of afford-able housing and often leads to better economic integration within regions. They include local inclusionary zoning mandates and incentives to developers to build affordable housing and mixed-income communities. These policies are discussed at length in Chapter 2. Regional tax sharing—sharing local taxes equally throughout metropolitan regions, addressing inequalities in revenue between cities and suburbs—can also be thought of as a fair share program in that it circumvents the fears among homeowners, particularly in affluent communities, that rental housing will lead to declining property values and thus tax revenue.

With the exception of the Gautreaux program, none of the policies discussed thus far explicitly address racial residential segregation. They favor class-based approaches that address the poor or poor neighborhoods. These policies address racial segregation only to the extent that the poor are disproportionately racial minorities. A final set of laws, however, explicitly aims to address racial discrimination and segregation in the U.S. housing market.

Fair Housing Policies

The Fair Housing Act of 1968, greatly strengthened by amendments in 1988, prohibits racial discrimination by real estate agents and other housing market professionals. It also aims to further racial integration in housing affirmatively. The Home Mortgage Disclosure Act of 1975 and Community Reinvestment Act of 1977 increased mortgage and insurance access to racial minorities. Recent legislation also aims to prevent predatory lending among minority communities. However, criticisms of fair housing enforcement abound. An estimated 0.75 percent of all instances of discrimination are reported, and of those, only about a third result in a legal remedy (National Commission on Fair Housing and Equal Opportunity 2008; Silverman and Patterson 2012). As the National Commission on Fair Housing and Equal Opportunity reports, "Literally millions of acts of rental, sales, lending, and insurance discrimination, racial and sexual harassment discrimination, and zoning and land use discrimination go virtually unchecked" (National Commission on Fair Housing and Equal Opportunity 2008).

Part of the problem with fair housing enforcement is that, until 2015, it was often left to state and local governments and nonprofit organizations; the federal government provided very little funding and guidance for uncovering discrimination or affirmatively furthering housing integration. For example, less than 1 percent of HUD's total budget is allocated to fair housing programs (U.S. Department of Housing and Urban Development 2015b). In addition, until 2015, HUD required much more proof than is necessary under the Fair Housing Act to issue charges of discrimination after reviewing complaints, and delays in fair housing investigations resulted in dismissal of cases. Over the decades HUD greatly underutilized its ability to launch systemic investigations into housing discrimination (National Commission on Fair Housing and Equal Opportunity 2008).

Even when fair housing lawsuits are heard in court, litigation has produced very limited change in the housing market. The Supreme Court has decided very few housing discrimination cases, leaving much of the interpretation of fair housing law up to appeals and district courts. It has also generally ruled against fair housing claims and interpreted fair housing law very narrowly, requiring intent to discriminate—rather than inequality in impact—to rule in favor of fair housing claims (Seabrook, Lamb, and Wilk 2012).

The summer of 2015 marked a potential sea change in fair housing enforcement, when HUD announced its new plans to require localities to provide evidence of affirmatively furthering fair housing in a systematic way. The Supreme Court also ruled that year that evidence of disparate impact— evidence that a policy or practice results in segregation without evidence of intent to discriminate on the part of policymakers or practitioners—is enough to prove discrimination. HUD's new final rule and the Supreme Court's ruling on disparate impact provide a new, more powerful foundation for fair housing enforcement in the U.S.

Case Study: HOPE VI in Atlanta

Dedicated by President Franklin Delano Roosevelt, Atlanta's Techwood Homes and nearby Clark Howell Homes were the nation's first slum-clearance public housing developments built in 1936. Once touted as a shining example of public housing, by 1993 over a third of their nearly 1,200 units were vacant, and the developments almost exclusively housed Black families. Built off the city's traditional grid system with a distinct architectural style from the surrounding neighborhoods, the projects' many interior streets and courtyards and vacant units attracted crime and vandalism. Poor public management and lax maintenance led to deplorable conditions, including outdated utility systems and lingering lead-based paint in units. The surrounding neighborhood had a poverty rate of 75 percent, high unemployment, and a high crime rate. The neighborhood school was among the most poorly performing schools in the city, and the local library was closed and abandoned. About half of the projects' units were one-bedroom or studio apartments, too small for families that desperately needed good quality, low-rent housing (Turbov and Piper 2005).

Touted as an overarching solution to a host of social ills, the Atlanta Housing Authority demolished Techwood and Clark Howell using the first HOPE VI grant issued in the U.S. and erected the mixed-income Centennial Place in their place between 1995 and 2000. Between 1994 and 2004, the Atlanta Housing Authority demolished thirteen public housing projects, displacing 25,000 residents, and replacing the old projects with ten new mixed-income projects using a combination of federal HOPE VI, local, and private funding sources (Oakley *et al.* 2011). Atlanta became the first city in the nation to demolish all of its public housing buildings (Oakley *et al.* 2011).

Centennial Place consists of 738 units of two and three-story townhomes and houses: 300 low-income households interspersed with market-rate and middle-income (up to 60 percent of median income) residents. While Techwood and Clark Howell were nearly 100 percent Black, Centennial Place is 60 percent Black and 40 percent white and Asian. It is privately managed and boasts a host of amenities: playgrounds, community spaces, a pool, parking, and a brand-new, high-performing elementary school that includes a gym with new equipment, computers, corporate and university-sponsored tutoring programs, and a Montessori preschool. The development includes three- and four-bedroom units, two-thirds of which are reserved for low-income households. A new boys-and-girls club and preschool are nearby (Turbov and Piper 2005).

Redevelopment of the neighborhood has not been limited to Centennial Place. At least $356 million in private funds have been invested in the surrounding neighborhood, mostly in condo construction (21 percent) and rentals (8 percent), office, mixed-use and retail developments (30 percent), and hotel developments (41 percent). These investments are anchored by new social services and the high-performing elementary school. Between 1993 and 2001, the neighborhood saw a 76 percent decline in crime and a 150 percent increase in median income. Rents rose in surrounding neighborhoods, but the lowest rents rose only slightly and still remained much lower than those in the city as a whole, while rents greater than the median quadrupled between 1990 and 2000. Thus, some researchers have concluded that rents in the neighborhood remain affordable to low-income families but competitive for higher-income households (Turbov and Piper 2005).

There is no question that Centennial Place provides dramatically improved conditions for current residents. But the model of redevelopment and social policy it exemplifies is not without criticism. First, only about a third of low-income tenants at Centennial Place are former Techwood/Clark Howell residents. When Techwood and Clark Howell were slated to be demolished, residents were given the choice of temporary housing vouchers for use in the private market, permanent housing vouchers, or alternative public housing units. The vast majority of residents chose vouchers and spread out in the sprawling Atlanta metropolitan region. The Atlanta Housing Authority reports that the alarmingly low return rates of former residents are due to residents not wanting to move again, bad memories of the former development, or failing to meet the eligibility criteria for return to Centennial Place. The patterns of return at Centennial Place mirror those in other HOPE VI projects: by the early 2000s, less than 20 percent of original residents of Atlanta's public housing returned to the redeveloped mixed-income communities that replaced them (Oakley *et al.* 2011). And while many of Atlanta's former public housing residents relocate to slightly less poor, safer neighborhoods, these places are as racially segregated as previous public housing (Oakley *et al.* 2013b).

Second, some Atlanta leaders claim that HOPE VI is a racially discriminatory program, unfairly targeting the Black population of Atlanta in violation of the Fair Housing Act (Cardinale 2007). Cities that have pursued HOPE VI projects tend to have disproportionate numbers of Black residents in public housing (Goetz 2013). In the wake of the Techwood/Clark Howell demolitions and Centennial Place construction, the surrounding neighborhood became more diverse, but it was led mostly by Black out-migration. The Black population decreased by a quarter between 1990 and 2000 while the white population nearly doubled during the same period (Turbov and Piper 2005).

A further criticism of HOPE VI is that eligibility requirements for return restrict the population of returnees to the most advantaged low-income households. Former Techwood/Clark Howell residents could return to Centennial Place only if they are current on their rent and utility payments, are employed, participating in a self-sufficiency program, or in school, and have committed no crimes in the past five years.

The redevelopment of the former Techwood/Clark Howell site and its surrounding neighborhood also relied strongly on private sector investment and private sector models. Only about a quarter of the financing needed came from HOPE VI. Another 20 percent came from the city, 11 percent came from LIHTC, 8 percent from Atlanta public schools, 3 percent from private philanthropy, 11 percent from 221(d) federal mortgage insurance, and the remainder from conventional financing. The leadership behind the transformation of the former Techwood/Clark Howell site had extensive corporate law and private sector real estate experience, and the Atlanta Housing Authority partnered with private housing development firms to realize the redevelopment plans (Turbov and Piper 2005).

Low return rates of public housing residents, eligibility requirements, the resegregation of former residents, and the role of the private sector in redevelopment leads some to characterize HOPE VI as a thinly veiled gentrification program (Bridge *et al.* 2011; Fraser *et al.* 2012). The fact that the former Techwood/Clark Howell site was chosen for Olympic Village when Atlanta won the bid for the 1996 summer Olympics only swelled this suspicion (Oakley *et al.* 2011).

The Centennial Place story is extraordinarily significant given that Atlanta was among the first cities in the country to build public housing, it was the first to receive HOPE VI funds, and it was the first to demolish all of its public housing. The city served as a laboratory for deconcentration and revitalization policies at the same time that it experienced intense gentrification, intimately tying policy experiments to market forces. Other cities have increasingly looked to Atlanta as a model of how to remedy residential segregation and disinvestment. Whether the Atlanta model represents a success story or a cautionary tale remains to be seen.

Terms

Restrictive covenant
Two-tier housing policy
Redlining
White flight
Racial steering
Deindustrialization
Blockbusting
Place stratification theory
Spatial assimilation theory
Fair housing
Exclusionary zoning
Mobility programs
Revitalization programs
Disparate impact

Discussion Questions

What are some explanations for racial and economic segregation in housing in the U.S.? How do individual preferences fit in?

Is residential segregation a social problem? Why or why not?

How have methods of racial and economic discrimination changed over time?

What are the costs and benefits of desegregation policies? Which do you think are most effective? Why?

What are the barriers to fair housing enforcement?

*could be
The end
project*

Application

You are an elected leader that represents an urban neighborhood that is 75 percent Black and Latino. One nearby public housing project provides much-needed affordable housing, but continues to have high rates of crime and vandalism that spills over to the adjoining blocks. You have led meaningful community meetings in your neighborhood to get the opinions of a diverse set of your constituents—homeowners, public housing residents, parents, local merchants, renters, police officers, and the homeless—to identify the most pressing problems the neighborhood faces. Your community has identified poverty, segregation, distrust of police officers, poor schools, high

5 meetings -- two weeks
to work

incarceration rates, high housing costs, and poor housing quality as the issues that need to be addressed.

You have come together with representatives from other similar neighborhoods to advise the city's newly established Committee for Urban Social Problems and Policy. The mayor has given your committee a $30 million budget with a mission to create and adopt innovative policy solutions to ongoing urban social problems. The mayor will support any set of policies that you endorse as long as it is strongly supported by academic research.

You must choose from the following policy options. You must choose at least one. You can choose to adopt as many as you want, but you cannot go over your budget. Explain how each policy choice will remedy the major problems your constituents say they face. Explain the benefits and limitations of your policy choice(s) using at least two sources of scholarly research from the text. Finally, identify a policy that you would not support under any circumstances and explain why, using at least one scholarly source.

group work outside of class in off weeks

Policy Options

- Purchase or build apartment buildings that are publicly maintained and operated in which rents are capped at 30 percent of tenants' incomes that are equally distributed among all neighborhoods (at least one building for every five to ten blocks, mandated by the city) ($30 million).
- Create a permanent city department to audit the private housing market continuously with paired testers to check for racial discrimination and punish violators with fines ($25 million).
- Demolish and redevelop the public housing project, temporarily relocating residents to private housing using housing vouchers and offering 20 percent of them units in the redeveloped project ($20 million).
- Demolish the public housing project and relocate residents to the private housing market using housing vouchers ($15 million).
- Lobby the federal government to mandate that developers build a "fair share" of housing for low-income households in middle-class and affluent communities with no guarantee of results ($15 million).
- Provide low-interest loans to property owners for home improvements ($10 million).
- Increase funding for the public housing authority to use at its discretion ($10 million).
- Donate a portion of your budget to federal fair housing programs (any amount).

References

Acevedo-Garcia, Dolores and Osypuk, Theresa L. 2008. "Impacts of Housing and Neighborhoods on Health: Pathways, Racial/Ethnic Disparities, and Policy

Directions." In J. H. Carr and N. K. Kutty, eds, *Segregation: The Rising Costs for America*, pp. 197–236. New York, NY: Routledge.

Adelman, Robert M. 2005. "The Roles of Race, Class, and Residential Preferences in the Neighborhood Composition of Middle-Class Blacks and Whites." *Social Science Quarterly* 86(1): 209–228.

Alba, Richard D. and Logan, John R. 1992. "Assimilation and Stratification in the Homeownership Patterns of Racial and Ethnic Groups." *International Migration Review* 26: 1314–1341.

Alba, Richard D. and Logan, John R. 1993. "Minority Proximity to Whites in Suburbs: An Individual-Level Analysis of Segregation." *American Journal of Sociology* 98(6): 138–1427.

Alba, Richard D., Logan, John R., and Stults, Brian J. 2000. "How Segregated Are Middle-Class African Americans?" *Social Problems* 47(4): 543–588.

Avery, R. B., Brevoort, K. P., and Canner, G. B. 2006. "High-Priced Home Lending and the 2005 HMDA Data." *Federal Reserve Bulletin* 8: 123–166.

Avery, R. B., Brevoort, K. P., and Canner, G. B. 2007. "The 2006 HMDA Data." *Federal Reserve Bulletin* 93: 73–109.

Barr, M. S., Dokko, J. K., and Keys, B. J. 2011. "Exploring the Determinants of High-Cost Mortgages to Homeowners in Low- and Moderate-Income Neighborhoods." In S. M. Wachter and M. M. Smith, eds, *The American Mortgage System: Crisis and Reform*, pp. 60–86. Philadelphia, PA: University of Pennsylvania Press.

Baxandall, Rosalyn and Ewen, Elizabeth. 2000. *Picture Windows: How the Suburbs Happened*. New York, NY: Basic Books.

Bischoff, Kendra and Reardon, Sean F. 2013. *Residential Segregation by Income, 1970–2009*. Providence, RI: US2010. Retrieved September 5, 2015. www.s4.brown.edu/us2010/Data/Report/report10162013.pdf.

Bocian, Debbie Gruenstein, Li, Wei, Reid, Carolina, and Quercia, Roberto G. 2011. *Lost Ground 2011: Disparities in Mortgage Lending and Foreclosures*. Durham, NC: Center for Responsible Lending.

Borchert, James. 1980. *Alley Life in Washington: Family, Community, Religion, and Folklife in the City, 1850–1970*. Urbana, IL: University of Illinois Press.

Bridge, Gary, Butler, Tim, and Lees, Loretta. 2011. *Mixed Communities: Gentrification by Stealth?* Bristol: Policy Press.

Briggs, Xavier de Souza, Popkin, Susan J., and Goering, John. 2010. *Moving to Opportunity: The Story of an American Experiment to Fight Ghetto Poverty*. Oxford: Oxford University Press.

Brown University Spatial Structures in the Social Sciences, U.S. 2010 American Communities Project, Diversity and Disparities. https://s4.ad.brown.edu/projects/diversity/Data/data.htm.

Bullard, Robert D. 1990. *Dumping in Dixie: Race, Class, and Environmental Quality*. Boulder, CO: Westview Press.

Calem, Paul S., Gillen, Kevin, and Wachter, Susan. 2004. "The Neighborhood Distribution of Subprime Lending." *Journal of Real Estate Finance and Economics* 29(4): 393–410.

Cardinale, Matthew. 2007. "HUD Investigates Atlanta Public Housing Complaint." *Atlanta Progressive News*, September 23. http://atlantaprogressivenews.com/2007/

9/23/exclusive-hud-investigates-atlanta-public-housing-complaint/. Retrieved on December 1, 2016.

Carr, James H. and Kutty, Nandinee K. 2008. *Segregation: The Rising Costs for America.* New York, NY: Routledge.

Castells, Nina. 2010. "HOPE VI Neighborhood Spillover Effects in Baltimore." *City-scape* 12(1): 65–98.

Charles, Camille Z. 2000. "Neighborhood Racial-Composition Preferences: Evidence from a Multiethnic Metropolis." *Social Problems* 47(3): 379–407.

Charles, Camille Z. 2003. "The Dynamics of Racial Residential Segregation." *Annual Review of Sociology* 29: 167–207.

Charles, Camille Z. 2006. *Won't You Be My Neighbor? Race, Class, and Residence in Los Angeles.* New York, NY: Russell Sage.

Chudacoff, Howard P., Smith, Judith E., and Baldwin, Peter C. 2015 [1981]. *The Evolution of American Urban Society.* Upper Saddle River, NJ: Pearson.

Clampet-Lundquist, Susan. 2004. "HOPE VI Relocations: Moving to New Neighbor-hoods and Building New Ties." *Housing Policy Debate* 15(2): 415–447.

DeNavas-Walt, Carmen and Proctor, Bernadette D. 2014. *Income and Poverty in the United States: 2013 (Current Population Reports).* Washington, DC: U.S. Census Bureau.

Ellen, Ingrid Gould. 2000. *Sharing America's Neighborhoods: The Prospects for Stable, Racial Integration.* Cambridge, MA: Harvard University Press.

Ellen, Ingrid Gould, Steil, Justin P., and De La Roca, Jorge. 2016. "The Significance of Segregation in the 21st Century." *City & Community* 15(1): 8–13.

Emerson, Michael O., Yancey, George, and Chai, Karen J. 2001. "Does Race Matter in Residential Segregation? Exploring the Preferences of Whites." *American Sociological Review* 66: 922–935.

Farley, Reynolds and Frey, William H. 1994. "Changes in the Segregation of Whites from Blacks during the 1980s: Small Steps Towards a More Integrated Society." *American Sociological Review* 59: 23–45.

Farley, Reynolds, Fielding, Elaine L., and Krysan, Maria. 1997. "The Residential Preferences of Blacks and Whites: A Four-Metropolis Analysis." *Housing Policy Debate* 8(4): 763–800.

Flippen, Chenoa A. 2001. "Racial and Ethnic Inequality in Homeownerhsip and Housing Equity." *The Sociological Quarterly* 42(2): 121–149.

Flippen, Chenoa A. 2004. "Unequal Returns to Housing Investments? A Study of Real Housing Appreciation among Black, White, and Hispanic Households." *Social Forces* 82(4): 1523–1551.

Florida, Richard and Mellender, Charlotta. 2015. *Segregated City: The Geography of Economic Segregation in America's Metros.* Toronto: Martin Prosperity Institute. Retrieved on August 15, 2015. http://martinprosperity.org/media/Segregated%20 City.pdf.

Florida, Richard, Matheson, Zara, Adler, Patrick, and Brydges, Taylor. 2014. *The Divided City and the Shape of the New Metropolis.* Toronto: Martin Prosperity Institute. Retrieved on August 15, 2015. http://martinprosperity.org/media/ Divided-City_NEW_v02.pdf.

Fraser, James Curtis, Brown Burns, Ashley, Bazuin, Joshua Theodore, and Oakley, Deirdre A. 2012. "HOPE VI, Colonization, and the Production of Difference." *Urban Affairs Review* 49(4): 525–556.

Friedman, Samantha, Reynolds, Angela, Scovill, Susan, Brassier, Florence R., Campbell, Ron, and Ballou, McKenzie. 2013. *An Estimate of Housing Discrimination Against Same-Sex Couples*. Washington, DC: U.S. Department of Housing and Urban Development.

Fullilove, Mindy Thompson. 2004. *Root Shock: How Tearing Up City Neighborhoods Hurts America, and What We Can Do About It*. New York, NY: One World.

Goetz, Edward. 2003. *Clearing the Way: Deconcentrating the Poor in Urban America*. Washington, DC: Urban Institute Press.

Goetz, Edward. 2013. *New Deal Ruins: Race, Economic Justice, and Public Housing Policy*. Ithaca, NY: Cornell University Press.

Hartman, Chester and Squires, Gregory D. 2010. *The Integration Debate: Competing Futures for American Cities*. New York, NY: Routledge.

Hirsch, Arnold. 1983. *Making the Second Ghetto: Race and Housing in Chicago 1940–1960*. Chicago, IL: University of Chicago Press.

Iceland, Joh, and Wilkes, Rima. 2006. "Does Socioeconomic Status Matter? Race, Class, and Residential Segregation." *Social Problems* 53: 248–273.

Jackson, Kenneth T. 1985. *Crabgrass Frontier: The Suburbanization of the United States*. New York, NY: Oxford University Press.

Jargowsky, Paul A. 2014. "Segregation, Neighborhoods, and Schools." In A. Lareau and K. Goyette, eds, *Choosing Neighborhoods, Choosing Schools*, pp. 97–136. New York, NY: Russell Sage Foundation.

Jargowsky, Paul. 2015. *Architecture of Segregation*. New York, NY: The Century Foundation. http://apps.tcf.org/architecture-of-segregation.

Kleit, Rachel Garshick and Manzo, Lynne C. 2006. "To Move or Not to Move: Relationship to Place and Relocation Choices in HOPE VI." *Housing Policy Debate* 17(2): 271–308.

Krivo, Lauren J. and Kaufman, Robert L. 2004. "Housing and Wealth Inequality: Racial-Ethnic Differences in Home Equity in the U.S." *Demography* 41(3): 585–605.

Krysan, Maria and Farley, Reynolds. 2002. "The Residential Preferences of Blacks: Do They Explain Persistent Segregation?" *Social Forces* 80: 937–980.

Lewis, Valerie A., Emerson, Michael O., and Klineberg, Stephen L. 2011. "Who We'll Live With: Racial Composition Preference of Whites, Blacks, and Latinos." *Social Forces* 89(4): 1385–1407.

Logan, John. 2002. *Separate and Unequal: The Neighborhood Gap for Blacks and Hispanics in Metropolitan America*. Albany, NY: Lewis Mumford Center for Comparative Urban and Regional Research.

Logan, John R. and Alba, Richard D. 1993. "Locational Returns to Human Capital: Minority Access to Suburban Community Resources." *Demography* 30(2): 243–268.

Logan, John and Stults, Brian J. 2011. "The Persistence of Segregation in the Metropolis: New Findings from the 2010 Census." US2010 Project Report. www.s4.brown.edu/us2010/Data/Report/report2.pdf.

Massey, Douglas S. and Denton, Nancy A. 1993. *American Apartheid: Segregation and the Making of the Underclass*. Cambridge, MA: Harvard University Press.

Massey, Douglas S., Albright, Len, Casciano, Rebecca, Derickson, Elizabeth, and Kinsey, David N. 2013. *Climbing Mount Laurel: The Struggle for Affordable Housing and Social Mobility in an American Suburb*. Princeton, NJ: Princeton University Press.

Massey, Douglas S., Rugh, Jacob S., Steil, Justin P., and Albright, Len. 2016. "Riding the Stagecoach to Hell: A Qualitative Analysis of Racial Discrimination in Mortgage Lending." *City & Community* 15(2): 118–136.

Mauer, Marc. 2010. "Two-Tiered Justice: Race, Class, and Crime Policy." In C. Hartman and G. D. Squires, eds, *The Integration Debate*, pp. 169–184. New York, NY: Routledge.

McClure, K., Schwartz, A., and Taghavi, L. B. 2012. "Housing Choice Voucher Location Patterns a Decade Later." Paper presented at the annual meetings of the Association of Collegiate Schools of Planning, Cincinnati, OH, November 2.

Meltzer, Rachel. 2013. "Do Homeowners Associations Affect Citywide Segregation? Evidence from Florida Municipalities." *Housing Policy Debate* 23(4): 688–713.

Miller, Reuben Jonathan. 2014. "Devolving the Carceral State: Race, Prisoner Reentry, and the Micro-Politics of Urban Poverty Management." *Punishment & Society* 16(3): 305–335.

National Commission on Fair Housing and Equal Opportunity. 2008. *The Future of Fair Housing: Report of the National Commission on Fair Housing and Equal Opportunity*. Washington, DC: National Commission on Fair Housing and Equal Opportunity. Retrieved on September 2, 2015. www.nationalfairhousing. org/Portals/33/reports/future_of_fair_Housing.pdf.

National Housing Law Project, Poverty & Race Research Action Council, Sherwood Research Associates, and Everywhere and Now Public Housing Residents Organizing Nationally Together. 2002. *False HOPE: A Critical Assessment of HOPE VI Public Housing Redevelopment Program*. Washington, DC: National Housing Law Project.

Oakley, Deirdre. 2008. "Locational Patterns of Low-Income Housing Tax Credit Developments: A Sociospatial Analysis of Four Metropolitan Areas." *Urban Affairs Review* 43(5): 599–628.

Oakley, Deirdre, Ruel, Erin, and Reid, Lesley. 2013a. "Atlanta's Last Demolitions and Relocations: The Relationship Between Neighborhood Characteristics and Resident Satisfaction." *Housing Studies* 28(2): 205–234.

Oakley, Deirdre, Ruel, Erin, and Reid, Lesley. 2013b. "'It Was Really Hard.... It Was Alright.... It Was Easy.' Public Housing Relocation Experiences and Destination Satisfaction in Atlanta." *Cityscape* 15(2): 183–192.

Oakley, Deirdre, Ward, Chandra, Reid, Lesley, and Ruel, Erin. 2011. "The Poverty Deconcentration Imperative and Public Housing Transformation." *Sociology Compass* 5(9): 824–833.

Oliver, Melvin L. and Shapiro, Thomas. 2006 [1995]. *Black Wealth/White Wealth: A New Perspective on Racial Inequality*. New York, NY: Routledge.

Pais, Jeremy, South, Scott J., and Crowder, Kyle. 2012. "Metropolitan Heterogeneity and Minority Neighborhood Attainment: Spatial Assimilation or Place Stratification?" *Social Problems* 59(2): 258–281.

Pattillo, Mary. 2007. *Black on the Block: The Politics of Race and Class in the City*. Chicago, IL: University of Chicago Press.

Pattillo-McCoy, Mary. 1999. *Black Picket Fences: Privilege and Peril among the Black Middle Class*. Chicago, IL: University of Chicago Press.

Pendall, Rolf. 2000. "Local Land Use Regulation and the Chain of Exclusion." *Journal of the American Planning Association* 66(2): 125–142.

Pendall, Rolf, Theodos, Brett, and Hildner, Kaitlin. 2014. "Why High-Poverty Neighborhoods Persist: The Role of Precarious Housing." *Urban Affairs Review,* January 2016 vol. 52(1): 33–65.

Radford, Gail. 1996. *Modern Housing for America: Policy Struggles in the New Deal Era.* Chicago, IL: University of Chicago Press.

Rosenbaum, James E. 1995. "Changing the Geography of Opportunity by Expanding Residential Choice: Lessons from the Gautreaux Program." *Housing Policy Debate* 6(1): 231–269.

Ross, Stephen L. and Yinger, John. 2002. *The Color of Credit: Mortgage Discrimination, Research Methodology, and Fair-Lending Enforcement.* Cambridge, MA: MIT Press.

Rothwell, Jonathan T. 2011. "Racial Enclaves and Density Zoning: The Institutionalized Segregation of Racial Minorities in the United States." *American Law and Economics Review* 13(1): 290–358.

Rothwell, Jonathan T. and Massey, Douglas S. 2009. "The Effect of Density Zoning on Racial Segregation in U.S. Urban Areas." *Urban Affairs Review* 44: 799–806.

Rothwell, Jonathan T. and Massey, Douglas S. 2010. "Density Zoning and Class Segregation in U.S. Metropolitan Areas." *Social Science Quarterly* 91: 1123–1143.

Sampson, Robert J. and Wilson, William Julius. 1995. "Toward a Theory of Race, Crime, and Urban Inequality." In J. Hagan and R. D. Peterson, eds, *Crime and Inequality,* pp. 37–56. Stanford, CA: Stanford University Press.

Sanbonmatsu, Lisa, Ludwig, Jens, Katz, Larry F., Gennetian, Lisa A., Duncan, Greg J., Kessler, Ronald C., Adam, Emma, McDade, Thomas W., and Tessler Lindau, Stacy. 2011. *Moving to Opportunity for Fair Housing Demonstration Program: Final Impacts Evaluation.* Washington, DC: U.S. Department of Housing and Urban Development.

Schwartz, Alex F. 2015. *Housing Policy in the U.S.,* third edition. New York: Routledge.

Seabrook, Nicholas R, Lamb, Charles M, Wilk, Erik M. 2011 "Federal Courts and Fair Housing Policy," in *Fair and Affordable Housing in the U.S.: Trends, Outcomes, Future Directions,* ed. Robert Mark Silverman and Kelly L. Patterson, Boston: Brill.

Shapiro, Thomas. 2004. *The Hidden Cost of Being African American: How Wealth Perpetuates Inequality.* New York, NY: Oxford University Press.

Silverman, Robert and Patterson, Kelly. 2012. *Fair and Affordable Housing in the U.S.: Trends, Outcomes, Future Directions.* Chicago, IL: Haymarket Books.

Squires, Gregory D. 1994. *Capital and Communities in Black and White: The Intersections of Race, Class, and Uneven Development.* Albany, NY: SUNY Press.

Squires, Gregory D. and Kubrin, Charis E. 2006. *Privileged Places: Race, Residence, and the Structure of Opportunity.* Boulder, CO: Lynne Rienner.

Squires, Gregory D. and O'Connor, Sally. 2001. *Color and Money: Politics and Prospects for the Community Reinvestment Movement in Urban America.* Albany, NY: SUNY Press.

Sugrue, Thomas J. 1993. "The Structures of Urban Poverty: The Reorganization of Space and Work in Three Periods of American History." In Michael B. Katz, ed., *The "Underclass" Debate: Views from History,* pp. 85–117. Princeton, NJ: Princeton University Press.

Taylor, Paul, and Fry, Richard. 2012. *The Rise of Residential Segregation by Income.* Washington, DC: Pew Research. Retrieved September 1, 2015. www.pewsocial-trends.org/files/2012/08/Rise-of-Residential-Income-Segregation-2012.2.pdf.

Turbov, Mindy and Piper, Valerie. 2005. *HOPE VI and Mixed-Finance Redevelopments: A Catalyst for Neighborhood Renewal—Atlanta Case Study.* Washington, DC: Brookings Institution.

Turner, Margery Austin, Herbig, Carla, Kaye, Deborah, Fenderson, Julie, and Levy, Diane. 2005. *Discrimination Against Persons with Disabilities: Barriers at Every Step.* Washington, DC: U.S. Department of Housing and Urban Development.

Turner, Margery Austin, Santos, Rob, Levy, Diane K., Wissoker, Doug, Aranda, Claudia, and Pitingolo, Rob. 2013. *Housing Discrimination Against Racial and Ethnic Minorities 2012.* Washington, DC: U.S. Department of Housing and Urban Development.

United Church of Christ. 1987. *Toxic Wastes and Race in the United States.* New York, NY: United Church of Christ Commission for Racial Justice.

U.S. Census Bureau. 2014. *Housing Vacancies and Homeownership (CPS/HVS).* Table 22: Homeownership Rates by Race and Ethnicity of Householder: 1994–2014. Washington, DC: U.S. Department of Commerce. Retrieved on July 1, 2015. www.census.gov/housing/hvs/data/ann14ind.html.

U.S. Department of Housing and Urban Development. 2015a. "Affirmatively Furthering Fair Housing." Federal Register 80, no. 136, July 16: 42272. www.gpo.gov/fdsys/pkg/FR-2015-07-16/pdf/2015-17032.pdf. Retrieved December 1, 2016.

U.S. Department of Housing and Urban Development. 2015b. Budget Authority by Program Comparative Summary, Fiscal Years 2013–2015. http://portal.hud.gov/hudportal/documents/huddoc?id=fy15cj_bdgt_auth_tbl.pdf.

U.S. General Accounting Office. 1983. *Siting of Hazardous Waste Landfills and Their Correlation with Racial and Economic Status of Surrounding Communities.* Washington, DC: Government Printing Office. Retrieved December 1, 2016.

Williams, David R. and Collins, Chiquita. 1995. "U.S. Socioeconomic and Racial Differences in Health: Patterns and Explanations." *Annual Review of Sociology* 21: 349–386.

Wilson, William Julius. 1978. *The Declining Significance of Race: Blacks and Changing American Institutions.* Chicago, IL: University of Chicago Press.

Wilson, William Julius. 1987. *The Truly Disadvantaged: The Inner City, the Underclass, and Public Policy.* Chicago, IL: University of Chicago Press.

Wilson, William Julius. 1996. *When Work Disappears.* New York, NY: Alfred A. Knopf.

Woldoff, Rachael A., and Ovadia, Seth. 2009. "Not Getting Their Money's Worth: African-American Disadvantages in Converting Income, Wealth, and Education into Residential Quality." *Urban Affairs Review* 45(1): 66–91.

CHAPTER 4

Homelessness

In August of 2015, more than one-third of the rooms in a motel on the far-east side of Madison, WI were occupied by homeless families and individuals, including twenty-five school-aged children. While many parents were working full time at places like Oscar Mayer, they could not find affordable housing in the area—leaving them to pay more than $800 a month for motel rooms. The competition for affordable housing in Madison is intense, and vulnerable families often contend with bad credit histories, criminal convictions, or prior evictions that prevent them from securing adequate housing (Erickson and Mosiman 2016). The popular images of homelessness—older men, often with mental illnesses, sleeping on urban streets—is increasingly challenged by the reality of homelessness in America. Families make up nearly 40 percent of the homeless population on any given night in the U.S., and the states with the largest increases in homelessness in recent years are rural.

Our best counts estimate that about a half a million people are homeless on any given night in America. While homelessness has abated somewhat at the national level since the 1980s, it has skyrocketed in New York City, Los Angeles, and beyond. Why? What contributes to homelessness? How do we make sense of how families end up staying in motels? Is homelessness a matter of choice or of circumstance? And why does the distinction matter? Do we have an obligation to address homelessness, and if so, how? This chapter explores the major trends and social debates surrounding homelessness and related social policies in the U.S.

Defining and Determining the Extent of Homelessness

At the outset of any earnest study of homelessness, two fundamental questions must be answered: who counts as homeless?; and how many homeless people are there? The very definition of homelessness has changed over time and social context, as have our methods of determining its extent. Both questions are central to determining the causes, extent of, and potential solutions to the homelessness problem (Treglia 2016).

The simplest definition of homelessness includes anyone without a home. But this is deceptively straightforward, and it has not historically been the definition used. In fact, during the era of the "tramp" in the late 1800s and early 1900s and in the "skid row" post-World War II era, people (primarily single men) were considered homeless if they had few social attachments, moved frequently, or drank heavily (Bahr and Caplow 1974). More recent definitions of homelessness emphasize the inherent poverty in the condition of homelessness. We don't generally consider affluent households that lose their home in a fire homeless, because these households can generally find new housing fairly easily. A common definition used since the 1980s has been "not having customary and regular access to a conventional dwelling" (Rossi 1989).

This definition may seem straightforward until we consider what we mean by "conventional." Clearly sidewalks, parks, and subway tunnels are not considered "conventional" dwellings, so people inhabiting those places would easily be considered homeless (Lee *et al.* 2010). But what about people who are squatting in abandoned houses? Or people staying for extended periods in single-room occupancy dwellings or motels? Furthermore, how long must a person not have a "conventional dwelling" to be considered homeless? Some people are temporarily homeless while transitioning between stable, conventional housing, others have episodes of homelessness in which they cycle in and out of homelessness over short periods, and others are chronically or permanently homeless (Culhane *et al.* 2007).

None of these definitions considers people who are "precariously" or "marginally" housed: people and families at risk of becoming homeless, including people with high rent burdens; people in trailers or RVs; or those who are temporarily or permanently "doubling up" with friends or family (Lee *et al.* 2010). They also do not include people living in jails, psychiatric hospitals, or other institutions (Treglia 2016).

In an attempt to address all of these issues with the definition of homelessness, as of 2009, the federal government defines homelessness as

> individuals and families who lack a fixed, regular, and adequate nighttime residence ... individuals and families who will imminently lose their primary residence ... [and] individuals and families who are fleeing, or attempting to flee, domestic violence, dating violence, sexual

assault, stalking, or other dangerous or life-threatening conditions that relate to violence against the individual or a family member.
(U.S. Department of Housing and Urban Development 2011)

Trends in Homelessness

Based on the current government definition of homelessness, how many people are homeless in America? How can we even count a population that is often hidden from plain view in motels, cars, and on the couches and floors of friends and families? Federal and local government agencies, as well as academics and homeless advocates, have employed a wide range of methodologies to count the homeless population in the U.S. Currently, local housing shelters and agencies are required to perform three counts and submit the counts to the Department of Housing and Urban Development: the number of homeless individuals they serve on a given night in January (known as point-in-time (PIT) estimates), the number of individuals served in an entire year (known as homeless management information system (HMIS) estimates), and the number of beds available to homeless individuals over ten nights in January. PIT estimates count both sheltered and unsheltered people, while HMIS estimates focus on the sheltered homeless (U.S. Department of Housing and Urban Development 2014a).

The Geography of Homelessness

As of 2015, more than 560,000 people are homeless on any given night in the U.S. The number has been steadily declining since 2007 (U.S. Department of Housing and Urban Development 2014a). Homelessness is geographically concentrated, particularly in California and New York. California has the largest homeless population in the U.S., followed by New York, Florida, Texas, Washington, Georgia, Oregon, Tennessee, Nevada, and Hawaii (Figure 4.1). While California is home to about 12 percent of the U.S. population, it holds about a fifth of the nation's entire homeless population, more than 60 percent of which is unsheltered. Indeed, a staggering 43 percent of the entire nation's unsheltered homeless population is in California alone (U.S. Department of Housing and Urban Development 2016; U.S. Census Bureau 2016). Following California, New York has the second-largest homeless population in the U.S. (15 percent of the homeless population is in New York), but the vast majority (95 percent) is sheltered—a major distinction. New York holds about a fifth of the entire nation's sheltered homeless population (U.S. Department of Housing and Urban Development 2016).

It is not surprising that California and New York have the largest homeless populations given that they are highly populated. But even when we take into account the underlying share of the population living in states with the

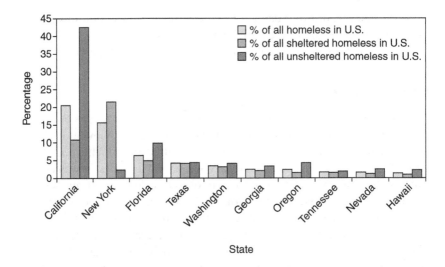

Figure 4.1 Percentage of sheltered and unsheltered homeless among states with top ten largest homeless populations

Source: U.S. Department of Housing and Urban Development 2016.

largest homeless populations, California and New York remain centers of homelessness, although a slightly different portrait of homelessness also emerges when we take underlying population counts into account. Relative to the size of its population, the District of Columbia leads the nation in homelessness, followed by Hawaii, New York, Oregon, Massachusetts, Nevada, California, Washington, Alaska, and Vermont.

Homelessness is often thought of as a distinctly urban problem. More than a third of California's homeless population, for example, is in Los Angeles. Similarly, more than 85 percent of Nevada's homeless population is in Las Vegas, 85 percent of New York's is in New York City, more than 60 percent of Hawaii's is in Honolulu, more than half of Washington's is in Seattle, and 40 percent of Tennessee's homeless are in Nashville and Memphis.

But homelessness is not confined to the nation's cities. The states with the largest increases in homeless populations between 2007 and 2015 are largely rural: North Dakota; South Dakota; Montana; Wyoming; Vermont; and Mississippi (Figure 4.2). Moreover, many of the states with the highest rates of homelessness have homeless populations that are widely dispersed, like Florida's. A third of Texas' homeless population, more than 40 percent of Oregon's, and more than 40 percent of Georgia's are in rural areas (U.S. Department of Housing and Urban Development 2016).

Some of the states with the largest homeless populations have the necessary resources (i.e. beds) to provide a foundation of aid. Others—such as

California, Oregon, Nevada, Hawaii, Vermont, Florida, Georgia, South Carolina, Montana, and Maryland—have very few beds relative to the size of their homeless populations (Figure 4.3).

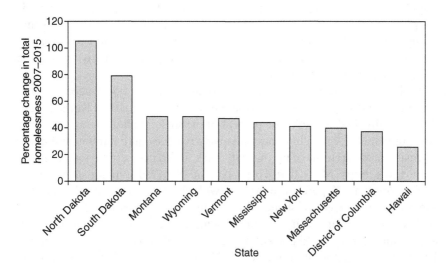

Figure 4.2 U.S. states with the ten largest increases in homeless population 2007–2015

Source: U.S. Department of Housing and Urban Development 2016.

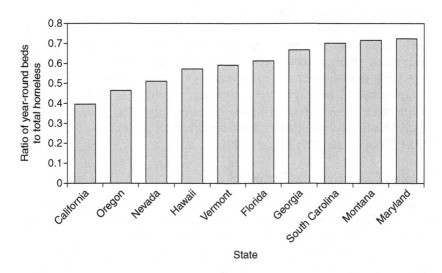

Figure 4.3 U.S. states with the lowest ratios of year-round beds to total homeless population

Source: U.S. Department of Housing and Urban Development 2016.

Characteristics of the Homeless Population

The typical person who was homeless on a given night in January in 2014 was a Black, middle-aged man with no disability in a U.S. city. But the homeless population is obviously much more diverse than this "typical" case. Practically speaking, the homeless population is often divided into two distinct groups: single adults and families with children. This division is not arbitrary: the two populations differ in significant ways, particularly among the sheltered and unsheltered populations.

Sheltered individuals are disproportionately male, middle-aged, African American, and single (U.S. Department of Housing and Urban Development 2014a). Individuals make up 66 percent of the sheltered homeless population (the population for which we have relatively reliable data); families and unaccompanied children make up the rest. Stark differences can be seen between these two groups. More than 70 percent of sheltered individuals are male, while more than 70 percent of families with children are headed by females. More than 45 percent of sheltered individuals are white; only 24 percent of sheltered families are white. Homeless families are disproportionately Black and Latino. And while 45 percent of sheltered individuals have a disability, of heads of homeless families only about 20 percent have a disability. Furthermore, prior to entering shelters, homeless individuals are more likely to report that they were previously staying in "places not meant for human habitation," while homeless families are more likely to report that they were previously staying in rental units or with family (U.S. Department of Housing and Urban Development 2014b).

While data on the unsheltered homeless population is limited, individual research teams have attempted to collect data on this hard-to-reach population, mostly through social service agencies (Treglia 2016). These studies suggest that unsheltered people and families tend to be chronically homeless, unemployed, and have low education levels (Shern *et al.* 2000). They also tend to have higher rates of behavioral issues, substance abuse issues, and physical health problems than sheltered individuals and families (Shern *et al.* 2000; O'Toole *et al.* 1999; Tsai *et al.* 2014).

History of Homelessness in the U.S.

Certainly there have always been homeless people in America. But the nature, scope, and reaction to homelessness have varied over time. Early evidence of concern about homelessness is found in reports of seventeenth-century town meetings in New England. Colonial settlers distinguished between the "settled" and "transient" poor, reserving small payments and places in poorhouses for the settled poor. Transient people received relatively little help and were often forced to move (Rossi 1989). The distinction—and the unequal benefits system on which it was based—was overturned only in 1969.

Homelessness increased after the Civil War, as the new railroad and commercial agriculture industries demanded transient labor. A set of severe economic downturns exacerbated the problem. "Tramps," "bums," and "hobos," mostly single men, increasingly populated the cities. In New York, the homeless were provided small payments and spaces in poorhouses for shelter. These policies were hotly debated, as politicians and the public argued over the cost and whether aid essentially subsidized laziness (Katz 1986). The homeless in New York could also go to any city police station for nightly shelter without any punishment. Shantytowns on the outskirts of cities grew during this period, only to be removed during large-scale urban redevelopment projects such as New York's Central Park and Chicago's Grant Park (Rossi 1989).

Skid rows also developed during this time, full of hotels, rooming houses, restaurants, goods, and services. These catered to needs of transient single male laborers in the lumber, railroad, agriculture, and construction industries, which all required seasonal manual labor. As Rossi argues, homelessness during this period did not mean one did not have shelter. Instead, "Homelessness marked off persons who were living transient lives outside conventional family contexts" (Rossi 1989).

Homelessness skyrocketed during the Great Depression, particularly among young, single men for whom unemployment would likely be permanent (Anderson 1940). But the booming wartime and postwar economy brought more workers into the employment fold, homelessness abated somewhat, and skid rows shrunk. The populations of the nation's skid rows shrunk by half between 1950 and 1970, particularly in places where the unskilled labor market declined (Lee 1980).

But homelessness, and the urban districts that catered to the homeless, did not disappear after World War II. While smaller than they once were, skid rows continued to house single men—particularly white, middle-aged men, many (but not all) of whom had disabilities, mental illnesses, or addictions—in rooming houses and flophouses (Bogue 1963; Bahr and Caplow 1974). As federal and local officials looked to build up and beautify the nation's downtowns, new, modern office and residential buildings began to rub up against existing skid row districts. Cities all over the country began to try to find ways to tear down the run-down rooming houses and single-room occupancy (SRO) hotels that housed the homeless in order to repurpose the landscape for business purposes (Rossi 1989). At the same time, more generous social security and housing benefits for the aged and disabled opened up additional housing opportunities for some who would have otherwise found homes on skid row (Rossi 1989).

During the 1970s, as Rossi (1989) notes, "What had been a minor form of homelessness became more prevalent: literal homelessness began to grow and at the same time to become more visible to the public." Over the 1970s, for example, New York City's poverty rate grew by nearly 40 percent while skid row districts shrank, and old rooming houses, flophouses, and SRO hotels closed down (Nunez and Sribnick 2013). This was partially the result of well-intentioned campaigns by homeless advocates to improve the housing conditions of the very poor (Vitale 2008). The U.S. had also begun the process of deinstitutionalization, whereby state-run psychiatric hospitals were closed, and mental health services transferred to community-based care. At the same time New York City and other places decriminalized public drunkenness and other minor "quality of life" offenses.

The population of homeless families rose in the early 1980s as the economy stagnated and welfare retrenchment began. A large-scale shift in the American economy from a manufacturing base to a service base beginning in the 1960s led to widespread job losses and declines in wages. There were 538,600 manufacturing jobs in 1977 in New York City, for example, and only 360,600 in 1989. Income inequality grew (Nunez and Sribnick 2013).

The election of President Ronald Reagan ushered in a new era in social welfare policy. A sweeping attack on welfare assistance throughout the 1980s and 1990s was buttressed by the widespread ideology that poor Americans had become too dependent on government aid, undermining their self-sufficiency and wellbeing. While full-scale welfare reform would not take place until 1996 under President Clinton, the Reagan administration drastically cut funding for welfare benefits, including low-income housing and food stamps, almost immediately. In the two years immediately after Reagan took office, for example, New York City lost $600 million in federal low-income housing funding (Nunez and Sribnick 2013).

These changes contributed to the migration of more and more homeless people to the streets of American cities. The homeless population skyrocketed during the 1980s to the highest level since the Great Depression. By 1985, the homeless population was four times as big as it had been in the previous decades (Rosenthal and Foscarinis 2006). Between 1985 and 1990, 3 percent of the U.S. population had been homeless at one point; in 2015, the rate is 0.2 percent (Link *et al.* 1994).

While there are fewer sheltered and unsheltered homeless people today than in the late 1980s, the characteristics of the homeless population remain significantly different from those of the "tramps," "hobos," and "bums" of earlier eras. The homeless population today has fewer housing options than in generations past, is more visible on the street, includes more women and people of color, is less concentrated in particular urban neighborhoods, and is less employed (Rossi 1989). The homeless population of today is also increasingly criminalized through local restrictions on sleeping or sitting in public spaces, anti-begging laws, and police sweeps, particularly of tourist areas in large cities (Foscarinis *et al.* 1999; Vitale 2008).

Major Debates: Causes of and Solutions to Homelessness

A set of fundamental debates over rights and responsibilities shapes our understanding of and response to homelessness. What causes homelessness? Do we have an obligation to address it? If so, how? Each of these questions is hotly debated in American society and politics.

Causes of Homelessness

As the homeless population grew and grew more visible through the 1980s, an obvious question emerged: why? Two sets of theories developed: those that emphasize the individual actions and behaviors of homeless people; and those that emphasize the social forces beyond individuals' control. The debate over the causes of homelessness has shaped our orientation toward solving the homelessness problem.

Early theories emphasized individual behaviors and characteristics as the root causes of homelessness: mental illness, addiction, or lifestyle choices. An early theory posited in the 1970s suggested that "disaffiliation"—the withdrawal of individuals from society—was the root cause of homelessness (Bahr 1973). Some research lends some support for this theory. Higher rates of homelessness are associated with fewer and more superficial social ties (Toohey *et al.* 2004), and veterans have higher rates of homelessness than the general population (Fargo *et al.* 2012). But mental illness and substance abuse contribute much less to homelessness than is commonly believed. The rates of mental illness and substance abuse, for example, are higher in the homeless population than in the general population, but much smaller than is often perceived (Montgomery *et al.* 2013b). Furthermore, by the late 1980s the homeless population had grown so tremendously that it became increasingly hard to argue that mental illness, for example, had grown that much more common.

Structural explanations developed to account for this massive growth in homelessness—particularly because of the large-scale economic shifts in the 1960s and 1970s. Research in the 1990s began to show that homelessness was a common stage that very poor families passed through, rather than a permanent state. About 80 percent of families who had entered a shelter had their own apartment five years later, the vast majority stably housed (Shinn *et al.* 1998). It turned out that homeless families who were able to access permanent housing were able to stay housed (Stojanovic *et al.* 1999), suggesting that individual characteristics did not account for the homeless condition.

Researchers began to advance the idea of involuntary displacement, or displacement of people "from housed lives by large social processes over which they had little control" (Rosenthal and Foscarinis 2006). They emphasized the scarcity of low-income housing, unemployment, deinstitutionalization, changes in the welfare system, and other social, economic, and political changes that contributed to rising homelessness in America. Deindustrialization—the economic shift away from a manufacturing-based economy to a service-based economy—has led to decreasing wages, benefits, and job security for American workers, a decline in union power, and widespread job losses due to automation (Wright 1997). Indeed, the homeless rate increases when the economy (employment, earnings, and extent of work) suffers (O'Flaherty and Wu 2006). The homeless can be thought of as a kind of surplus that the labor market will not accommodate (Willse 2015).

And the decrease in the low-rent housing supply is particularly significant. The income–rent gap grew dramatically in the 1970s, particularly for the poorest Americans. At the same time that the largest number of housing units have been lost at the lowest rent levels—like the SRO units (Hartman and Zigas 1991). As we saw in Chapter 2, soaring housing costs impact poor households most: nearly 80 percent of extremely low-income working households spend more than half of their monthly budget on housing (Viveiros and Sturtevant 2014). In 2013, one in eight poor renting families in the U.S. were unable to pay their rent in full (Desmond 2016). About 15 percent of renters are evicted every year in Milwaukee alone (Desmond 2016). Research repeatedly shows that homelessness is greater in places with higher rents and fewer vacancies (Byrne et al. 2013; Lee, Price-Spratlen, and Kanan 2003; Quigley and Raphael 2001). Indeed, 72 percent of city officials across the country report lack of affordable housing as the primary cause of homelessness among families with children (United States Conference of Mayors 2008).

Furthermore, individuals with unstable housing situations, those who have used shelters in the past, and those facing eviction are most likely to enter a homeless shelter or become homeless (Byrne et al. 2015; Shinn et al. 1998; Shinn et al. 2013). Those that exit homeless shelters with a rental subsidy are less likely to return to homelessness (Allgood and Warren 2003; Byrne et al. 2015; Shinn et al. 1998; Wong et al. 1997). Tax laws that reward housing speculation and contribute to rising housing prices and the paltry budget of the Department of Housing and Urban Development are contributing factors to the lack of affordable housing (see Chapter 2), as are local redevelopment efforts that shuttered SROs but provided no alternative housing for their residents.

Changes in social welfare policy also contributed to an increase in homelessness. While families with children could still rely on cash assistance from welfare programs in the 1970s, for example, the real value of that aid decreased at the same time that housing prices rose. By the early 1980s, the rise in the number of homeless families with children began to alarm officials (Nunez and Sribnick 2013). The result was massive retrenchment of social welfare aid, as Americans and their elected leaders—particularly President

Ronald Reagan—increasingly blamed government for making the poor dependent on welfare. By 1985 the average welfare payment was about 60 percent of its 1968 value, and the federal government massively cut aid for low-income housing (Nunez and Sribnick 2013). Welfare retrenchment culminated in the 1996 welfare reform act, which severely limited cash assistance and prevented people with drug and alcohol addictions from seeking disability payments through Social Security (Rosenthal and Foscarinis 2006).

None of the structural explanations for homelessness disputes the fact that personal circumstances may make some individuals more likely to end up without shelter. But without enough low-rent housing units to go around, those individuals will be more likely than those without mental illness, for example, to go without permanent shelter (Rosenthal and Foscarinis 2006). As Main aptly notes, "Structural features of the housing market and the economy determine the essential fact that there will be a certain amount of homelessness, while individual characteristics explain precisely who will make up the homeless" (Main 2016). Thus, by the late 1980s, public opinion and policy tended to favor the more structural explanations for homelessness (Rosenthal and Foscarinis 2006). Americans consider homelessness more a product of structural problems and bad luck than individual factors (Link *et al.* 1995).

Approaches to Policy

If homelessness is primarily the result of individual choices or actions, perhaps we have no obligation to address it, or should address it punitively. If, on the other hand, homelessness is primarily the result of a scarcity in very low-income housing, deinstitutionalization, employment opportunities, or other socioeconomic factors, a strong argument exists that we are obligated to help those for whom our shared social system is not functioning properly. Moreover, homelessness costs society financially, as homeless people are in close contact with emergency health services and the criminal justice system (Kuno *et al.* 2000; Kushel *et al.* 2001; Salit *et al.* 1998). But what if, as many scholars argue, homelessness is probably the product of a combination of individual and social factors (Jencks 1994; Main 1998; O'Flaherty and Wu 2006; O'Flaherty 1996; Shlay and Rossi 1992)? What if, as Main (2016) argues, the political economy of the U.S. ensures that a certain amount of the population will be homeless, and individual characteristics determine who they will be? What shape should our policies toward homelessness take?

One option is to treat homelessness as a matter of choice and punish those without shelter, particularly in public places. New "quality of life" policing campaigns designed to clean up urban areas, particularly for tourist use, rely on harsh policing of small offenses like public drinking, loitering, and turnstile jumping on subways to keep the homeless out of public spaces (Vitale 2008). This tactic is fundamentally linked to the redevelopment of urban America, as cities attempt to refashion themselves and compete with each other to attract capital in the service economy (Wright 1997). In this view, a visible homeless population could undermine economic growth. Thus, homeless people are excluded from certain physical areas and repressed—"forcibly removed, punished, or harassed for occupying space or communicating in ways not sanctioned by authority" (Wright 1997: 183). The ethics of the policing approach to homelessness is hotly debated, as the fundamental civil rights of homeless people are often ignored (Foscarinis *et al.* 1999). Furthermore the question of whether this approach solves the homelessness problem and the literal costs of these measures—in arrests and other processing costs in the criminal justice system—may make this approach impractical.

Another option is to try to determine whether all homeless people deserve help. Are some people homeless because of choice, and others as the result of factors beyond their control? Making this distinction, essentially between the "undeserving" and the "deserving" poor, has a long history in American social policy (Katz 2013). It can be seen in early colonial policies toward the homeless: "transient" homeless were removed (at times forcibly) from local jurisdictions, while "local" homeless were offered small payments and rooms (Rossi 1989). Ethics of this distinction aside, it is hard to employ when the combination of individual and social risk factors for homelessness are so intertwined.

A final option is to consider the right to housing fundamental to all people. Some researchers argue that a fundamental right to housing in the U.S. is not only just but also pragmatic given that decent housing is linked to better health and personal safety, employment opportunities, education, and security. A right to housing might also help ameliorate the troubling trends in income and wealth inequality (Bratt *et al.* 2006). Indeed, other countries, ranging from the Netherlands to South Africa to Argentina, guarantee the right to adequate housing for their citizens (Van Bueren 2016).

Proponents of a fundamental right to housing stress that any earnest attempt to eradicate homelessness must focus on prevention. Preserving low-cost housing is the main concern, either by preventing the destruction of low-cost units in the private market or preventing the destruction of public housing units without a one-for-one replacement guarantee. Tenants must also be protected from unlawful eviction, and in some cases be offered emergency rental and utility assistance (Rosenthal and Foscarinis 2006). In addition, demand-side housing assistance like Section 8 has done little to spur new housing construction at the low end of the market; proponents of the right to housing argue that it would be far more efficient to build public housing (Rosenthal and Foscarinis 2006). They also note that local exclusionary zoning policies must be repealed, and fair housing should be better enforced (for a further discussion, see Chapters 2 and 3).

Beyond housing-specific goals, proponents of a right to housing argue that additional policy changes in the employment, public assistance, social services, and health services arenas are necessary to address homelessness as a social problem. Full employment, a living wage, training, and education are required, as is a more robust social safety net that is easier to navigate. Furthermore, they argue, we need to improve care for mental illness and substance abuse, including universal health care coverage, or, failing that, improvements in access to and care under Medicare and Medicaid (Rosenthal and Foscarinis 2006).

While the focus must be on prevention, we cannot ignore ameliorative and exit-oriented goals for those already homeless, sheltered and unsheltered. Proponents of a right to housing argue, first, for an immediate placement in a shelter with a quick transition to permanent housing, followed by food, clothing, centralized access to social services, health care (particularly preventative health care), and opportunities to work. Underlying all of these steps should be a basic respect for the civil rights of homeless people (Rosenthal and Foscarinis 2006).

Historical and Contemporary Homelessness Policies

Policy toward the homeless has only very recently focused on homelessness as a distinct social problem. Early policies and practices focused on how to alleviate poverty, then what to do about skid row, and most recently on how to combat urban decline. Only very recently have federal policies and local practices been oriented toward alleviating homelessness by addressing some of its root causes.

Until the homeless population exploded in the 1980s, local (usually religious) soup kitchens and shelters were the only services for the homeless (Rosenthal and Foscarinis 2006; Nunez and Sribnick 2013). Initial government involvement was at the local level, beginning in New York City (Rosenthal and Foscarinis 2006). The federal government first responded to homelessness as a distinct problem in 1983, when Congress first appropriated money to be specifically used to aid the homeless via FEMA (Federal Emergency Management Agency). The Stewart B. McKinney Homeless Assistance Act followed in 1987, which changed seven existing programs and created fifteen new homeless assistance programs. The programs were centered on emergency relief; prevention-oriented aspects of the original legislation were not enacted (Rosenthal and Foscarinis 2006). Early implementation was spotty and sometimes required litigation to be enacted; some aspects, like a program to aid local entities in accessing underutilized properties to aid the homeless, were entirely ignored (Rosenthal and Foscarinis 2006).

Changes to the McKinney Act in the early 1990s shifted the federal response to homelessness from emergency aid to exit and prevention. The

Clinton administration, building on a set of amendments to the McKinney Act, adopted the "continuum of care" approach, which essentially requires local coordination and linking of housing services and related social services. Emergency shelter grants continued, but new programs were adopted, such as Supportive Housing (for families and disabled people), Shelter Plus Care (for disabled homeless people), and Section 8 Moderate Rehabilitation Single Room Occupancy Program (to increase the supply of SRO units) (Rosenthal and Foscarinis 2006). These programs were essentially transitional, designed to get people placed in permanent housing elsewhere. By 2000, Congress mandated that 30 percent of McKinney Act funds be directed toward permanent housing for homeless individuals.

At the same time, perhaps counterintuitively, local police departments in the nation's largest cities and beyond began a new approach to policing focused on "quality of life." This mode of policing cracked down on small "quality of life" offenses such as drinking or urinating in public, blocking subway entrances or stairs, and sleeping in public parks, to name a few. This approach to policing effectively criminalized homelessness in an effort to "restore civility" to the nation's cities, many of which had been in economic decline due to deindustrialization (Vitale 2008: 2). Criminalization has been the dominant policy toward the homeless at the local level despite relatively progressive goals behind federal funding initiatives.

Reflecting public opinion, homelessness policies have evolved to focus more on prevention in an effort to eliminate the need for shelter for those who are at risk for becoming homeless, have recently become homeless, or contend with chronic homelessness (Burt et al. 2005; Culhane et al. 2011). Service providers now typically aid those who have recently become homeless or who are at imminent risk of becoming homeless with a flexible set of tools that can include rental and utility assistance, move-in costs and security deposits, and mainstream assistance like Medicaid and Temporary Assistance for Needy Families (TANF) (Treglia 2016). Termed "homelessness prevention and rapid re-housing," this short-term, flexible assistance was first developed at the local level in places such as New York City, Philadelphia, Columbus, OH, and in Minnesota and Massachusetts. It was codified in the federal American Recovery and Reinvestment Act of 2009 and made more permanent in the HEARTH Act in the same year, which amended the original McKinney Act (Byrne et al. 2015; Wong et al. 1999). Initial evidence suggests that prevention and rapid rehousing is working, although permanent housing is needed to prevent recidivism (Rolston et al. 2013; Byrne et al. 2015; Rodriguez 2013; Taylor 2014).

Aid for the chronically homeless has taken a different form since the mid-1980s, one that emphasizes permanent supportive housing (PSH). A landmark study from the late 1990s showed that the chronically homeless made up about 10 percent of a shelter population but consumed about

50 percent of its resources (Kuhn and Culhane 1998). Providing permanent housing to the chronically homeless, then, would reduce much of the need for emergency shelter, and likely cost less. PSH programs, then, provide housing as well as voluntary support services to people over eighteen years of age with some source of income (usually social security). Residents of PSH can be permanent tenants, the units are affordable, and tenants' preferences are taken into account. They also have tenants' rights (Rog *et al.* 2014). Research thus far overwhelmingly shows that the costs of PSH programs are generally offset by savings to criminal justice, hospitals, and other emergency services (Culhane *et al.* 2002; Treglia 2016).

One version of PSH, called Housing First, is gaining popularity. Based on the notion that every person has a fundamental right to housing rather than housing being something one must earn, these programs operate in New York City, Washington, DC, Philadelphia, Seattle, Los Angeles, New Orleans, Minneapolis, Denver, San Francisco, Atlanta, Salt Lake City, and other places, including smaller cities, across the country. Residents of Housing First communities do not have to be sober or enroll in services, which many other programs require. They must actively choose their housing characteristics, such as location of the apartment, whether to have roommates, etc. Their housing is not contingent on receiving services; likewise, if evicted, they can still access services. And while Housing First programs can be oriented toward recovering from drug or alcohol abuse, residents' personal goals are central, rather than clinicians' assessments. Perhaps most importantly, people live in apartments of their choosing among non-homeless households, facilitating greater social integration (Tsemberis 2010). So far, research suggests that Housing First programs decrease homelessness, contributing greatly to housing retention and stability for individuals and families (Montgomery *et al.* 2013a; Rog *et al.* 2014; Leff *et al.* 2009; Martinez and Burt 2006; Tsemberis *et al.* 2004, Tsemberis 2010).

The Department of Housing and Urban Development also recently changed its definition of homelessness in 2009 under the HEARTH Act to include

> individuals and families who lack a fixed, regular, and adequate night-time residence ... individuals and families who will imminently lose their primary residence ... individuals and families who are fleeing, or attempting to flee, domestic violence, dating violence, sexual assault, stalking, or other dangerous or life-threatening conditions that relate to violence against the individual or a family member
>
> (U.S. Department of Housing and Urban Development 2011)

Such changes reflect—to some extent—a more nuanced understanding of homelessness.

While much of the current policy approach to homelessness embraces the spirit of a right to housing, many of its key tenets are ignored, including its recommendations regarding the construction of housing, employment, and health care. Furthermore, at the local level, implementing policies that address homelessness often face great resistance.

This resistance usually takes two forms: the "magnet theory" and the "cost argument" (Rosenthal and Foscarinis 2006). Local governments often argue that improving services for the homeless will attract homeless people. While the homeless are no more mobile than the housed, they may consider the availability of services when choosing where to go after entering homelessness (Burt 2001). To prevent a concentration of homeless people, some right to housing proponents suggest we focus on prevention as well as regional rather than localized strategies (Rosenthal and Foscarinis 2006). Local governments often cite the costs associated with supportive housing programs to justify taking little action on homelessness. But the current approach to homelessness—increased policing and spotty services—incurs significant costs to local governments through emergency room services and criminal justice management (Rosenthal 1994).

Thus, while our general approach to homelessness has shifted away from punitive measures toward the Housing First model, with great success, the number of permanent supportive housing and rapid rehousing programs lags behind what is needed. Furthermore, local resistance to building supportive housing tends to prevent any large-scale solution to the homelessness problem.

Extended Case Study: Homelessness Policy in New York City

Yvonne McCain and her three children resided at the Martinique, a so-called welfare hotel near Manhattan's Herald Square, for four years in the early 1980s. The room's mattresses were stained with urine, and although the room was on the eleventh floor the windows had no bars to protect her young children. She became one of the plaintiffs in a Legal Aid Society lawsuit against the city that spurred a massive overhaul in the city's treatment of the homeless. In response to the suit, the court issued an initial order in 1983 that once families were considered eligible for emergency shelter, New York City was required to "assure, insofar as practicable, that such housing meets specified minimal standards of health, safety, and decency suitable for young children" (Nunez and Sribnick 2013: 248).

But thirty years later, the *New York Times* profiled an eleven-year-old named Dasani, who lived with her parents and seven siblings at the Audobon shelter in Brooklyn, NY. Dasani and her family resided at Audobon for almost three years despite the shelter's repeat citations for "deplorable conditions, including sexual misconduct by staff members, spoiled food, asbestos exposure, lead paint, and vermin," and inoperable smoke alarms and permits (Elliott 2013). An inspector noted that the family's room was infested with mice.

It seems as though the treatment of homeless families in New York City had changed very little over thirty years. Indeed, New York City has served as an epicenter of homelessness for decades and a laboratory for approaches to alleviate it. The city is one of few places in the U.S. with a court-ordered enforceable policy that it must provide shelter to anyone who requests it (Main 2016). The city has tried various approaches to providing a basic right to shelter, offering lessons for other localities nationwide.

Almshouses and private charity organizations aided the city's poorest residents from its inception. The city and private charities provided some shelters during the Great Depression's homelessness epidemic, and homeless and alcoholic men populated Bowery flophouses and motels in the postwar period. But homeless families were relatively rare in New York until the late 1960s, when a critical mass of such families led the Lindsay administration to begin sheltering them in decrepit hotels, the city's so-called welfare hotels (Main 2016; Nunez and Sribnick 2013). In 1970, about 1000 families lived in forty such hotels. Most had experienced an emergency that rendered their living situation uninhabitable; the rest simply could not find housing at a low enough rate for their welfare allowance (Nunez and Sribnick 2013). At the same time, the city continued to run a small system of shelters, particularly for men, including the Men's Shelter on E. Third Street in Manhattan and in an abandoned mental institution on Wards Island (Main 2016).

In the summer of 1981, a consent decree was signed in the *Callahan v. Carey* case such that New York City recognized "with the force of law a right to shelter" (Main 2016). The city scrambled to provide shelter for the ballooning homeless population, opening new makeshift shelters at area armories, including two for women at the Flushing and Lexington Avenue Armories. Between 1980 and 1983 the population of single sheltered homeless adults doubled, and the city's budget for dealing with homelessness increased by more than six times, from $6.8 million in 1978 to $38 million in 1983 (Main 2016). The city relied on these low-quality shelters for more than a decade as officials tried to formulate workable plans to house the homeless. The quality and safety of the shelters was questionable at best; New York City shelter clients rated prisons higher than emergency shelters in safety, cleanliness, and food quality in 1982 (Crystal and Goldstein 1982). New York City shelters remained municipally run during this time; in other cities religious organizations such as the Salvation Army operated emergency shelters for the homeless. City officials also continued to house homeless families in welfare hotels all over the city and as far as New Jersey (Nunez and Sribnick 2013).

While the homeless population skyrocketed during the 1980s to the highest level since the Great Depression, city officials debated how to solve the problem. The discussion centered on the causes of homelessness. Was the limited supply of low-rent housing to blame? Or was it individual deficiencies? On one hand advocates argued that the homelessness crisis was essentially a housing crisis, and providing more low-income housing would go a long way toward solving the problem. Another set of officials argued that high-quality shelters were more important, coupled with social services and training that would help people "resolve the issues that had pushed them into homelessness in the first place and ensure greater economic opportunity for the future" (Nunez and Sribnick 2013: 249). This debate would haunt homelessness policy in New York City and in countless localities across the country for decades.

The Koch administration of the 1980s never came down on one side of the debate, splitting the difference. The administration planned to provide more than 250,000 low-income housing units within ten years, 10 percent of which would be set aside for homeless families. They also offered incentives to landlords who rented to homeless families. City officials also began seizing tax-delinquent properties and rehabilitating them to rent to homeless families. The city housed more than 2,400 homeless families in such apartments in 1985, and more than 3,600 in 1987, a small fraction of the estimated 26,000–68,000 homeless individuals in New York City between 1986 and 1988 (Main 2016). The remainder of the homeless population could find shelter in new temporary and permanent barracks-style shelters and in welfare hotels until the late 1980s.

Opposition mounted to the Koch strategy, particularly from the Manhattan Borough President—later mayor—David Dinkins. Funding transitional shelters, he and the Brooklyn, Bronx, and Queens borough presidents argued, was simply wasteful. The city should instead invest in even more low-income housing and increase the welfare shelter allowance (Nunez and Sribnick 2013: 251). After Dinkins won the 1990 mayoral election, the City Council passed a law that the city must stop using barracks-style shelters by the summer of 1992. The city began providing more apartments to homeless families, aided in particular by an agreement with the city's public housing agency that one in four vacant public housing units go to homeless families (Main 2016).

Designed with the underlying Dinkins-era philosophy that providing more low-income housing—rather than social services and temporary shelter—would go a long way toward solving the homelessness problem, this policy instead began to violate the "economic mix" ethos of public housing in New York. For decades the city prioritized a makeup of a third elderly, a third working poor, and a third on public assistance to prevent the concentration of the very poor in public housing. The policy of giving homeless families an advantage for public housing units resulted in a drastic shift in the public housing population, as the share of very low-income families (on public assistance) in public housing increased from 32 percent to 54 percent between 1985 and 1991 (Main 2016). City officials also began to criticize this policy with the view that it created incentives for families to move into the transitional barracks-style shelters to receive priority in public housing, thus increasing the shelter population, though this view was later proven unfounded by rigorous research (Main 2016).

In the meantime, the view that homelessness was caused not primarily by a lack of low-income housing but instead by individual deficiencies on the part of the homeless gained traction. A resurgence in neoconservative views on social welfare led to the reduction of federal welfare benefits under the Reagan, Bush, and Clinton administrations. Local politicians like Rudy Giuliani—elected mayor in 1993—represented a new strategy toward the homeless. Giuliani hoped to increase the quality of life in New York City by cracking down on minor crimes and offenses like loitering, public urination, and the activities of the so-called squeegee men in their attempts to garner tips from motorists. The Giuliani administration's policies toward the homeless were motivated primarily by increasing the safety of the city and spurring economic development and the idea that personal deficiencies were at the root of homelessness.

The Giuliani administration thus adopted a two-pronged approach toward homelessness: cut social welfare spending on this population while requiring some effort of self-help for aid; and shift the provision of homeless services from the city to nonprofits. The Giuliani administration cut the city's budget for social services for the poor and made eligibility requirements much stricter, leading to a 30 percent decline in the welfare and food stamp caseloads between 1995 and 1998 (Nunez and Sribnick 2013). The administration led a similar effort to limit the number of people to whom the city provided emergency shelter. Requiring strict proof of need, the city increased the number of families rejected from emergency shelter from 894 in 1996 to 7,747 in 1997, and 14,401 in 1998—an increase of 700 percent in the first year and 85 percent the second (Nunez and Sribnick 2013).

The city also privatized homeless shelters under Giuliani, shifting their operation to nonprofits. These organizations were free to impose all kinds of requirements on the homeless population in exchange for shelter, including work or rehabilitation. The city was still required by law to provide shelter to anyone who asked for it, but the rise of nonprofit shelter management meant that behavior-oriented strategies could be implemented without worries of lawsuits, since anyone who refused to comply with nonprofit shelter requirements could go back to a few city-run shelters (Main 2016). While the Giuliani administration's crackdown on social services for the homeless certainly decreased the numbers of people receiving aid, it did nothing to the size of the homeless population.

By the time Michael Bloomberg was elected in 2001, homelessness was again on the rise. His election marked a sea change in the city's homelessness policies. Despite decades of attempting to manage homelessness in New York City, in 2004 homelessness reached its highest level since the Great Depression (Elliott 2013). That same year, Mayor Michael Bloomberg announced a radical and unprecedented goal of eradicating homelessness in New York City.

First, the Bloomberg administration aimed to provide supportive housing to the chronically homeless, who had been found to use a disproportionate share of social services (Kuhn and Culhane 1998). Supportive housing is "subsidized housing for people with various sorts of disabilities who are provided medical and social services on-site so that they can live independently off the streets" (Main 2016: 8). In contrast to the Giuliani-era nonprofit shelters, supportive housing was permanent housing governed by an ethos of "housing first," meaning residents did not have to be sober or engage in any social services to receive housing. Supportive housing received the most funding to date under the Bloomberg administration.

Second, the administration sought to prevent homelessness, primarily by reducing the shelter population. Arguing that the shelter population was growing because of the city's policy of giving homeless families priority in public housing and housing vouchers, the administration ended the policy in 2004. Rather than being given priority for low-income housing, the city would provide rental assistance grants for up to five years, with the amount shrinking by 20 percent each year, in addition to a host of other requirements. The policy reflected the larger trends in social welfare retrenchment the country had seen since Reagan. Still, by 2009, the city's shelter population had grown rather than shrunk (Main 2016).

When this initial policy failed by several measures, a new program—called Advantage—replaced it. Advantage provided only a one-year rental subsidy with a possible second-year extension with a host of other work and shelter requirements. Advantage was a failure on multiple fronts. It was poorly administered, incited landlord fraud, and, perhaps most importantly, 25 percent of Advantage families ended back up in the shelter system once their second-year subsidy ran out (Main 2016).

In all, while the Bloomberg administration advanced the most ambitious policy goal to date to eradicate homelessness through supportive housing and prevention, homelessness in the city reached an all-time high in 2013 (Elliott 2013). Providing supportive housing did seem to make a dent in the chronically homeless population: the population of homeless people sleeping on the street decreased by about a quarter between 2005 and 2014 (Main 2016), but the shelter population grew to unprecedented levels.

The eradication of priority referrals to public housing and housing vouchers for homeless families under Bloomberg undermined the larger goal to prevent homelessness in New York by embracing the notion that the policy created perverse incentives. When homeless families were given priority for permanent low-income housing, only 11.5 percent ended up back in shelters within five years, but 25 percent of Advantage families ended up back in shelters within two years (Elliott 2013; Main 2016). Among them was Dasani's family, profiled by the *New York Times* and discussed earlier in this section.

When the Bloomberg administration instituted its ambitious plan to eradicate housing in New York City in 2004, the shelter population was 36,399 (Main 2016). By the time Bill de Blasio took office in 2014, the number of men, women, and children in city shelters was 60,939 (Routhier 2016)—an increase of more than 65 percent. By 2013, more than 20,000 children were homeless in New York City—the highest number since the Great Depression (Elliott 2013).

Mayor de Blasio's approach to homelessness is considered to be the most progressive in more than a generation. It largely reaffirms the efficacy of the Housing First model, established by more than a decade of empirical research. The de Blasio administration adopted the ambitious goal of building 15,000 new units of supportive housing by 2026 (New York City Office of the Mayor 2016). The city also established the Living in Communities (LINC) program—a temporary rental subsidy program similar to Advantage but extendable for five years and available to a larger constituency.

But the de Blasio administration considers homelessness prevention from a very different angle than Bloomberg's—one that emphasizes the significance of the underlying economy. The fact that median household income in New York City rose by 2 percent, while median rents rose by 14 percent between 2010 and 2014 (Routhier 2016) underscores the administration's general approach toward homelessness. For example, the administration reinstated priority in public housing and housing vouchers for homeless families; it is also aggressively combating illegal evictions of poor households from apartments with rising values. Perhaps most widely publicized is the administration's ambitious goal to construct or preserve 200,000 units of affordable housing by 2026 (Figure 4.4). Such policies reflect a more robust understanding of the underlying economic causes of homelessness. Their impact is, of course, to be determined.

The three distinct phases of homelessness policy in New York City—what Main (2016) calls entitlement, paternalism, and post-paternalism—offer great lessons to other locales grappling with homelessness. The entitlement phase, exemplified largely under Mayor Koch in the 1980s, focused on how to implement the immediate right to shelter, with the construction of temporary and permanent shelters the dominant policy. The paternalism phase, exemplified during the 1990s Giuliani era, focused on the supposed deficiencies of homeless individuals that were thought to be the primary cause of homelessness, with welfare rollbacks and self-help requirements the primary policies. The post-paternalism phase, advanced in the Bloomberg age of the first decade of the millennium, abandoned the notion that homelessness was

Figure 4.4 New affordable housing construction in New York City, 2016

Source: Ken Gould.

caused by individual deficiencies, instead advancing the Housing First model for the chronically homeless. But the Bloomberg administration also retained the neoconservative view that housing aid should be accompanied by some sort of self-help on the part of recipients by instituting a time limit on housing aid and requiring work hours, and abolishing the policy of granting priority in public housing to homeless families. The de Blasio area can be best characterized by a fundamental recognition that underlying economic conditions, including the housing market, are primarily responsible for homelessness, with policies meant to address economic inequality and increase housing aid to New Yorkers.

The extent to which the New York City experience can be applied to other localities varies greatly. New York is by no means alone in the amount of low-income housing it has lost over the decades. Other locales face similar, if not worse, challenges. But it is relatively distinct in that its housing costs are among the highest in the nation—a factor that exacerbates homelessness—and in that it retains the largest and most robust public housing in the country, an asset that many other locales do not have. Certainly the debates around the root causes of homelessness and their attendant policies, as well as the linkage of homelessness policy to urban economic policy, have been echoed in countless communities across the country. Whether other places learn from New York's mistakes is to be determined.

Terms

Homelessness
Precariously or marginally housed
Social welfare retrenchment
Disaffiliation theory
Involuntary displacement
Magnet theory
Cost argument
"Quality of life" policing

Discussion Questions

What are some problems with the ways we define homelessness? What is the best definition of homelessness?

What are the problems with the ways we count the homeless population? What might be a better way?

What characterizes the homeless population today? How did the characteristics of the homeless population in the U.S. change over time?

What contributed to the rise in street homelessness in the 1970s?

What are the foundational social debates around homelessness? Which position(s) have shaped policy the most? Why?

How would you characterize our current policies toward the homeless? What should be changed?

Pick a locality in the U.S. How does its homelessness problem compare to New York's?

Can the lessons from New York's homeless policies over the years apply to other places? Why or why not?

Application

You are a caseworker at a city shelter. A young mother with two children—one school aged, the other a toddler—comes to the shelter for the first time and meets with you. What do you suggest as a plan of action? Peruse the homeless assistance programs available at HUD's website and through local housing and social service agencies and craft a case plan for your client. Next, craft an assessment of the federal and local governments' approach to homelessness as it pertains to your client. What do you recommend continue or be changed, and why?

Next, you see a middle-aged male individual, a chronically homeless addict with a history of mental illness. What do you suggest as a plan of action? What is your assessment of the federal and local approaches to homelessness as they relate to this client? What would you recommend continue or be changed, and why?

Did your plans or critiques of homelessness policy change when dealing with different clients? If so, how and why? What does this suggest about our current policies toward the homeless?

References

Allgood, Sam and Warren, Ronald S. 2003. "The Duration of Homelessness: Evidence from a National Survey." *Journal of Housing Economics* 12: 273–290.

Anderson, Nels. 1940. *Men on the Move.* Chicago, IL: University of Chicago Press.

Bahr, Howard M. and Caplow, Theodore. 1974. *Old Men: Drunk and Sober.* New York, NY: New York University Press.

Bahr, Howard. 1973. *Skid Road.* New York, NY: Oxford University Press.

Bogue, Donald B. 1963. *Skid Row in American Cities.* Chicago, IL: Community and Family Study Center, University of Chicago.

Bratt, Rachel G., Stone, Michael E., and Hartman, Chester. 2006. *A Right to Housing: Foundation for a New Social Agenda.* Philadelphia, PA: Temple University Press.

Burt, Martha R. 2001. "What Will It Take to End Homelessness? Washington, DC: Urban Institute." Retrieved December 1, 2016. www.urban.org/research/publication/what- will-it- take-end- homelessness/view/full_report.

Burt, Martha R., Pearson, Carol L., and Montgomery, Ann Elizabeth. 2005. *Strategies for Preventing Homelessness.* Washington, DC: Urban Institute. Retrieved May 13, 2016. www.urban.org/research/publication/strategies-preventing-homelessness.

Byrne, Thomas, Munley, Ellen A., Fargo, Jamison D., Montgomery, Ann E., and Culhane, Dennis P. 2013. "New Perspectives on Community-Level Determinants of Homelessness." *Journal of Urban Affairs* 35(5): 607–625.

Byrne, Thomas, Treglia, Dan, Culhane, Dennis P., Kuhn, John, and Kane, Vincent. 2015. "Predictors Of Homelessness Following Exit From Homelessness Prevention And Rapid Re-Housing Programs: Evidence From The Department Of Veterans Affairs Supportive Services For Veteran Families Program." *Housing Policy Debate,* December: 1–24.

Crystal, Stephen, and Goldstein, Merv. 1982. "Chronic and Situational Dependency: Long Term Residents in a Shelter for Men." Human Resources Administration, New York, NY.

Culhane, Dennis P., Metraux, Stephen, and Byrne, Thomas. 2011. "A Prevention-Centered Approach to Homelessness Assistance: A Paradigm Shift?" *Housing Policy Debate* 21: 295–315.

Culhane, Dennis P., Metraux, Stephen, and Hadley, Trevor. 2002. "Public Service Reductions Associated with Placement of Homeless Persons with Severe Mental Illness in Supportive Housing." *Housing Policy Debate* 13(1): 107–162.

Culhane, Dennis P., Metraux, Stephen, Park, Jung Min, Schretzman, Maryanne, and Valente, Jesse. 2007. "Testing a Typology of Family Homelessness Based on

Patterns of Public Shelter Utilization in Four U.S. Jurisdictions: Implications for Policy and Program Planning." *Housing Policy Debate* 18: 1–28.

Desmond, Matthew. 2016. *Evicted: Poverty and Profit in the American City*. New York, NY: Crown.

Elliott, Andrea. 2013. "Invisible Child: Girl in the Shadows, Dasani's Homeless Life." *New York Times* December 9, 2013. Retrieved December 1, 2016. www.nytimes. com/projects/2013/invisible-child/#/?chapt=1.

Erickson, Doug and Mosiman, Dean. 2016. "A Knock on the Door Brings Help for Homeless Families." *Wisconsin State Journal*, July 17. Retrieved August 16, 2016. http://host.madison.com/wsj/news/special/homeless/a-knock-on-the-door-brings-help-for-homeless-families/article_096c36c0-2faa-5289-83ba-476724c94962.html.

Fargo, Jamison, Metraux, Stephen, Byrne, Thomas, Munley, Ellen, Montgomery, Ann E., Jones, Harlan, Sheldon, George, Kane, Vincent, and Culhane, Dennis P. 2012. "Prevalence and Risk of Homelessness Among US Veterans." *Preventing Chronic Disease* 9: 110–112.

Foscarinis, Maria, Cunningham-Bowers, Kelly, and Brown, Kristen E. 1999. "Out of Sight—Out of Mind?: The Continuing Trend Toward the Criminalization of Homelessness." *Georgetown Journal on Poverty Law & Policy* 6(2): 145–164.

Hartman, Chester, and Zigas, Barry. 1991. "What's Wrong with the Housing Market." In J. H. Kryder-Coe, L. M. Salomon, and J. M. Molnar, eds, *Homeless Children and Youth*. New Brunswick, NJ: Transaction Publishers.

Hunger and Homelessness Survey: Status Report on Hunger and Homelessness in America's Cities, a 25-City Survey. Retrieved December 1, 2016. www.usmayors. org/pressreleases/documents/hungerhomelessnessreport_121208.pdf

Jencks, Christopher. 1994. *The Homeless*. Cambridge, MA: Harvard University Press.

Katz, Michael B. 1986. *In the Shadow of the Poorhouse: A Social History of Welfare in America*. New York, NY: Basic Books.

Katz, Michael B. 2013. *The Undeserving Poor: America's Enduring Confrontation with Poverty*. Oxford: Oxford University Press.

Kuhn, Randall and Culhane, Dennis P. 1998. "Applying Cluster Analysis to Test a Typology of Homelessness by Pattern of Shelter Utilization: Results from the Analysis of Administrative Data." *American Journal of Community Psychology* 26: 207–232.

Kuno, Eri, Rothbard, Aileen B., Averyt, June, and Culhane, Dennis. 2000. "Homelessness Among Persons With Serious Mental Illness in an Enhanced Community-Based Mental Health System." *Psychiatric Services* 51(8): 1012–1016.

Kushel, Margot B., Vittinghoff, Eric, and Haas, Jennifer S. 2001. "Factors Associated with the Health Care Utilization of Homeless Persons." *JAMA* 285(2): 200–206.

Lee, Barrett A. 1980. "The Disappearance of Skid Row: Some Ecological Evidence." *Urban Affairs Quarterly* 16(1): 81–107.

Lee, Barrett A., Price-Spratlen,Townsand, and Kanan, James W. 2003. "Determinants of Homelessness in Metropolitan Areas." *Journal of Urban Affairs* 25(3): 335–356.

Lee, Barrett A., Tyler, Kimberly A., and Wright, James D. 2010. "The New Homelessness Revisited." *Annual Review of Sociology* 36: 501–521.

Leff, H. Stephen, Chow, Clifton M., Pepin, Renee, Conley, Jeremy, Allen, Isabel E., and Seaman, Christopher A. 2009. "Does One Size Fit All? What We Can and

Can't Learn from a Meta-Analysis of Housing Models for Persons with Mental Illness. *Psychiatric Services* 60(4): 473–482.

Link, Bruce, Susser, Ezra, Stueve, Anne, Phelan, Jo, Moore, Robert E., and Struening, Elmer. 1994. "Lifetime and Five-Year Prevalence of Homelessness in the United States." *American Journal of Public Health* 84: 1907–1912.

Link, Bruce G., Schwartz, Sharon, Moore, Robert, Phelan, Jo, Struening, Elmer, Stueve, Ann, and Colten, Mary Ellen. 1995. "Public Knowledge, Attitudes, and Beliefs About Homeless People: Evidence for Compassion Fatigue?" *American Journal of Community Psychology* 23(4): 533–555.

Main, Thomas. 1998. "How to Think About Homelessness: Balancing Structural and Individual Causes." *Journal of Social Distress and the Homeless* 7(1): 41–54.

Main, Thomas J. 2016. *Homelessness in New York City: Policymaking from Koch to de Blasio.* New York, NY: New York University Press.

Martinez, Tia E. and Burt, Martha R. 2006. "Impact of Permanent Supportive Housing on the Use of Acute Care Health Services by Homeless Adults." *Psychiatric Services* 57(7): 992–999.

Montgomery, Ann E., Metraux, Stephen, and Culhane, Dennis. 2013. "Rethinking Homelessness Prevention Among Persons with Serious Mental Illness." *Social Issues and Policy Review* 7(1): 58–82.

Montgomery, Ann E., Hill, Lindsay L., Kane, Vincent, and Culhane, Dennis P. 2013. "Housing Chronically Homeless Veterans: Evaluating the Efficacy of a Housing First Approach to HUD-VASH." *Journal of Community Psychology* 41(4): 975–991.

New York City Office of the Mayor. 2016. "At Visit to Supportive Housing, Mayor de Blasio Announces Task Force to Help Deliver 15,000 New Units." Retrieved August 14, 2016. www1.nyc.gov/office-of-the-mayor/news/043-16/at-visit-supportive-housing-mayor-de-blasio-task-force-help-deliver-15-000-new.

Nunez, Ralph da Costa and Sribnick, Ethan G. 2013. *The Poor Among Us: A History of Family Poverty and Homelessness in New York City.* New York, NY: White Tiger Press.

O'Flaherty, Brendan. 1996. *Making Room: The Economics of Homelessness.* Cambridge, MA: Harvard University Press.

O'Flaherty, Brendan and Wu, Ting. 2006. "Fewer Subsidized Exits and a Recession: How New York City's Family Homeless Shelter Population Became Immense." *Journal of Housing Economics* 15: 99–125.

O'Toole, T. P., Gibbon, J. L., Hanusa, B. H., and Fine, M. J. 1999. "Utilization of Health Care Services Among Subgroups of Urban Homeless and Housed Poor." *Journal of Health Politics, Policy and Law* 24: 91–114.

Quigley, John M. and Steven Raphael. 2001. "The Economics of Homelessness: The Evidence from North America." *European Journal of Housing Policy* 1(3): 323–336.

Rodriguez, Jason. 2013. "Homelessness Recurrence in Georgia." Georgia Department of Community Affairs: State Housing Trust Fund for the Homeless. Retrieved on May 13, 2016. www.dca.state.ga.us/housing/specialneeds/programs/downloads/homelessnessrecurrenceingeorgia.pdf.

Rog, Debra J., Marshall, Tina, Dougherty, Richard H., George, Preethy, Daniels, Allen S., Ghose, Sushmita S., and Delphin-Rittmon, Miriam E. 2014. "Permanent Supportive Housing: Assessing the Evidence." *Psychiatric Services* 65: 287–294.

Rolston, Howard, Geyer, Judy, and Locke, Gretchen. 2013. "Final Report: Evaluation of the Homebase Community Prevention Program." NYC Department of Homeless Services, New York. Retrieved on May 13, 2016. www.abtassociates.com/AbtAssociates/files/cf/cf819ade-6613-4664-9ac1-2344225c24d7.pdf.

Rosenthal, Rob. 1994. *Homeless in Paradise: A Map of the Terrain.* Philadelphia: Temple University Press.

Rosenthal, Rob and Foscarinis, Maria. 2006. "Responses to Homelessness: Past Policies, Future Directions, and a Right to Housing." In R. G. Bratt, M. E. Stone, and C. Hartman, eds, *A Right to Housing: Foundation for a New Social Agenda,* pp. 316–339. Philadelphia, PA: Temple University Press.

Rossi, Peter H. 1989. *Down and Out in America: The Origins of Homelessness.* Chicago, IL: University of Chicago Press.

Routhier, Giselle. 2016. *State of the Homeless 2016.* New York, NY: Coalition for the Homeless.

Salit, Sharon A., Kuhn, Evelyn M., Hartz, Arthur J., Vu, Jade M., and Mosso, Andrew L. 1998. "Hospitalization Costs Associated with Homelessness in New York City." *The New England Journal of Medicine* 338: 1734–1740.

Shern, David L., Tsemberis, Sam, Anthony, William, Lovell, Anne M., Richmond, Linda, Felton, Chip J., Winarski, Jim, and Cohen, Mikal. 2000. "Serving Street-Dwelling Individuals with Psychiatric Disabilities: Outcomes of a Psychiatric Rehabilitation Clinical Trial." *American Journal of Public Health* 90(12): 1873–1878.

Shinn, Marybeth, Greer, Andrew L., Bainbridge, Jay, Kwon, Jonathan, and Zuiderveen, Sara. 2013. "Efficient Targeting of Homelessness Prevention Services for Families." *American Journal of Public Health* 103: 324–330.

Shinn, Marybeth, Weitzman, Beth C., Stojanovic, Daniela, Knickman, James R., Jiménez, Lucila, Duchon, Lisa, James, Susan, and Krantz, David H. 1998. "Predictors of Homelessness among Families in New York City: From Shelter Request to Housing Stability." *American Journal of Public Health* 88: 1651–1657.

Shlay, Anne, and Rossi, Peter H. 1992. "Social Science Research and Contemporary Studies of Homelessness." *Annual Review of Sociology* 18: 129–160.

Stojanovic, Daniela, Weitzman, Beth C., Shinn, Marybeth, Labay, Larissa E., and Williams, Nathaniel P. 1999. "Tracing the Path Out of Homelessness: The Housing Patterns of Families after Exiting Shelter." *Journal of Community Psychology* 27(2): 1651–1657.

Taylor, Jamie. 2014. "Housing Assistance for Households Experiencing Homelessness." National Conference on Family & Youth Homelessness. Retrieved May 13, 2016. www.endhomelessness.org/page/-/files/NOLA%20Housing%20Assistance%20as%20Support%20for%20Households%20Experiencing%20Homelessness.pdf.

Toohey, Siobhan M., Shinn, Marybeth, and Weitzman, Beth C. 2004. "Social Networks and Homelessness among Women Heads of Household." *American Journal of Community Psychology* 33: 7–20.

Treglia, Dan. 2016. "Homelessness in the United States." In Anacker, K., Carswell, A. T., Kirby, S., and Tremblay, K., eds, *Introduction to Housing.* Athens, GA: University of Georgia Press.

Tsai, J., Kasprow, W. J., Kane, V., and Rosenheck, R. A. 2014. "Street Outreach and Other Forms of Engagement with Literally Homeless Veterans." *Journal of Health Care for the Poor and Underserved* 25(2): 694–704.

Tsemberis, Sam. 2010. "Housing First: Ending Homelessness, Promoting Recovery, and Reducing Costs." In B. O'Flaherty and I. G. Ellen, eds, *How to House the Homeless*, pp. 37–56. New York, NY: Russell Sage Foundation.

Tsemberis, Sam, Gulcur, Leyla, and Nakae, Maria. 2004. "Housing First, Consumer Choice, and Harm Reduction for Homeless Individuals with a Dual Diagnosis." *American Journal of Public Health* 94(4): 651–656.

U.S. Census Bureau. 2016. "Annual Estimates of the Resident Population: April 1, 2010 to July 1, 2015." Retrieved April 21, 2016. http://factfinder.census.gov/faces/tableservices/jsf/pages/productview.xhtml?pid=PEP_2015_PEPANNRES&src=pt.

U.S. Conference of Mayors. 2008. "Hunger and Homelessness Survey: A Status Report on Hunger and Homelessness in America's Cities." Available at www.usmayors.org.

U.S. Department of Housing and Urban Development. 2011. "Homeless Emergency Assistance and Rapid Transition to Housing: Defining 'Homeless.'" *Federal Register* 76(233): 75994.

U.S. Department of Housing and Urban Development. 2014a. "The 2014 Annual Homeless Assessment Report (AHAR) to Congress." Retrieved April 21, 2016. www.hudexchange.info/onecpd/assets/File/2014-AHAR-Part-2.pdf.

U.S. Department of Housing and Urban Development. 2014b. "2014 AHAR HMIS Estimates of Homelessness." Retrieved April 21, 2016. www.hudexchange.info/resource/4828/2014-ahar-part-2-estimates-of-homelessness/.

U.S. Department of Housing and Urban Development. 2016. "HUD Exchange: PIT and HIC Data Since 2007." Retrieved April 21, 2016. www.hudexchange.info/resource/3031/pit-and-hic-data-since-2007/.

Van Bueren, Geraldine. 2016. "A Right to Housing Should Be Part of UK Law." *The Guardian*, March 1. Retrieved August 20, 2016. www.theguardian.com/society/2016/mar/01/right-to-housing-uk-law-homelessness.

Vitale, Alex S. 2008. *City of Disorder: How the Quality of Life Campaign Transformed New York Politics*. New York, NY: New York University Press.

Viveiros, Janet and Sturtevant, Lisa. 2014. *Housing Landscape 2014*. Washington, DC: National Housing Conference.

Willse, Craig. 2015. *The Value of Homelessness: Managing Surplus Life in the United States*. Minneapolis, MN: University of Minnesota Press.

Wong, Yin-Ling I., Culhane, Dennis P., and Kuhn, Randall. 1997. "Predictors of Exit and Reentry among Family Shelter Users in New York City." *Social Service Review* 71(3): 441–462.

Wong, Yin-Ling I., Koppel, Meg, Culhane, Dennis P., Metraux, Stephen, Eldridge, David E., Hillier, Amy, and Lee, Helen R. 1999. "Help in Time: an Evaluation of Philadelphia's Community-Based Homelessness Prevention Program." Retrieved December 1, 2016. http://repository.upenn.edu/spp_papers/145/.

Wright, Talmadge. 1997. *Out of Place: Homeless Mobilizations, Subcities, and Contested Landscapes*. Albany, NY: State University of New York Press.

CHAPTER 5

Homeownership and Home Financing

In July of 2016 an NBC headline alarmingly proclaimed: "Millennials Cause Home Ownership to Drop to Its Lowest Level Since 1965" (Olick 2016). The American homeownership rate reached its highest level in history in the first decade of the millennium, before the housing crisis and Great Recession led to the loss of millions of Americans' homes. News story after news story describe dramatic changes in the housing market, as millennials, saddled with student debt and delaying marriage and children, postpone or eschew homeownership altogether. What will become of our homeownership society? And why the panic over the changes in the housing market?

Homeownership is a central component of the American Dream. It is also the most important source of long-term wealth building for Americans. But property values and the homeownership rate have fallen significantly in recent years, and researchers continue to debate whether homeownership is personally, economically, and/or socially beneficial, particularly in the wake of the recent housing crisis. Homeownership requires substantial debt for the vast majority of Americans, and homeownership benefits some social groups more than others. Yet the federal government continues to incentivize homeownership for Americans as we work toward a "homeownership society," and highly complex financial markets fund home purchases and refinances.

Why is homeownership so venerated in American society? How does the government encourage homeownership—and more importantly, should it? What are the characteristics and potential problems with our current system of housing finance? Are markets—financial markets in particular—the best way to provide social goods such as homes? This chapter examines the

significance of homeownership in American society, changes in homeownership patterns over time, the benefits and pitfalls of homeownership, and how
we as a society manage and encourage homeownership.

Homeownership in the Twenty-First Century

The majority of Americans have owned their homes for nearly seventy years.
Home equity—the value of a home—remains the single largest part of the
vast majority of Americans' wealth (McCabe 2016). In 2014 about 65 percent
of Americans owned their homes, down from a high of 69 percent in 2004
(U.S. Census 2015). America's homeownership rate is about average compared to other countries; it is 80 percent in Spain, for example, while less
than 40 percent of households in Switzerland own their own homes
(Andrews and Sánchez 2011). The recent foreclosure crisis seems to have
done little to shake Americans' fundamental faith in homeownership: more
than 80 percent of renters hope to own a home someday (Belsky 2013).

Homeownership remains a near-universal ideal in American society, and
research shows that homeownership may provide a set of associated social,
economic, physical, and psychological benefits. Certainly Americans have
great confidence in homeownership as a safe financial investment strategy,
even despite the recent dramatic crash in housing prices and home equity
(Joint Center for Housing Studies 2012; McCabe 2016). But large questions
remain about the mechanisms of the supposed social, physical, and psychological benefits of homeownership. Simply put, it is very difficult to tease out
whether homeownership provides social and psychological advantages, or
whether people who are already advantaged seek out homeownership.

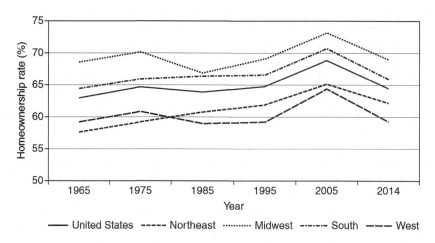

Figure 5.1 U.S. homeownership rates 1965–2014

Source: U.S. Census Current Population Survey/Housing Vacancy Survey, Series H-111.

There is also evidence that homeownership benefits some social groups more than others. Certainly homeownership has traditionally benefited working-class, middle-class, and affluent households, but there are other social inequalities that can be reinforced through homeownership. Regional and racial differential benefits are especially clear. Because housing prices in the Midwest and the South have generally been more affordable for the typical American, homeownership rates have been consistently higher there (Figure 5.1). White households have always had higher than average rates of homeownership, while the Black and Latino homeownership rate has lagged behind considerably (Figure 5.2). In 2014 nearly 73 percent of white households owned their homes, while only 45 percent of Latino households and 43 percent of Black households were homeowners (Table 5.1). The Black and Latino homeownership rates increased from 1995 to 2005—though they never approached the rate of whites—only to decrease again during the foreclosure crisis that began roughly in 2007 (Figure 5.2).

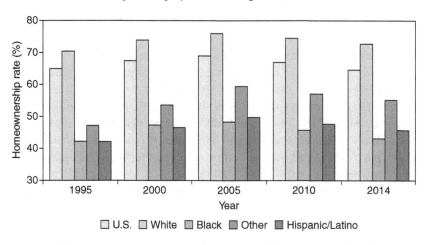

Figure 5.2 U.S. homeownership rate by race and ethnicity 1995–2014

Source: U.S. Census Current Population Survey/Housing Vacancy Survey, Series H-111.

Table 5.1 Homeownership rate (%) by race and ethnicity of householder 1995–2014

| | Race/Ethnicity of Householder | | | | |
	White	Black	Other	Hispanic/Latino	U.S.
1995	70.4	42.2	47.1	42.1	64.8
2000	73.8	47.2	53.6	46.3	67.4
2005	75.8	48.2	59.4	49.5	68.9
2010	74.5	45.4	57.0	47.5	66.9
2014	72.7	43.0	55.0	45.4	64.5

Source: U.S. Census Current Population Survey/Housing Vacancy Survey, Series H-111.

The Housing Crisis

Despite lingering questions over how and to whom homeownership provides benefits, the federal government aimed to increase homeownership among Americans in the early 1990s. At the same time that public policy worked to support homeownership for more and more Americans, the financial industry developed a new array of mortgage options designed to elicit additional streams of profit. While some of these new mortgages enabled more Americans to own homes, others had such burdensome features that they were almost certain to end in default, and therefore lost homes. These new mortgages were designed to open new channels for profit from home lending rather than extend the benefits of homeownership to a larger segment of Americans per se. As the financial industry created new mortgage types and more people could finance homeownership, the housing, construction, and related industries boomed. By 2005, housing construction, remodeling, and sales accounted for more than 6 percent of the U.S.'s gross domestic product—a significant increase over the 4.7 percent reported in 1990 (National Association of Home Builders 2015).

The new mortgage products that fueled such dramatic economic growth, however, were very risky. Often referred to as "subprime" loans, these mortgages were developed to provide loans to people with more credit risk—traditionally people with FICO scores below 640 (Lo 2012). These loans had higher interest rates and/or unique features that brought higher costs to borrowers, such as adjustable rather than fixed rates, pre-payment penalties, and balloon payments. Designed to compensate for the higher default risk of people with average credit, these features could raise interest rates, charge high costs if borrowers paid more than was owed on the mortgage, or require a large one-time payment to clear the mortgage in addition to the loan amount, respectively. Because lenders made a higher profit with subprime loans, they were heavily marketed to prime borrowers—people with excellent credit—as well.

This highly lucrative but ultimately tenuous housing finance system, coupled with enormously inflated housing values, led to widespread foreclosures. Foreclosure occurs when a lender repossesses a property after the owner has failed to make mortgage payments for a particular period of time. The high-cost features associated with subprime loans, rising unemployment, and dramatically falling housing prices caused many households to miss mortgage payments, in the late 2000s.

Between 2007 and August 2010, banks seized more than three million homes through foreclosure nationwide (Bohan and Daly 2010; see Figure 5.3). At the peak of the housing crisis, a full quarter of all American homeowners owed more on their homes than they were worth, and the share of U.S. households in foreclosure was more than 5.5 percent (Belsky 2013; see

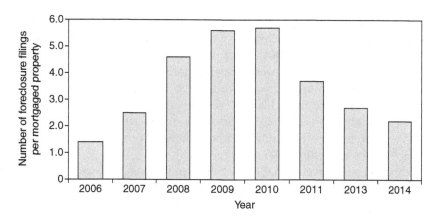

Figure 5.3 U.S. foreclosure rate 2006–2014

Source: RealtyTrac, U.S. Census American Community Survey (2008–2012 5-Year Estimates, DP04).

Figure 5.4). In 2008, one in fifty-four U.S. households received a foreclosure filing, and one in forty-five households received a filing at the peak of the housing crisis in 2009 (RealtyTrac 2009, 2010). In the hardest-hit state of Nevada, one in ten households received a foreclosure filing (RealtyTrac 2010). Households holding subprime and other high-cost loans were much more likely to enter foreclosure than those with prime or fixed-rate mortgages. The prime, fixed-rate mortgage foreclosure rate peaked at around 6 percent at the end of 2009; at the same point in time, the prime adjustable-rate mortgage foreclosure rate stood at nearly 14 percent, the subprime fixed-rate mortgage rate was more than 25 percent, and the subprime adjustable foreclosure rate was about 29 percent (Federal Reserve Bank of Richmond 2011).

Subprime loans were much more likely to be held by Black and Latino households than white households, increasing their risk of foreclosure. While Blacks and Latinos and Black and Latino neighborhoods in the postwar era and throughout the 1980s still suffered from redlining, or the unfair denial of credit, in the last two decades Blacks and Latinos have been more likely to receive credit, but at extremely high costs compared to their white counterparts. Black borrowers were the most likely of all racial and ethnic groups to receive high-cost loans between 2004 and 2007 (Schmidt and Tamman 2009). Wyly *et al.* (2009) found that African Americans were 1.6 times as likely as whites to have subprime credit in 2004, and 2.3 times more likely in 2006. Casey, Glasberg, and Beeman report similar results (Casey *et al.* 2011).

Research has uncovered that these patterns are not due to differential credit scores or income levels. Even after taking into account borrower income, neighborhood profile, and other borrower and neighborhood characteristics, Blacks and Latinos were more likely to receive subprime loans (Gruenstein-Bocian *et al.* 2008; Smith and Hevener 2014). In fact, higher-income Blacks and Latinos were actually more likely to receive subprime loans than their lower-income counterparts; in contrast, higher-income white borrowers were more likely to receive prime loans than their lower-income counterparts (Faber 2013). Similarly, the racial divide in mortgage terms was even more pronounced among homebuyers with higher credit scores (Brooks and Simon 2007).

Research has uncovered that Black and Latino homebuyers were systematically steered to subprime lenders even when they qualified for prime loans (Apgar, Bedimerad, and Essene 2007). These results were echoed at the neighborhood level as well: subprime loan rates were higher in minority communities, and higher in higher-income minority communities than low-income (Calem *et al.* 2004; Kingsley 2009). Recent research suggests that predominantly Black and Latino neighborhoods, particularly in cities and declining inner-ring suburbs, have experienced the highest rates of foreclosure (Rugh and Massey 2010).

At the household level, the loss of a home through foreclosure damages credit and depletes wealth holdings, requires moving, and causes serious personal stress and disruption (Kingsley *et al.* 2009; Ross and Squires 2011). Experiencing foreclosure may also impact mental and physical health, particularly among older people and households with children (Kingsley *et al.* 2009). Concentrated foreclosures can have rippling negative effects at the neighborhood level: they are associated with increased crime rates, vacancies, and decreased property values for neighbors; they also reduce tax revenues that fund school systems and basic municipal services. Foreclosures are liable to require inspections, legal fees, and other expenses that can cost municipalities tens of thousands of dollars (Harding *et al.* 2009; Immergluck and Smith 2006a, 2006b; Molina 2012; Schuetz *et al.* 2008).

Despite the widespread and varied negative effects of the recent housing collapse, American faith in homeownership remains strong. Between 2006 and 2011 home prices fell by more than a third nationwide; Americans lost more than $8 trillion in home equity (Joint Center for Housing Studies 2012). Confidence in homeownership as a financial investment strategy fell during the housing crisis, but it has rebounded considerably since the end of the recession (Belsky 2013; Taylor *et al.* 2011; MacArthur Foundation 2013). Nearly three-quarters of respondents in a recent survey thought that homeownership was a wise investment (Belsky 2013).

Homeownership: The Debates

Three sets of debates surround the role of homeownership in American society in the wake of the housing crisis. First, is homeownership personally, economically, and/or socially beneficial? Second, is the American housing finance system functional and sustainable? Finally, should the U.S. government encourage homeownership, and if so, how? These debates have gained new import in the wake of the Great Recession.

The Benefits of Homeownership?

Despite the fact that encouraging and facilitating homeownership has been a central strategy of American housing policy, researchers continue to disagree about the extent to which homeownership is personally, economically, and/ or socially beneficial, particularly as we recover from the housing crisis.

The idea that property owners make better citizens has a long history in America. Indeed, in early America, property ownership was required to vote in elections (McCabe 2016). Political leaders thought that property owners were more independent and unbiased and more invested in social, political, and economic affairs (Keyssar 2009; Krueckeberg 1999; McCabe 2016). Later, political and civic leaders in the early twentieth century espoused homeownership in an effort to curtail growing urban political and social radicalism and to ensure a docile workforce (Karolak 2000; McCabe 2016). In contemporary times political leaders and ordinary citizens across the political spectrum widely believe that "homeownership anchors citizens in their neighborhoods, generates shared interests in those places, and fortifies the social bonds that are central to safe, vibrant communities" (McCabe 2016: 8).

A good deal of research confirms these contemporary beliefs, as well as other benefits of homeownership. Homeowners tend to be more satisfied with life, have higher self-esteem, have better physical health, vote more in elections, and participate in voluntary organizations and some political activities at higher rates (Ahlbrandt and Cunningham 1979; Blum and Kingston 1984; Cox 1982; DiPasquale and Glaeser 1999; Guest and Oropesa 1986; Lyons and Lowery 1989; McCabe 2013; 2016; Rohe and Stegman 1994a, b; Rossi and Weber 1996). Children of homeowners tend to have higher test scores, more educationally stimulating and supportive home environments, lower high school dropout rates, fewer emotional and behavioral problems, and lower poverty and teen pregnancy rates than children of renters (Boyle 2002; Cairney 2005; Essen *et al.* 1978; Green and White 1997; Harkness and Newman 2002; Haurin *et al.* 2002). Homeownership can have positive effects on neighborhoods too: neighborhoods with more homeowners are more stable and have higher property values than those with more renters, and neighborhoods with low homeownership rates tend to have more social problems (Galster *et al.* 2000; Rohe and Stewart 1996).

However, the extent to which these supposed benefits of homeownership are due to owning a home or to other characteristics of people who own their homes is unresolved (Grinstein-Weiss *et al.* 2012; Holupka and Newman 2012; Newman 2008; Rohe *et al.* 2002). In fact, research that attempts to account for all of these confounding factors suggests that homeownership itself brings no benefits to households (Barker and Miller 2009; Holupka and Newman 2012; Mohanty and Raut 2009). Furthermore, homeowners are no more engaged in most political activities and informal neighborhood activities than renters (McCabe 2016).

Other research also casts doubt on the supposed benefits of homeownership. The financial payoff of homeownership, for example, depends heavily on the type of mortgage, the length of time in a home, and the characteristics of the surrounding neighborhood (McCabe 2016). Homeownership is surely a sound financial investment for homeowners with a single thirty-year, fixed-rate mortgage who live in their home long-term and whose neighborhood has low poverty rates (Di *et al.* 2007; Grinstein-Weiss *et al.* 2013; Herbert *et al.* 2013). On the other hand, homeownership can act as a trap for homeowners in distressed neighborhoods, for example, or whose property values fall—particularly for low-income, female-headed, elderly, and Black households (Burkhauser *et al.* 1995; South and Deane 1993; South and Crowder 1997; 1998a, b).

The recent foreclosure crisis, for example, is considered by many to be "the greatest loss of wealth for communities and individuals of color in modern US history" (Rivera *et al.* 2008). The historic racial wealth gap—the result of discriminatory policies and practices—continues to be reinforced through the housing market (Oliver and Shapiro 2006). Between 2005 and 2009, Latinos' wealth holdings fell by 66 percent and Blacks' wealth holdings by 53 percent, compared to 16 percent of whites', due almost entirely to disproportionate losses in home equity during the recession (Kochhar *et al.* 2011). Asian and Latino homeowners suffered the worst losses in home equity nationally, followed by Black households (Kochhar *et al.* 2011). Furthermore, Latinos experienced the greatest decline among all groups in homeownership between 2005 and 2009, dropping from 51 percent to 47 percent (Kochhar *et al.* 2011; Kochhar *et al.* 2009). Black households had the lowest rate of homeownership in 2009, followed by Latinos and Asians, reversing years of gains (Kochhar *et al.* 2009; Kochhar *et al.* 2011).

As a result, the Black–white and Latino–white wealth gaps are at their highest levels since data have been collected. Whites' median net worth is $92,000, compared to Blacks' median net worth of $4,900 and Latinos' of $6,325 (Kochhar *et al.* 2011). The dramatic and disproportionate wealth loss among Black and Latino households has been attributed largely to the collapse of the housing market and loss of home equity. These consequences will continue to affect future generations, as lost wealth cannot be translated into investments in children's education, medical care, and safe and affordable housing. Damaged credit can limit people's ability to secure student loans, car loans, and other forms of credit that enable upward mobility, particularly for children.

Thus, homeownership does convey some social and economic benefits, although research shows that those benefits may be somewhat exaggerated (McCabe 2016). Furthermore, the benefits are not distributed equally in American society. They depend largely on underlying social positions. The most advantaged groups in society reap the most benefits from homeownership, and while homeownership in some cases may help the most disadvantaged, it also has the potential to hurt them.

The American System of Housing Finance

Even as debates about the benefits of homeownership continue, the vast majority of Americans own or hope to own a home one day (Belsky 2013). Among the most prominent markers of American citizenship—if not the most prominent—is homeownership, which most often means debt.

The financial system that facilitates home purchases has undergone massive changes in the past thirty years, reflecting and sparking debates about the efficacy and sustainability of the American housing finance system. Today banks, private mortgage companies, and other lenders offer mortgages and sell them to other financial institutions, including private and government-sponsored private institutions like Fannie Mae, Freddie Mac, and Ginnie Mae. Those institutions then package mortgages together in large pools and sell shares in them to global investors as financial products, not unlike stocks and bonds. This process is called securitization, and it integrates mortgage lending and American homes fully into the global economy.

It has not always been so, and critics note that the risks associated with the financialization of mortgage lending outweigh the benefits. The demand for mortgage-backed investments can impede the market for homeownership, increase housing prices for ordinary Americans, and indeed perversely incentivize the sale of bad mortgages to ordinary homeowners (Sassen 2009). The transformation of mortgage lending in the U.S. is one component of a larger economic transformation based on neoliberalism,

> a theory of political economic practices that proposes that human well-being can best be advanced by liberating individual entrepreneurial freedoms and skills within an institutional framework characterized by

strong private property rights, free markets, and free trade. The role of the state is to create and preserve an institutional framework appropriate to such practices.... It holds that the social good will be maximized by maximizing the reach and frequency of market transactions, and it seeks to bring all human action into the domain of the market.

(Harvey 2005: 2)

The transformation of mortgage lending from small savings and loans to securitization is one component of the larger neoliberal transformation of the American economy. Mortgage securitization is one aspect of financialization—or "the increasing role of financial motives, financial markets, financial actors and financial institutions in the operation of the domestic and international economies" (Epstein 2005). The widespread economic consequences of the recent collapse of the mortgage lending industry calls into question the American system of housing finance—in particular, the integration of mortgage lending into the global economy—and raises criticisms of financialization and neoliberalism more generally. Are markets—financial markets in particular—the best ways to provide social goods like homes?

For example, the demand for mortgage-backed investments, the boom in housing construction, and the ever-present housing affordability crisis led to the most recent transformation in home lending: a series of new mortgage inventions in the early 2000s. These exotic loans contained features that provided higher rates of profit to investors, but ultimately translated into higher costs for borrowers. "Subprime" loans (mortgages with higher interest rates to compensate for borrowers with higher risk), adjustable-rate mortgages, negative amortization mortgages, very low or zero down payment loans, stated-income loans, and loans with balloon payments and/or prepayment penalties all entered the mortgage marketplace and enabled more and more people to finance property with almost no attendant consumer protections or government regulation.

As housing prices rose all over the country, ordinary people needed to find ways to afford homes. Rising property values all over the country increased demand for exotic loans, which in turn contributed to rising prices in a vicious cycle (Immergluck 2009). Lenders and brokers steered more and more borrowers to higher-cost loans than they were entitled to because of the higher profit they earned (Immergluck 2009). Lenders and brokers operated with virtually no regulation, and fraudulent practices—including lying about borrowers' incomes—proliferated during the subprime boom (Fligstein and Roehrkasse 2016; Immergluck 2009). As Immergluck explains:

In highly competitive home loan markets, originators, including brokers and retail loan officers paid on commission, competed less by helping the borrower find the loan with the lowest interest rate or fees and more by finding the loan—no matter how poorly structured—that would deliver the largest amount of principal per dollar of income.

(Immergluck 2009: 88)

The FBI estimates that instances of mortgage fraud increased by more than 270 percent between 2004 and 2008 (Federal Bureau of Investigation 2008). The fraud was widespread—not simply limited to a few "bad apple" firms. Fligstein and Roehrkasse (2016) show that thirty-two of the largest sixty financial firms in the mortgage business have recently settled lawsuits over fraud during the housing boom.

Lenders and brokers had little incentive to offer stable loan terms to borrowers, as the loans they originated would be sold immediately, and investors—not lenders—ultimately bore the risk. The agencies responsible for rating these mortgage-backed investments received compensation for higher ratings, thus misrepresenting their high risk to investors (Immergluck 2009). As more and more borrowers could not meet these loan terms, the investments in them also tanked, causing a widespread economic collapse not seen since the Great Depression. American taxpayers funded a bailout of major financial institutions holding mortgage-backed investments to a tune of $700 billion to avoid a global catastrophe (Immergluck 2009).

As Stone argues, the recent housing collapse reflects

a very real problem rooted ultimately in the inability of U.S. capitalism to solve the problem of housing affordability through a system of profit-driven mortgage-debt financing, which inevitably passes much of the costs and risks of financial instability and insecurity onto housing consumers and the government

(Stone 2006a: 90)

One problem is that no other sector of the American economy is as dependent—indeed, overly dependent—on debt as housing, rendering such a crucial social good fragile (Bratt 2006; Stone 2006a).

A second problem is that many of the mortgage products offered in the U.S. throughout its history—the first high-cost, short-term mortgages, and thirty-year fixed-rate mortgages offered by savings and loans, and the FHA and VA (discussed in the next section), mortgage-backed investments, and exotic mortgages—have proven to be unsustainable without heavy government support and/or financial bailouts in the billions. The sustainability of the current housing finance system, in which securitization remains dominant and mortgage origination, servicing, and investment are handled by different entities—all with profit as the underlying motive—is unclear, but the economic outcomes thus far suggest that without strong government regulation and intervention they will fail with attendant negative consequences for American households and the national and global economies (Immergluck 2009).

Homeownership Policy: A Historical Perspective

Until the 1930s, very few Americans purchased homes with mortgages; they almost exclusively purchased or built homes with cash, savings, small personal loans, and/or mortgages that typically covered a very small part of home prices, carried high fees, and needed to be repaid in no more than eleven years (Immergluck 2009). As a result, homeownership—even financed partially with a mortgage—was accessible only to affluent Americans until the Great Depression.

With help from the federal government, a massive transformation of private mortgage lending was necessary to make it possible for the average American to own a home and therefore create a homeownership society (McCabe 2016). As noted in Chapter 3, the federal government under the Roosevelt administration first created the Home Owners Loan Corporation and later the Federal Housing Administration to insure a brand-new mortgage designed for the average American worker: an affordable mortgage loan that was fully paid off in thirty years.

Beginning in 1933, the Home Owners Loan Corporation (HOLC) refinanced mortgages to prevent foreclosure for more than a million households. It developed and perfected the long-term, self-amortizing mortgage characterized by low down payments and relatively low interest rates, and this financed homeownership for generations. Modeled after the HOLC, the Federal Housing Administration (FHA) supported the recovery of housing-related industries in the wake of the Great Depression by insuring mortgages under certain criteria, effectively removing lending risk from financial institutions and making them more likely to provide mortgages. At the same time, the Veterans Administration aided military workers returning from World War II to buy homes by assisting with down payments and mortgages. The FHA famously protected existing patterns of residential segregation in its policies, insuring mortgages only in exclusively white, homogeneous communities, particularly in the burgeoning suburbs (Jackson 1985). Because the FHA would not insure mortgages in communities of color, integrated communities, or urban neighborhoods, financial institutions were not inclined to issue mortgages there either, all but ensuring their economic decline (see Chapter 3).

The FHA's policies and influences made homeownership affordable for the largest segment of American households in the country's history (Oliver and Shapiro 2006). Homeownership boomed as a result of this new loan product with the full backing of the U.S. government. By 1950, 55 percent of Americans were homeowners; by 1960, it had increased to 62 percent (McCabe 2016).

After the advent of the low-cost, thirty-year mortgage, home lending was under the near-exclusive purview of the FHA, VA, and local banks (savings and loans) that were insured by the federal government (Immergluck 2009). Local savings and loan banks offered home loans to homebuyers at prevailing interest rates, covering the loans with savings deposits from their communities. In the 1960s, however, as mortgage demand grew but savings deposits waned, this system of housing finance verged on collapse (Stone 2006a). To prevent catastrophe, the federal government led a second major change to the housing finance system by expanding so-called secondary mortgage markets between 1968 and 1970 (Stone 2006a).

Rather than being solely funded by savings deposits, local banks could sell the mortgages they held to other entities—commercial banks, insurance companies, pension funds, and government-sponsored private entities (GSEs) such as Fannie Mae, Ginnie Mae, and Freddie Mac—ensuring a steady stream of cash for more loans, a process called securitization. Larger financial institutions found mortgages to be a lucrative investment—people generally pay their mortgages reliably, so the investment tends to be very safe—but left the logistics of mortgage applications, appraisal, and collection to local banks (Stone 2006a). Some of these large financial institutions, particularly Ginnie Mae, Fannie Mae, and Freddie Mac, then pooled individual federally insured mortgages together and sold shares in them to individual investors, with insurance from the federal government. Thus, individual investors could now purchase shares in sets of household mortgages—what we now call residential mortgage-backed securities, or RMBS—just like stocks and bonds, funneling money back to local banks for more mortgage originations (Stone 2006a). This set of policy and industry changes marked the housing finance system's first step to full integration in national capital markets, as a teachers' pension fund, for example, could now invest in and therefore provide money for home mortgages.

At the same time, the federal government instituted a set of policies designed partly to remedy the discriminatory FHA policies of the generation before and increase homeownership among disadvantaged social groups. Initiated in 1968, the federal Section 235 program helped more than 400,000 families buy homes by 1972 but was embroiled in scandal as housing industry players colluded to inflate housing prices falsely (Gotham 2000; Welfield 1998). The Home Mortgage Disclosure Act (1975), designed to encourage more transparency and combat discrimination in mortgage lending patterns, requires financial institutions to report each mortgage they issue with borrower characteristics. The Community Reinvestment

Act, passed in 1977, requires financial institutions receiving FDIC insurance to provide mortgages in all communities where they do business—including low- and moderate-income neighborhoods that were previously redlined or denied mortgages and other loans based on their demographic composition. The federal government passed these acts, along with the Equal Credit Opportunity Act (1974), to remove barriers to homeownership for qualified households.

While mortgage lending made homeownership a reality for millions more Americans than ever, it merely "created the illusion of homeownership through the reality of debt" (Stone 2006a: 83). The option to finance a home purchase at reasonable terms created demand that boosted the home construction and related industries, but by the early 1980s the overall American economy failed to keep pace such that average households could afford their mortgage payments. More and more of Americans' stagnating income went to housing debts (Stone 2006a).

To address this pitfall in housing finance and save the savings and loan industry, a third set of major policy changes throughout the 1980s further transformed mortgage lending in America. A whole set of new laws and policies, including the Depository Institutions Deregulation and Monetary Control Act (1980), the Alternative Mortgage Transaction Parity Act (1982), the Garn-St Germain Act (1982), the Secondary Mortgage Market Enhancement Act (1984), the Tax Reform Act (1986), and the Financial Institutions Reform Recovery and Enforcement Act (1989) effectively nudged the old savings and loans out of the mortgage business and allowed new, largely unregulated private mortgage companies backed by the GSEs and private investors in RMBS and other related investment products to take their place (Immergluck 2009). Encouraged by these new laws, the savings and loans exited the mortgage loan business and entered other more lucrative but risky ventures. By 1989 this new system failed to save them, and American taxpayers shelled out at least $124 billion to bail out local savings and loan banks and avoid economic collapse (Immergluck 2009).

As mortgage securitization gained increased footing in the 1980s and steam in the 1990s, private companies increasingly bought and sold shares in mortgage loans in increasingly complicated ways that pooled risk and allowed investors to choose between different mortgage-backed financial products with differing risks and rates of return (Immergluck 2009). At the same time, George W. Bush's administration and the Clinton administration's National Homeownership Strategy in particular aimed to increase homeownership, especially among groups with traditionally less access to the mortgage market by facilitating public-private partnerships between federal agencies such as the Federal Housing Administration, Fannie Mae, and Freddie Mac, and private mortgage lenders. In addition to these new policies, the demand for mortgage-backed financial products fueled growing homeownership rates in the 1990s and 2000s, leading into the subprime crisis discussed earlier in this chapter.

Contemporary Homeownership Policy

In the wake of the housing crisis, the policies designed to increase homeownership under the Clinton and Bush administrations have come under fire. Critics argue that the Community Reinvestment Act, National Homeownership Strategy, and other federal homeownership policies pushed homeownership onto households that could not afford it, contributing to the overall collapse of the housing market. Research has shown that the deregulated mortgage market rather than these policies is more to blame (Aalbers 2009).

Federal Homeownership Policy

Despite some criticisms, the goal of a "homeownership society" still reigns in the U.S. Several programs exist to make homeownership affordable to working Americans. The federal government augmented the Housing Choice Voucher program (see Chapter 2) to subsidize home purchase costs for low-income households. The federal government covers the difference between 30 percent of participants' income and monthly homeowner costs, which includes a financed down payment. Homeowners are responsible for upkeep, repairs, and home-related costs beyond the mortgage payment. Local public housing authorities, which administer housing vouchers, can choose whether to offer this program. As a result, this program has been relatively limited in scale, supporting only about 21,000 mortgages in 2012 (Schwartz 2015). Other subsidy programs offer second mortgages to finance down payments, rent-to-own programs in which monthly rents go toward a down payment that can be used for purchase, and individual development accounts in which government or nonprofit agencies match individual contributions toward a down payment (Schwartz 2015).

High housing prices and prevailing housing finance trends like down payment requirements can serve as a barrier to homeownership for even moderate-income households who would be otherwise qualified. One U.S. Census study found that nationally only 2 percent of renters who could not afford to purchase a home only lacked the income to qualify for a mortgage —the vast majority had qualifying incomes but lacked substantial down payments or funds for closing costs (Savage 2009). The Federal Housing Administration—now a part of the Department of Housing and Urban Development—offers down payment assistance to qualified buyers by insuring loans that require only 3.5 percent of the asking price as a down payment.

The Good Neighbor Next Door program discounts properties in designated "revitalization zones" by 50 percent for teachers, firefighters, and EMTs in exchange for residing in purchased homes for at least three years (U.S. Department of Housing and Urban Development 2016).

State and Local Policy

The vast majority of federal funding to aid low- and moderate-income households to purchase homes is administered and distributed by state and local governments and nonprofits. The HOME Investments Partnerships Program (HOME) is the largest of these "block grant"—federal funding distributed at the local level—programs for affordable housing. A little more than 40 percent of HOME funding went toward home purchase aid, counseling, and rehabilitation of owner-occupied housing between 1992 and 2012 (Schwartz 2015). The Self-Help Home Ownership Opportunity Program (SHOP), authorized in 1996, helps local nonprofits purchase properties for renovation by aspiring low-income homeowners. States offer tax-exempt bonds and mortgage revenue bonds to investors to finance low-interest mortgages to first-time homebuyers and investors in multi-family housing. And many localities also have housing trusts that offer housing counseling and down payment assistance to low- and moderate-income households (Schwartz 2015).

Tax Incentives

While these relatively small programs explicitly aim to increase homeownership, the single largest incentive to own a home is in the nation's tax code: the mortgage interest deduction. Homeowners can deduct all of the interest paid on mortgages or home equity loans from their tax burden. In 2012, a staggering 86 percent of federal tax expenditures went to homeowners, largely through the mortgage interest tax deduction (Schwartz 2015). The tax code also incentivizes homeownership in other ways. Homeowners can deduct their property taxes as well as any capital gains from home sales (Schwartz 2015). While there is no evidence that these tax incentives were created explicitly to encourage homeownership, they remain the biggest public incentives for homeownership (Howard 1997; McCabe 2016; Schwartz 2015).

There are at least three major criticisms of tax credits for homeownership. First, they disproportionately benefit higher-income homeowners, because the deductions are worth more to higher-income households. Taking the deduction often doesn't pay off for lower-income homeowners if it is less than the standard tax deduction. For example:

When mortgage interest and property tax payments, combined with state and local income taxes, non-reimbursed medical expenses, charitable donations, and other deductible expenses are less than the standard deduction, taxpayers receive no tax benefit at all from their homeowner expenses.

(Schwartz 2015: 120)

Homeowners with incomes over $100,000 file 19 percent of all tax returns but receive 77 percent of the $68.2 billion in mortgage interest deductions (Schwartz 2015), and homeowners earning more than $100,000 account for 75 percent of property tax deductions (Schwartz 2015). Moreover, households earning more than $200,000 a year—fewer than 5 percent of American households—reap 35 percent of the benefit (McCabe 2016). Mortgage credit certificates, issued by state and local governments, attempt to remedy this by issuing additional tax credits to low- and moderate-income households, but these are grossly underused (Schwartz 2015). As a result, the tax code incentivizes spending more on housing for wealthy Americans, which in turn can raise housing prices for everyone, particularly in tight markets.

A second criticism of the homeowner tax incentives is they favor homeowners over renters within the same income groups who should, ostensibly, have the same tax burdens. A final criticism is that the mortgage interest and property tax deductions coupled with the exclusion of home sales from capital gains taxes encourages speculation in the housing market, ultimately making housing less affordable for Americans (Schwartz 2015).

The criticisms of homeowner tax deductions have led to a development of proposals to reform or eliminate them. Proposals include capping the mortgage loan amount on which homeowners can deduct interest, offering a one-time-only credit for first time homebuyers, and limiting it to only primary residencies (McCabe 2016). But despite the criticisms, new proposals, and the fact that homeowner-related deductions cost Americans more than $68 billion a year (dwarfing the entire budgets of the Departments of Homeland Security, Housing and Urban Development, and Education) most of which goes to the highest-income households, nearly two-thirds of Americans oppose reforming or eliminating the deductions (McCabe 2016).

Alternative Policies

One of the major criticisms of American housing policy, in particular the homeownership society ideal, is that it relies far too much on the volatility of the private market. American taxpayers continuously bail out financial institutions that trade in housing as a commodity for profit, while housing expenses rise for the average American. One alternative would be better regulation of the housing finance industry to help protect the American public from the wild volatility of capital markets and help the housing and lending markets operate more efficiently (Ellen and Willis 2011; Van Order 2011).

Another criticism of homeownership policy is that it rewards speculation, which increases housing prices unnecessarily. An alternative would be to decommodify housing, partially or completely, and treat it as a crucial social good rather than an avenue for profit. The overall goal is to ensure housing security and affordability (Stone 2006b). One option might be to incentivize forms of social ownership of housing through cooperatives, community land trusts, and other shared-ownership models (see Chapter 2). Rather than further reinforcing privatism, social ownership can build community resources beyond individual wealth that help households withstand economic volatility, with investment in playgrounds, day cares, clinics, and recreation opportunities (Radford 2000: 116). A large market for cooperative housing could gain a foothold in the overall housing market, making it less dependent on wild fluctuations in property values and lending markets.

Another possibility would be to encourage social financing of housing, or "financing that is not motivated exclusively, primarily, or even at all on the basis of earning market rates of return" (Swack 2006). Social financing of housing can provide finance to households and communities that the private market has eschewed, shield some of the housing market from global market volatility, make housing more affordable by lessening the cost of debt service, and provide opportunities for social consciousness and accountability to financial institutions (Swack 2006). Examples include federal grants for housing financing, similar to the CDBG and HOME programs but with fewer restrictions, federal loans for housing such as those administered by state and local housing finance agencies, incentives in the form of tax credits such as the Low-Income Housing Tax Credit (see Chapter 2), and a strong regulatory system to govern the private home lending market (Swack 2006).

Case Study: The National Foreclosure Crisis

There is no better example of the rise—and perils—of the financialization of homeownership than the recent home foreclosure crisis. Households, families, communities, and cities all over the U.S. still bear the consequences of the rise of risky lending practices, as more instances of mortgage discrimination and fraud are discovered years after they occurred and well after countless households lost their homes through foreclosure.

At the height of the foreclosure crisis in 2009, suburban Modesto, CA, an hour and a half's drive east of San Francisco, had the fifth-highest foreclosure rate in the country behind Las Vegas, NV, Merced, CA, Cape Coral, FL, and Stockton, CA (Pepitone 2009). Scores of foreclosed homes sat vacant in the best of circumstances as former homeowners scrambled to rent new homes and manage the stress of foreclosure. At worst, squatters occupied the modest dwellings of former homeowners, partying, hanging out, and in some cases burglarizing and vandalizing properties. Burglaries in Modesto increased by 26 percent from 2007 to 2008 (Kloberdanz 2008). Research shows that fore-closure vacancies create opportunities for crime, reduce tax revenues used for municipal services, and depress property values (and thus the wealth hold-ings) of residents in neighborhoods hard hit by foreclosures (Biswas 2012; Ellen *et al.* 2013; Harding *et al.* 2009; Immergluck and Smith 2006a, 2006b; Pfeiffer and Molina 2013; Schuetz *et al.* 2008; Whitaker and Fitzpatrick 2013).

Across the country in urban Baltimore, MD, newly foreclosed properties join the heaps of vacancies—products of deindustrialization, economic downturn, and depopulation—that have blighted the city's neighborhoods for decades. Communities already struggling under the weight of economic depression, poor schools, and high crime face a new wave of such severe blight that the state plans to bulldoze entire neighborhoods (Clark 2016). As other regional housing markets bounce back from the housing crisis, Balti-more's foreclosure rate is the eleventh-highest in the nation, joining places such as Atlantic City and Trenton, NJ, and Tampa Bay–St Petersburg and Clearwater, FL (Simmons 2016). The so-called "sunbelt" and mid-Atlantic regions face the most difficulty in recovering: in early 2016, New Jersey, Maryland, Florida, Nevada, and Delaware had the highest foreclosure rates in the nation (RealtyTrac 2016).

As two very different communities on opposite coasts grappled with the negative consequences of foreclosure on the ground, the Department of Justice filed suit against some of the financial institutions responsible for the devastation. A landmark suit uncovered that Wells Fargo operated specialized lending units to target Black borrowers for subprime loans, even if—*especially* if—they qualified for prime loans. They routinely referred to subprime loans as "ghetto loans" and to Black borrowers as "mud people" (Powell 2009). Wells Fargo settled in 2012, paying $175 million to the city of Baltimore and affected borrowers, and funding a down payment assistance program for homeowners with an average compensation for targeted borrowers of $15,000 (Broadwater 2012). More than half of Wells Fargo's foreclosures in Baltimore between 2005 and 2008 stood vacant in 2009 (Powell 2009).

The Department of Justice, as well as state and local governments, con-tinue to file scores of other suits with similar claims against other financial institutions (Calvey 2015; U.S. Department of Justice 2016). One of those recent suits focuses on discrimination within the foreclosure process among households in Modesto, alleging that three Modesto mortgage companies targeted Latino homeowners for faulty loan modifications that inevitably led to foreclosure (Gaona 2016).

Even as the weaknesses of the housing finance system continue to be exposed, the housing market continues to operate more or less as normal:

mortgages are issued, securitized, invested in, and fully integrated into the global financial system, with very little regulation, as recent fraud cases illustrate. Real estate remains a source of significant financial speculation, particularly in the wake of the housing crisis, leaving neighborhoods at great risk when the market inevitably falters.

Terms

Subprime lending
Foreclosure
Securitization
Financialization
Neoliberalism

Discussion Questions

How have homeownership trends changed over time?

What are the benefits and pitfalls of homeownership for different groups in American society?

Why did we have a foreclosure crisis?

What are some problems with the current mortgage financing system? Should the housing finance system change? Why? How?

What is financialization and how does it impact homeownership?

Should the U.S. government encourage homeownership? Why? How?

Application

Choose an identity from the following options:

- Young multiracial family with a large student debt burden living in a small Midwestern city
- Young multiracial family with a large student debt burden living in a large coastal city
- CEO of a manufacturing company earning $650,000 per year
- Black household that lost their home to foreclosure
- New immigrant to the U.S., eager to own a home, living in a small Southern town
- New immigrant to the U.S., eager to own a home, living in a large Southwestern city
- Manager earning $80,000 year

- Very poor family of three living in public housing
- Homeowner earning $30,000 per year
- Single mother of two working at a retail shoe store
- Mortgage broker earning $110,000 per year
- Investor in rental properties in a mid-sized Midwestern city
- Investor in rental properties in a large coastal city

From this perspective, which of the following policies would you support, and why? You may only choose one. Why would you not support the other policies?

- A large federal grant program for down payment assistance
- Prohibit all mortgages that are not thirty-year, fixed-rate mortgages
- A federal grant program that offers 50 percent discounts on housing cooperative prices
- A large federal home financing program available to everyone
- Eliminate the exemption of property sales from capital gains taxes
- Large funding increases to the Departments of Justice and Housing and Urban Development, allowing them to check continuously for discrimination in the mortgage market
- Eliminate the mortgage interest tax deduction

Now choose a different identity. Which policy would you support, and why? Why would you not support the other policies?

Finally, taking into account both identities, which policy would you support? Why? Do you think it would be likely to be supported by a majority of Americans? Why or why not?

References

Aalbers, Manuel. 2009. "Why the Community Reinvestment Act Cannot Be Blamed for the Subprime Crisis." *City & Community* 8: 346–350.

Ahlbrandt, Roger S. and Cunningham, James V. 1979. *A New Public Policy for Neighborhood Preservation.* New York, NY: Praeger Publications.

American Farmland Trust. 2002. *Farming on the Edge: Sprawling Development Threatens America's Best Farmland.* Washington, DC. Retrieved December 7, 2016. www.farmlandinfo.org/sites/default/files/Farming_on_the_Edge_2002_1.pdf.

Andrews, Dan and Sánchez, Aida Caldera. 2011. "The Evolution of Homeownership Rates in Selected OECD Countries: Demographic and Public Policy Influences." *OECD Journal: Economic Studies:* 207–235.

Apgar, William, Bendimerad, Amal, and Essene, Ren S. 2007. *Mortgage Market Channels and Fair Lending: An Analysis of HMDA Data.* Cambridge, MA: Harvard University, Joint Center for Housing Studies.

Barker, David and Miller, Eric. 2009. "Homeownership and Child Welfare." *Real Estate Economics* 37(2): 279–303.

Blum, Terry C. and Kingston, Paul W. 1984. "Homeownership and Social Attachment." *Sociological Perspectives* 27(2): 159–180.

Belsky, Eric S. 2013. *The Dream Lives On: The Future of Homeownership in America.* Cambridge, MA: Joint Center for Housing Studies, Harvard University. Retrieved January 14, 2016. www.jchs.harvard.edu/sites/jchs.harvard.edu/files/w13-1_belsky_0.pdf.

Biswas, Arnab. 2012. "Housing Submarkets and the Impacts of Foreclosures on Property Prices." *Journal of Housing Economics* 21(3): 235–245.

Bohan, Caren and Daly, Corbett B. 2010. "White House Rejects Foreclosure Moratorium." *Reuters* October 12. Retrieved December 1, 2016. www.reuters.com/article/us-usa-foreclosures-idUSTRE69B4UY20101012.

Boyle, Michael H. 2002. "Homeownership and the Emotional and Behavioral Problems of Children and Youth." *Child Development* 73(3): 883–892.

Bratt, Rachel G., Stone, Michael E., and Hartman, Chester. 2006. *A Right to Housing: Foundation for a New Social Agenda.* Philadelphia: Temple University Press.

Broadwater, Luke. 2012. "Wells Fargo Agrees to Pay $175M Settlement in Pricing Discrimination Suit." *Baltimore Sun,* July 12. Retrieved January 26, 2016. http://articles.baltimoresun.com/2012-07-12/news/bs-md-ci-wells-fargo-20120712_1_mike-heid-wells-fargo-home-mortgage-subprime-mortgages.

Brooks, Rick and Simon, Ruth. 2007. "As Housing Boomed, Industry Pushed Loans to a Broader Market." *Wall Street Journal* A1. December. Retrieved December 1, 2016. www.wsj.com/articles/SB119662974358911035.

Burkhauser, Richard V., Butrica, Barbara A., and Wasylenko, Michael J. 1995. "Mobility Patterns of Older Homeowners: Are Older Homeowners Trapped in Distressed Neighborhoods?" *Research on Aging* 17(4): 363–384.

Cairney, John. 2005. "Housing Tenure and Psychological Well-Being during Adolescence." *Environment and Behavior* 37: 552–564.

Calem, Paul S., Gillen, Kevin, and Wachter, Susan. 2004. "The Neighborhood Distribution of Subprime Mortgage Lending." *Journal of Real Estate Finance and Economics* 29(4): 393–410.

Calvey, Marc. 2015. "City of Oakland Sues Wells Fargo Over Allegations of Predatory Lending." *San Francisco Business Times,* September 22. Retrieved January 26, 2015. www.bizjournals.com/sanfrancisco/blog/2015/09/wells-fargo-oakland-lawsuit-predatory-lending-wfc.html.

Casey, Colleen, Glasberg, Davita Silfen, and Beeman, Angie. 2011. "Racial Disparities in Access to Mortgage Credit: Does Governance Matter?" *Social Science Quarterly* 92(3): 782–806.

Clark, Patrick. 2016. "Can We Fix American Cities by Tearing Them Down?" *Bloomburg Business,* January 13. Retrieved January 26, 2016. www.bloomberg.com/news/articles/2016-01-13/can-we-fix-american-cities-by-tearing-them-down.

Cox, Kevin R. 1982. "Housing Tenure and Neighborhood Activism." *Urban Affairs Review* 18(1): 107–129.

Di, Zhu Xiao, Belsky, Eric, and Liu, Xiaodong. 2007. "Do Homeowners Achieve More Household Wealth in the Long Run?" *Journal of Housing Economics* 16(3–4): 274–290.

DiPasquale, Denise and Glaeser, Edward L. 1999. "Incentives and Social Capital: Are Homeowners Better Citizens?" *Journal of Urban Economics* 45(2): 354–384.

Ellen, Ingrid Gould and Willis, Mark A. 2011. "Improving U.S. Housing Finance Through Reform of Fannie Mae and Freddie Mac: A Framework for Evaluating Alternatives." In S. M. Wachter and M. M. Smith, eds, *The American Mortgage System: Crisis and Reform*, pp. 305–338. Philadelphia, PA: University of Pennsylvania Press.

Ellen, Ingrid Gould, Lacoe, Johanna, and Sharygin, Claudia Ayanna. 2013. "Do Foreclosures Cause Crime?" *Journal of Urban Economics* 74: 59–70.

Epstein, Gerald A. 2005. *Financialization and the World Economy*. Cheltenham: Edward Elgar.

Essen, Juliet, Fogelman, Ken, and Head, Jenny. 1978. "Childhood Housing Experiences and School Attainment. *Child Care, Health, and Development* 4(1): 41–58.

Faber, Jacob W. 2013. "Racial Dynamics of Subprime Mortgage Lending at the Peak." *Housing Policy Debate* 23(2): 328-349.

Federal Bureau of Investigation. 2008. "2008 Mortgage Fraud Report." Retrieved January 26, 2016. www.fbi.gov/stats-services/publications/mortgage-fraud-2008.

Federal Reserve Bank of Richmond. 2011. "U.S. Residential Mortgage Delinquency Rates." Retrieved December 30, 2015. www.richmondfed.org/~/media/richmondfedorg/banking/markets_trends_and_statistics/trends/pdf/delinquency_and_foreclosure_rates.pdf.

Fligstein, Neil, and Roehrkasse, Alexander F. 2016. "The Causes of Fraud in the Financial Crisis of 2007 to 2009: Evidence from the Mortgage-Backed Securities Industry." *American Sociological Review* 81(4): 617–643.

Galster, George C., Quercia, Roberto G., and Cortes, Alvaro. 2000. "Idenitifying Neighborhood Thresholds." *Housing Policy Debate* 11(3): 701–732.

Gaona, Elena. 2016. "HUD Files Charge Alleging California Foreclosure Rescue Companies Scammed Hispanic Homeowners." Retrieved January 26, 2016. http://portal.hud.gov/hudportal/HUD?src=/press/press_releases_media_advisories/2016/HUDNo_16-002.

Gotham, Kevin Fox. 2000. "Separate and Unequal: The Housing Act of 1968 and the Section 235 Program." *Sociological Forum* 15(1): 13–37.

Green, Richard and White, Michelle J. 1997. "Measuring the Benefits of Home Owning: Effects on Children." *Journal of Urban Economics* 41: 441–461.

Grinstein-Weiss, Michal, Williams Shanks, Trina R., Manturuk, Kim R., Key, Clinton C., Paik, Jong-Gyu, and Greeson, Johann K. P. 2010. "Homeownership and Parenting Practices: Evidence from the Community Advantage Panel." *Children and Youth Services Review* 32(5): 774–782.

Grinstein-Weiss, Michal, Key, Clinton, Guo, Shenyang, Yeo, Yeong Hun, and Holub, Krista. 2013. "Homeownership and Wealth among Low- and Moderate-Income Households." *Housing Policy Debate* 23(2): 259–279.

Gruenstein-Bocian, Debbie, Ernst, Keith S., and Li, Wei. 2008. "Race, Ethnicity, and Subprime Home Loan Pricing." *Journal of Economics and Business* 60(1–2): 110–124.

Guest, Avery M. and Oropesa, R. S. 1986. "Informal Social Ties and Political Activity in the Metropolis." *Urban Affairs Quarterly* 21(4): 550–574.

Harding, John, Rosenblatt, Eric, and Yao, Vincent W. 2009. "The Contagion Effect of Foreclosed Properties." *Journal of Urban Economics* 66(3): 164–178.

Harkness, Joseph and Newman, Sandra J. 2002. "Homeownership for the Poor in Distressed Neighborhoods: Does This Make Sense?" *Housing Policy Debate* 13(3): 597–630.

Harvey, David. 2005. *A Brief History of Neoliberalism*. Oxford: Oxford University Press.

Haurin, Donald R., Parcel, Toby L., and Haurin, R. Jean. 2002. "Does Homeownership Affect Child Outcomes?" *Real Estate Economics* 30: 635–666.

Herbert, Christopher E., McCue, Daniel T., and Sanchez-Moyano, Rocio. 2013. "Is Homeownership Still an Effective Means of Building Wealth for Low-income and Minority Households? (Was it Ever?)" Cambridge, MA: Harvard University Joint Center for Housing Studies. Retrieved on January 29, 2016. www.jchs.harvard.edu/sites/jchs.harvard.edu/files/hbtl-06.pdf.

Holupka, Scott and Newman, Sandra J. 2012 "The Effects of Homeownership on Children's Outcomes: Real Effects or Self-Selection?" *Real Estate Economics* 40(3): 566–602.

Howard, Christopher. 1997. *The Hidden Welfare State: Tax Expenditures and Social Policy in the United States*. Princeton, NJ: Princeton University Press.

Immergluck, Daniel. 2009. *Foreclosed: High-Risk Lending, Deregulation, and the Undermining of America's Mortgage Market*. Ithaca, NY: Cornell University Press.

Immergluck, Dan and Smith, Geoff. 2006a. "The External Costs of Foreclosure: The Impact of Single-Family Mortgage Foreclosures on Property Values." *Housing Policy Debate* 17(1): 57–79.

Immergluck, Dan and Smith, Geoff. 2006b. "The Impact of Single-Family Mortgage Foreclosures on Neighborhood Crime." *Housing Studies* 21(6): 851–866.

Joint Center for Housing Studies. 2012. *The State of the Nation's Housing 2011*. Cambridge, MA: Harvard University.

Karolak, Eric J. 2000. "'No Idea of Doing Anything Wonderful': The Labor-Crisis Origins of National Housing Policy and the Reconstruction of the Working-Class Community, 1917–1919." In J. F. Bauman, R. Biles, and K. M. Szylvian, eds, *From Tenements to the Taylor Homes: In Search of an Urban Housing Policy in Twentieth-Century America*, pp. 60–80. University Park, PA: Pennsylvania State University Press.

Keyssar, Alexander. 2009. *The Right to Vote: The Contested History of Democracy in the United States*. New York, NY: Basic Books.

Kingsley, G. Thomas. 2009. *High Cost and Investor Mortgages: Neighborhood Patterns*. Washington, DC: Urban Institute. Retrieved December 1, 2016. www.urban.org/research/publication/high-cost-and-investor-mortgages.

Kingsley, G. Thomas, Smith, Robin, and Price, David. 2009. "The Impacts of Foreclosures on Families and Communities." Washington, DC: Urban Institute for the Open Society Institute. Retrieved January 15, 2016. www.urban.org/research/publication/impacts-foreclosures-families-and-communities/view/full_report.

Kloberdanz, Kristin. 2008. "Foreclosed Homes: A Local Blight." *Time*, March 18. Retrieved on January 26, 2016. http://content.time.com/time/nation/article/0,8599,1723193,00.html.

Kochhar, Rakesh, Fry, Richard, and Taylor, Paul. 2011. "Wealth Gaps Rise to Record Highs Between Whites, Blacks, and Hispanics." Washington, DC: Pew Research Center.

Kochhar, Rakesh, Gonzalez-Barrera, Ana, and Dockterman, Daniel. 2009. "Through Boom and Bust: Minorities, Immigrants, and Homeownership." Washington, DC: Pew Hispanic Center.

Krueckeberg, Donald A. 1999. "The Grapes of Rent: A History of Renting in a Country of Owners." *Housing Policy Debate* 10(1): 9–30.

Lo, Andrew W. 2012. "Reading about the Financial Crisis: A Twenty-One Book Review." *Journal of Economic Literature* 50(1): 151–178.

Lyons, William E. and Lowery, David. 1989. "Citizen Responses to Dissatisfaction in Urban Communities: A Partial Test of a General Model." *Journal of Politics* 15(4): 841–868.

MacArthur Foundation. 2013. "How Housing Matters: Americans' Attitudes Transformed by the Housing Crisis and Changing Lifestyles." Retrieved January 14, 2016. www.macfound.org/media/files/HHM_Hart_report_2013.pdf.

McCabe, Brian. 2013. "Are Homeowners Better Citizens? Homeownership and Community Participation in the United States." *Social Forces* 91(3): 929–954.

McCabe, Brian J. 2016. *No Place Like Home: Wealth, Community, and the Politics of Homeownerhsip.* Oxford: Oxford University Press.

Mohanty, Lisa L. and Raut, Lakshmi K. 2009. "Homeownership and School Outcomes of Children: Evidence from the PSID Child Development Supplement." *Journal of Economics and Sociology* 68(2): 465–489.

Molina, Emily Tumpson. 2012. "Reversed Gains? The Foreclosure Crisis and African-American Neighborhoods in the Los Angeles Region, 2008–2009." In *Black California Dreamin': The Crises of California's African-American Communities,* edited by Ingrid Banks et al. Santa Barbara, CA: UCSB Center for Black Studies Research.

National Association of Home Builders. 2015. "Table 1: Housing's Contribution to GDP." Retrieved December 30, 2015. www.nahb.org/en/research/housing-economics/housings-economic-impact/housings-contribution-to-gross-domestic-product-gdp.aspx.

Newman, Sandra J. 2008. "Does Housing Matter for Poor Families? A Critical Summary of Research and Issues Still to be Resolved." *Journal of Policy Analysis and Management* 27(4): 895–925.

Olick, Diana. 2016. "Millennials Cause Home Ownership to Drop to Its Lowest Level Since 1965." *NBC News,* July 28. Retrieved August 15, 2016. www.nbcnews.com/business/real-estate/millennials-cause-home-ownership-drop-its-lowest-level-1965-n619056.

Oliver, Melvin L. and Shapiro, Thomas. 2006. *Black Wealth/White Wealth.* New York, NY: Routledge.

Pepitone, Julianne. 2009. "Foreclosures: Worst-Hit Cities." *CNN Money* October 28. Retrieved December 6, 2016. http://money.cnn.com/2009/10/28/real_estate/foreclosures_worst_cities/?postversion=2009102809.

Percent Change in Housing Units, 2000–2010. Social Explorer, www.socialexplorer.com/054be672f0/view (based on data from 2010 and 2000 U.S. Census Bureau accessed December 7, 2016).

Pfeiffer, Deirdre and Molina, Emily T. 2013. "The Trajectory of REOs in Southern California Latino Neighborhoods: An Uneven Geography of Recovery." *Housing Policy Debate* (13)1: 81–109.

Powell, Michael. 2009. "Bank Accused of Pushing Mortgage Deals on Blacks." *New York Times*, June 6. Retrieved January 26, 2016. www.nytimes.com/2009/06/07/us/07baltimore.html?_r=0.

Radford, Gail. 2000. "The Federal Government and Housing during the Great Depression." In J. F. Bauman, R. Biles, and K. M. Szylvian, eds, *From Tenements to the Taylor Homes: In Search of an Urban Housing Policy in Twentieth-Century America*, pp. 102–120. University Park, PA: Pennsylvania State University Press.

Realty Trac. 2009. "Foreclosure Activity Increases 81 Percent in 2008." Retrieved December 30, 2015. www.realtytrac.com/content/press-releases/foreclosure-activity-increases-81-percent-in-2008-4551.

Realty Trac. 2010. "2009 Year End Forelosure Report." Retrieved December 30, 2015. www.realtytrac.com/landing/2009-year-end-foreclosure-report.html.

RealtyTrac. 2016. "Foreclosure Rates for the Nation." Retrieved January 26, 2016. www.realtytrac.com/statsandtrends/foreclosuretrends.

Rivera, Amaad, Cotto-Escalera, Brenda, Desai, Anisha, Huezo, Jeannette, and Muhammad, Dedrick. 2008. *Foreclosed: State of the Dream*. Boston, MA: United for a Fair Economy.

Rohe, William M. and Stegman, Michael A. 1994a. "The Impacts of Homeownership on the Self-Esteem, Perceived Control, and Life Satisfaction of Low-Income People." *Journal of the American Planning Association* 60(1): 173–184.

Rohe, William M. and Stegman, Michael A. 1994b. "The Impact of Homeownership on the Social and Political Involvement of Low-Income People." *Urban Affairs Quarterly* 30 (September): 152–172.

Rohe, William M. and Stewart, Leslie S. 1996. "Homeownership and Neighborhood Stability." *Housing Policy Debate* 7(1): 37–81.

Rohe, William M., Van Zandt, Shannon, and McCarthy, George. 2002. "The Social Benefits and Costs of Homeownership: A Critical Assessment of the Research." In N. P. Retsinas and E. S. Belsky, eds, *Low Income Homeownership: Examining the Unexamined Goal*, pp. 381–406. Washington, DC: Brookings.

Ross, Lauren M. and Squires, Gregory D. 2011. "The Personal Costs of Subprime Lending and the Foreclosure Crisis: A Matter of Trust, Insecurity, and Institutional Deception." *Social Science Quarterly* 92(1): 140–163.

Rossi, Peter H. and Weber, Eleanor. 1996. "The Social Benefits of Homeownership: Empirical Evidence from National Surveys." *Housing Policy Debate* 7(1): 1–35.

Rugh, Jacob S. and Massey, Douglas S. 2010. "Racial Segregation and the American Foreclosure Crisis." *American Sociological Review* 75(5): 629–651.

Sassen, Saskia. 2009. "When Local Housing Becomes an Electronic Instrument: The Global Circulation of Mortgages—A Research Note." *International Journal of Urban and Regional Research* 332: 411–426.

Savage, Howard A. 2009. *Who Could Afford to Buy a Home in 2004?* Washington, DC: Census Housing Reports, H21/09-1. Retrieved December 6, 2016. www.census.gov/housing/affordability/data/2004/h121-09-01.pdf.

Schmidt, Susan and Tamman, Maurice. 2009. "Housing Push for Hispanics Spawns Wave of Foreclosures." *Wall Street Journal*, January 5. Retrieved March 20, 2012. http://online.wsj.com/article/SB123111072368352309.html.

Schuetz, Jenny, Been, Vicki, and Ellen, Ingrid Gould. 2008. "Neighborhood Effects of Concentrated Mortgage Foreclosures." *Journal of Housing Economics* 17(4): 306–319.

Schwartz, Alex F. 2015. *Housing Policy in the United States* (3rd Edition). New York, NY: Routledge.

Simmons, Melanie. 2016. "Maryland Foreclosure Rate Was Among the Highest in the U.S. in 2015." *Baltimore Business Journal*, January 14. Retrieved January 26, 2015. www.bizjournals.com/baltimore/blog/real-estate/2016/01/marylands-foreclosure-rate-was-among-the-highest.html.

Smith, Marvin M. and Hevener, Christy Chung. 2014. "Subprime Lending over Time: The Role of Race." *Journal of Economics and Finance* 38(2): 321–344.

South, Scott J. and Crowder, Kyle D. 1997. "Escaping Distressed Neighborhoods: Individual, Community, and Metropolitan Influences." *American Journal of Sociology* 102(4): 1040–1084.

South, Scott J. and Crowder, Kyle D. 1998a. "Residential Mobility between Cities and Suburbs: Race, Suburbanization, and Back-to-the-City Moves." *Demography* 34(4): 525–538.

South, Scott J. and Crowder, Kyle D. 1998b. "Avenues and Barriers to Residenital Mobility among Single Mothers." *Journal of Marriage and the Family* 60(4): 866–877.

South, Scott J. and Deane, Glenn D. 1993. "Race and Residential Mobility: Individual Determinants and Structural Constraints." *Social Forces* 72(1): 147–167.

Stone, Michael E. 2006a. "Pernicious Problems of Housing Finance." In R. G. Bratt, M. E. Stone, and C. Hartman, eds, *A Right to Housing: Foundation for a New Social Agenda*, pp. 82–104. Philadelphia, PA: Temple University Press.

Stone, Michael E. 2006b. "Social Ownership." In R. G. Bratt, M. E. Stone, and C. Hartman, eds, *A Right to Housing: Foundation for a New Social Agenda*, pp. 240–260. Philadelphia, PA: Temple University Press.

Swack, Michael. 2006. "Social Financing." In R. G. Bratt, M. E. Stone, and C. Hartman, eds, *A Right to Housing: Foundation for a New Social Agenda*, pp. 261–278. Philadelphia, PA: Temple University Press.

U.S. Census. 2012. *American Community Survey (2008–2012 5-Year Estimates, DP04)*. Washington, DC. Retrieved October 1, 2015. http://factfinder.census.gov/faces/tableservices/jsf/pages/productview.xhtml?src=bkmk.

U.S. Census. 2015. *Current Population Survey/Housing Vacancy Survey, Series H-111*. Washington, DC. Retrieved October 1, 2015. www.census.gov/housing/hvs/data/histtabs.html.

U.S. Department of Housing and Urban Development. 2016. Retrieved January 19, 2016. http://portal.hud.gov.

U.S. Department of Justice. 2016. Retrieved January 26, 2016. www.justice.gov/crt/housing-and-civil-enforcement-section-cases-1#lending.

Van Order, Robert. 2011. "Some Thoughts on What to Do with Fannie Mae and Freddie Mac." In S. M. Wachter and M. M. Smith, eds, *The American Mortgage System: Crisis and Reform*, pp. 339–357. Philadelphia, PA: University of Pennsylvania Press.

Welfield, Irving H. 1998. "Section 235: Home Mortgage Interest Deduction. In W. van Vliet, ed., *Encyclopedia of Housing*, pp. 514–515. Thousand Oaks: Sage.

Whitaker, Stephan and Fitzpatrick, Thomas J. IV. 2013. "Deconstructing Distressed-Property Spillovers: The Effects of Vacant, Tax-Delinquent, and Foreclosed Properties in Housing Submarkets." *Journal of Housing Economics* 22(2): 79–91.

Wyly, Elvin, Moos, Markus, Hammel, Daniel, and Kabahizi, Emanuel. 2009. "Cartographies of Race and Class: Mapping the Class-Monopoly Rents of American Subprime Capital." *International Journal of Urban and Regional Research* 33(2): 332–354.

CHAPTER **6**

Housing Development, Planning, and the Environment

Bordering the San Francisco Bay just east of Daly City, tiny Brisbane, CA sits squarely within the booming San Francisco Bay Area, one of the epicenters of the U.S.'s housing affordability crisis. San Francisco famously has the highest rents in the U.S., with nearby Oakland and San Jose not far behind. But most of the Bay Area's seven million residents are spread out across suburbs to the north, south, and east of San Francisco in a territory that encompasses nine counties and almost 7,000 square miles (Walker and Schafran 2015). Skyrocketing housing prices in and around San Francisco, Oakland, and San Jose have pushed people further and further outward in pursuit of affordable housing, despite incredibly long commutes. Indeed, sprawling, suburban single-family homes have dominated housing development in the Bay Area since World War II. But while housing sprawl is often regarded as a way to increase housing supply and therefore affordability, it has a number of significant negative environmental and social impacts, including housing people in areas at high risk for natural disasters like wildfires. Recognizing these hazards, many localities within the Bay Area have adopted policies designed to limit housing sprawl and growth. In the meantime, the housing affordability crisis worsens.

In Brisbane, the San Francisco-based University Paragon Corporation owns and plans to develop a 684-acre former railyard and landfill into more than 4,400 housing units and commercial space, a plan that could help to ease the housing affordability crisis but more than double Brisbane's population (Kinney 2016). So-called infill development like this—development of vacant or underused areas within urban and older suburban areas—is often seen as a more environmentally and socially sustainable way of housing Americans than the outward suburban sprawl that has dominated during the last half-century. However, it can meet a great deal of resistance at the local level as communities like Brisbane are dramatically changed.

The history of housing development in the Bay Area and the proposed development in Brisbane and local resistance to it illustrate fundamental issues in housing the American population. How and where should we build housing? Are our current strategies sustainable? How do we balance societal needs for housing with environmental concerns? This chapter explores recent trends in housing development and the relationship between housing development and environmental problems. After decades of housing sprawl outward from metropolitan areas, researchers and policymakers continue to debate the consequences of housing development and where to build future housing for the American population.

Housing Development in the U.S.

The dominant form of housing development in the last fifty years in the U.S. has been low-density housing in suburbs, exurbs, and some rural areas—single-family homes on relatively larger lots of land. Of course, new housing development is expected with an expanding population, as in the U.S. during the postwar period. But the extent and shape of housing development outpaces what is attributable to simple population growth (Cieslewicz 2002).

In fact, the characteristics of new housing development are relatively distinct. First, U.S. urban areas are among the most sprawled in the world (Kenworthy and Laube 1999), and new housing is larger than in previous eras (Dwyer 2009; U.S. Census Bureau 2016). Next, housing is less dense—that is, it tends to be on larger lots of land than in the past. Much of the new housing construction of large homes on large lots has occurred in the Southern and western regions of the country. Last, more Americans own multiple and seasonal homes than in previous generations. In 1940 there were 5.6 seasonal homes for every 1000 people; in 2000 that rate more than doubled to 12.8 seasonal homes for every 1000 people, representing about 3.6 million homes (Hammer *et al.* 2009).

Exurban Development

New housing development is concentrated in the nation's exurbs—places on the fringes of metropolitan areas characterized by low-density development, long commutes to urban centers, commercial strip development, single-use development (i.e. housing developments, business parks, etc. in separate zones), and so-called "leapfrog" or scattered, relatively unplanned development (Hamidi *et al.* 2015). Exurbs are also sometimes referred to as

Figure 6.1 Exurban development outside Houston, TX

Source: Ken Gould.

boomburbs (Lang and LeFurgy 2007) or edge cities (Garreau 1992). Popular examples are: parts of Fairfax, Montgomery, Loudon, and Prince George's counties outside Washington, DC; parts of the Inland Empire and Orange County east of Los Angeles; Henderson, Nevada; and even places like Steubenville, Ohio, once an industrial city in its own right, now a part of the Pittsburgh metropolitan area.

Despite the recent housing crisis, exurban housing development thrives, far outpacing housing development in other places. Between 2000 and 2010, the U.S. population increased by 10 percent, while the exurban population increased by 60 percent (Gardner and Marley 2016). The pattern is especially strong in the largest metropolitan areas, particularly in the Southwest. Phoenix's exurban population grew by 300 percent between 2000 and 2010, and Las Vegas' grew by 400 percent during the same period.

This trend toward low-density housing development in exurban areas is not limited to the last decade. The share of Americans living in low-density housing has steadily increased since 1970 (Figure 6.2). One way of ascertaining how much of the American population is living in very low-density communities relative to past periods is to calculate the sprawl index: the difference between the proportion of the population living in high-density and low-density census tracts (a proxy for neighborhoods) between 1970 and 2010 in all metropolitan areas in the U.S., to determine the change over time (Lopez 2014). The sprawl index has, indeed, steadily increased, from about 37 in 1970 to about 51 in 2010—an increase of 38 percent (Lopez 2014). The number of metropolitan areas with sprawl indices over 75—a very large difference between the number of people living in low- versus high-density tracts—increased by more than 250 percent between 1970 and 2010 (Figure 6.3).

Rural Housing Development

Indeed, much housing sprawl has simply extended the reach of metropolitan areas already in existence—exurban sprawl. But other housing sprawl has taken over previously rural land in non-metropolitan communities, a phenomenon better described as rural sprawl (Brown *et al.* 2005). New housing development grew nearly tenfold in counties adjacent to existing metropolitan areas in the U.S. between 1950 and 2000, reflecting exurbanization. But nearly equally significant is that new housing development increased nearly sevenfold in previously non-metropolitan areas, reflecting rural sprawl (Brown *et al.* 2005).

Together, exurban and rural sprawl reflect an overall "selective deconcentration" of the U.S. population (Johnson, Nucci, and Long 2005). Americans have been taking part in a "rural rebound" since around 1970, with a marked acceleration in the 1990s (Johnson and Beale 1994; Johnson 1999; Johnson *et al.* 2005). Much of the new housing development in rural places is near natural amenities like forests, mountains, lakes, and coasts and often provides second-home opportunities for middle-class and affluent Americans (Brown *et al.* 2005; McGranahan 1999). Rural sprawl tends to impact larger parcels of land than exurban sprawl (Brown *et al.* 2005).

Urban Housing Development

While the primary trend in American housing development over the past several decades has been sprawl, many American cities have experienced population resurgence and a dramatic redevelopment of the landscape. Nine of the ten largest cities in the U.S. have gained population over the last decade. After declining by a million between 1950 and 1980, New York City's

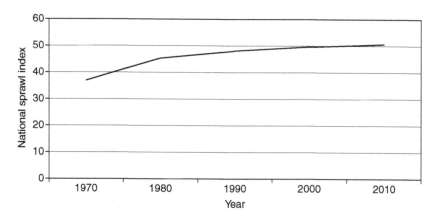

Figure 6.2 Housing sprawl in U.S. metropolitan areas 1970–2010

Source: Lopez 2014.

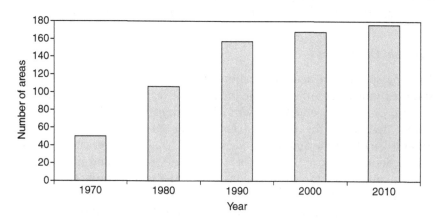

Figure 6.3 Number of U.S. metropolitan areas with sprawl indexes over 75, 1970–2010

Source: Lopez 2014.

population, for example, has increased by over one million since 1990 alone (Sander and Testa 2013). Gentrification—the transformation of working-class or vacant areas of central cities into middle-class residential and/or commercial uses—is a central socioeconomic engine in many cities nation-wide (Lees *et al.* 2010). Large urban centers such as San Francisco, New York, and Chicago as well as some smaller cities underwent major transformations in the built environment in recent decades, with new residential and com-mercial development in previously economically depressed communities. Some scholars argue that this represents a large-scale "back to the city" movement among millennials who want more walkable, less car-dependent, and more environmentally responsible lifestyles (Leinberger and Lynch 2014; Lucy 2010). Some have gone so far as to proclaim that we are witnessing the death of the suburbs (Gallagher 2014).

While particular cities have indeed witnessed large-scale gentrification, the national data unequivocally show that America is becoming less dense and more suburbanized (Boustan and Shertzer 2010; Sander and Testa 2013; Wilson *et al.* 2012). While white, college-educated households are more likely to live in central cities of large metropolitan areas, college-educated households of color are not—nor are college-educated households with children (Sander 2004; Sander and Testa 2013). The vast majority of Americans still prefer suburban living—even members of the millennial generation.

Thus, the dominant trends in housing development continue to be the simultaneous centralization and decentralization of housing and business. The exurban/rural fringe and the urban core experience concentrated housing development and investment relative to the older, postwar, inner-ring suburbs like Long Island's classic Levittown (Bruegmann 2005; Short *et al.* 2007).

Regional Differences

Housing sprawl is a decidedly national trend, but some areas have surely sprawled more than others. While the Rustbelt region—parts of the Northeastern, Great Lakes, and Midwestern U.S.—has experienced significant economic decline in the past half-century due to deindustrialization, the Sunbelt—parts of the Southern and Western U.S.—has experienced an economic boom due to growth in the agribusiness, energy, and military economies concentrated in those regions during the same period. These broad economic trends spurred an overall shift in residential patterns, away from old industrial and manufacturing centers in much of the North, East, and Midwest to new, fast-growing metropolitan regions in the South and West. While the population of all other contiguous states grew by 1.7 times between 1940 and 2000, the population of the West grew 4.5 times larger and the Southeast 4.8 times larger during the same period (Hammer *et al.* 2009).

As a result of these demographic trends, new housing development is more concentrated in the Sunbelt than in other regions, aided by a stream of migrants from the North and East seeking employment and lower costs of living, immigration, and corporate tax breaks. Between 1940 and 2000, the number of housing units in the West increased by a factor of 5.8 and in the Southeast by 7.6, while the number of housing units in the rest of the U.S. increased by a factor of 2.6 (Hammer *et al.* 2009). Since new housing construction has been concentrated in the Southern and Western regions, sprawl has disproportionately shaped the housing patterns of those regions. The top ten regions with the most housing sprawl are in the Sunbelt states (Table 6.1; see also Figure 6.4).

Table 6.1 Ten most sprawling metropolitan areas in the U.S.

1	Kingsport–Bristol–Bristol, TN–VA, metro area
2	Augusta–Richmond County, GA–SC, metro area
3	Greenville–Mauldin–Easley, SC, metro area
4	Riverside–San Bernardino–Ontario, CA, metro area
5	Baton Rouge, LA, metro area
6	Nashville–Davidson–Murfreesboro–Franklin, TN, metro area
7	Prescott, AZ, metro area
8	Clarksville, TN-KY, metro area
9	Atlanta–Sandy Springs–Marietta, GA, metro area
10	Hickory–Lenoir–Morgantown, NC, metro area

Source: Hamidi *et al.* 2015.

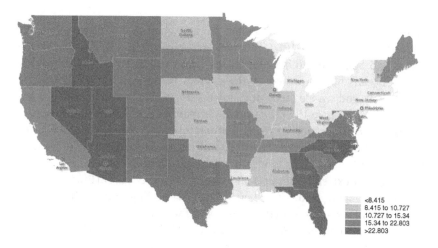

<8.415
8.415 to 10.727
10.727 to 15.34
15.34 to 22.803
>22.803

Figure 6.4 Percentage change in housing units 2000–2010

Source: Social Explorer, U.S. Census 2000 and 2010.

While sprawl has historically been concentrated in the so-called Sunbelt, it has largely leveled off or decreased in those regions. Housing is, in fact, becoming denser in many Western regions, for example. The San Francisco Bay Area, and the Santa Barbara, Santa Cruz, Miami, and Santa Ana regions, for example, are all in the top ten most compact regions in the U.S. (Table 6.2). In contrast, housing sprawl is increasing in many Midwestern regions.

Housing Sprawl and Natural Disasters

Housing has sprawled all over the U.S., but particularly in places at high risk for natural disasters such as wildfires and coastal storms, which are likely to

Table 6.2 Ten most compact metropolitan areas in the U.S.

1	New York–White Plains–Wayne, NY–NJ, metro division
2	San Francisco–SanMateo–Redwood City, CA, metro division
3	Atlantic City–Hammonton, NJ, metro area
4	Santa Barbara–Santa Maria–Goleta, CA, metro area
5	Champaign–Urbana, IL, metro area
6	Santa Cruz–Watsonville, CA, metro area
7	Trenton–Ewing, NJ, metro area
8	Miami–Miami Beach–Kendall, FL metro division
9	Springfield, IL, metro area
10	Santa Ana–Anaheim–Irvine, CA metro division

Source: Hamidi *et al.* 2015.

become more common given global climate change. By all accounts, the Earth has warmed since 1880, in large part since the 1970s (National Aeronautics and Space Administration 2016a). Absorbing much of this heat, the planet's oceans have warmed by 0.3 degrees Fahrenheit since 1969. As ice sheets shrink and sea ice melts, the global sea level has risen at about 3.4 millimeters per year since 1993 (National Aeronautics and Space Administration 2016b). The combination of rising temperatures and rising sea levels has led to stronger hurricanes in the North Atlantic, larger and more frequent wildfires in the Western U.S., longer droughts in some parts of the U.S., and more frequent extreme rain and snowstorms in other parts (Emanuel 2005; Madsen and Figdor 2007; Trenberth 2005; Westerling *et al.* 2006). Indeed, the number of weather-related disasters and the costs of those disasters in the U.S. have escalated since 1960 (see Figure 6.5; Cutter and Emrich 2005).

At the same time, Americans continue increasingly to inhabit areas at great risk for natural disasters. Fully 43 percent of Americans live in areas at high or very high risk of natural disasters (Figure 6.6). Despite the fact that hurricanes are the costliest natural disasters in the United States, the coastal population of the U.S. in particular continues to grow (Pielke and Landsea 1998). The U.S. population as a whole increased by thirty-six people per square mile between 1970 and 2010, but populations of coastal shoreline counties increased by nearly 3.5 times as many people (125 people per square mile), and those of coastal watershed counties by more than 2.5 times as many people (ninety-nine people per square mile) (U.S. Census Bureau 2013). As a result, 29 percent of Americans live in homes that are at high or very high risk level for hurricanes, with another 13 percent at moderate risk (Figure 6.7).

Similarly, the Western and Southeastern regions of the U.S. grew more rapidly in population and housing units between 1940 and 2000 than the rest

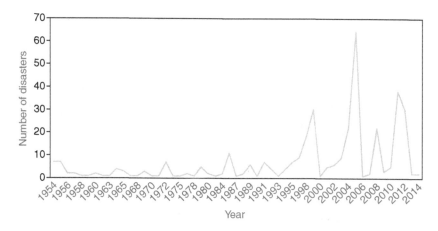

Figure 6.5 Federal hurricane and tropical storm disaster declarations 1954–2014

Source: Federal Emergency Management Agency 2016a.

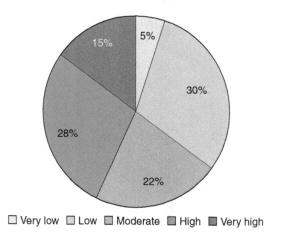

☐ Very low ☐ Low ☐ Moderate ◼ High ◼ Very high

Figure 6.6 Percentage of U.S. homes by natural disaster risk level 2015

Source: RealtyTrac 2015.

of the U.S., and those two regions account for 91 percent of the wildfire acres burned in 2007 (Hammer *et al.* 2009). In Southern California, wildfires in the "wilderness-urban interface"—the boundary between wilderness and human settlement—destroyed more than 3000 structures and cost the state $300 million in 2007 alone (Hammer *et al.* 2009). About 13 percent of the U.S. lives in areas currently at high or very high risk for wildfires, with another 23 percent at moderate risk (Figure 6.9).

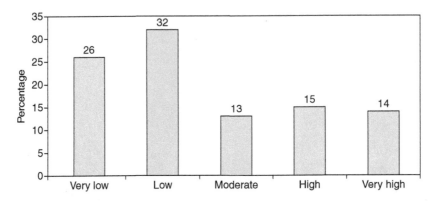

Figure 6.7 Percentage of U.S. homes by hurricane risk level 2015

Source: RealtyTrac 2015.

Figure 6.8 Coastal housing development in Chicago, IL

Source: Ken Gould.

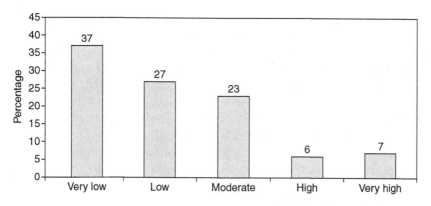

Figure 6.9 Percentage of U.S. homes by wildfire risk level 2015

Source: RealtyTrac 2015.

A Brief History of Sprawl

To some extent, the current shape of American housing development is simply an acceleration of longstanding patterns. But the extent and nature of its potential impacts are relatively new phenomena.

Historically, affluent and otherwise powerful families have held homes on the outskirts of nearly every major city to escape the congestion, hazards, and social problems of urban life (Bruegmann 2005). Indeed, suburbs have existed as long as cities have. But the *process* of suburbanization—the "systematic growth of fringe areas at a pace more rapid than that of core cities, as a lifestyle involving a daily commute to jobs in the center" (Jackson 1985)—has accelerated in relatively recent times. Suburbanization as a process began in the U.S. and Great Britain around 1815 (Jackson 1985). Between 1815 and 1865, New York, Philadelphia, and Boston "exhibited the most extensive changes on their residential peripheries yet witnessed in the world" (Jackson 1985: 13) as affluent Americans sought havens on the outskirts of major American cities.

The suburbanization of the U.S. ballooned in the wake of the development of mass transit at the close of the nineteenth century, particularly the streetcar and trolley systems. New York, Boston, Chicago, Philadelphia, Toronto, and Milwaukee, among other places, all developed streetcar systems at the turn of the twentieth century. U.S. suburbs developed and grew largely because of concerted efforts on the part of owners of land on the outskirts of cities to maximize their land value. They partnered with developers of mass transit to develop large swaths of urban land previously inaccessible by walking into new "streetcar suburbs." Prior to World War II, unprecedented economic growth, mass transit, and growing automobile ownership enabled many urban Americans to suburbanize into communities such as Floral Park on Long Island and Berwyn outside of Chicago (Bruegmann 2005).

Centralized planning of land use was virtually nonexistent in the U.S. during this early period of suburban boom. As a result, the metropolitan landscape was largely determined by real estate developers and their partners in transit development. But by the 1910s, the real estate industry began to push for land use planning that would designate residential, commercial, industrial, and other distinct areas of metropolitan regions (Weiss 1987). The division of land designated for particular uses and regulated in size and nature is known as zoning, a practice that officially took hold in the U.S. in the 1920s. After New York City adopted the nation's first zoning regulation in 1916 and the constitutionality of zoning was upheld by the Supreme Court in the 1926 *Village of Euclid, Ohio* v. *Amber Realty Co.* case, localities began to employ zoning to regulate everything from density to air rights to land purpose (Fischler 1998; Natoli 1971). But it was primarily employed to protect developers and homeowners from losses in the value of their land as a result of possible future unwanted land uses nearby (Fischel 2003).

U.S. suburban development exploded in the postwar period, aided by federal policies that encouraged homeownership, facilitated highway construction, and aided returning veterans to achieve their slice of the American Dream (see Chapters 2, 3, and 5). Suburban development did not differ much in kind from previous eras of human history, but the scope of postwar American suburbanization was unprecedented (Jackson 1985; Bruegmann 2005). The mass production of suburban homes on the outskirts of American cities by firms like William Levitt's (of Levittown, Long Island) coupled with large federal tax breaks and the transformation of mortgage lending led to the massive suburbanization of America in the 1950s and 1960s.

As more affluent Americans moved out of cities, so did jobs and recreational opportunities. Regional shopping centers/malls, industries, and businesses also located to the suburbs. By 1963 more than half of industrial jobs had moved to the suburbs (Gillham 2002). These new opportunities on the suburban frontier attracted more people, more money, and more development in a self-perpetuating cycle (Jackson 1985). Certainly many postwar suburbs maintained racial and economic exclusivity. Others largely housed the working classes, immigrants, and people of color in segregated suburban enclaves (Harris and Lewis 2001; Nicolaides 2002; Wiese 2004; see also Chapter 3).

Housing sprawl increasingly made its way into areas at high risk for natural disasters. The federal government enabled housing development in hazardous areas by providing funding for flood and hurricane protection works and subsidized disaster insurance. The fundamental idea behind these policies is that "land exposed to natural hazards can be profitably used if steps are taken to make it safe for human occupancy" (Burby 2006: 173). For example, Congress authorized the construction of levees around New

Orleans following devastating hurricane losses in 1947, and additional levees after Hurricane Betsy in 1965. Designed to protect residents, these policies actually encouraged continued housing development in very hazardous regions (Burby 2006).

Despite burgeoning worries over the various environmental impacts of sprawl, developers continued to build and Americans continued to move outward from central cities and into formerly rural areas throughout the 1970s.

Planning for Housing: The Debates

A host of debates surround American housing development, most of which are rooted in the nature of American urban planning. Debates from the causes and consequences of sprawl to whether to regulate housing development in disaster-prone areas touch on the nature, shape, and potential of land use regulation in the U.S. and how to balance the rights of private property owners with the public good.

Causes of Sprawl

The first two major debates around American housing development center on sprawl. The first focuses on its causes. There are five major sets of explanations for the development of sprawl in the U.S. The first centers on the relationship between land costs and commuting costs. The second focuses on factors important to residential choice in the metropolitan context, such as schools and crime. The third emphasizes the role of public policy; and the fourth the concomitant roles of anti-urban bias and racist and anti-immigrant sentiments. The last argues that sprawl is neither new nor uniquely American, and is simply the spatial expression of human desires. It is a mass phenomenon in the U.S. because of the country's relative affluence.

The Monocentric City Theory

First, the monocentric city theory posits that urban development patterns are the result of the trade-off between land costs/rents and commuting costs—in other words, affordability (Alonso 1964; Mills 1967; Muth 1969). Central-city land is more expensive than outlying land. As transportation costs have declined and allowed more people to buy and fuel cars and industry to transport goods cheaply using trucks, living in the exurbs is a viable option for many American households. The relative affordability of exurban housing trumps the cost of commuting. Real estate developers and homebuilders, then, can count on reaping great rewards from their investment on the urban fringe, especially as their costs and tax burdens are lower as well. Since the advent of New Deal-era homeownership incentives (see Chapter 5),

Americans have found "more for their money" and widespread economic opportunity for accruing wealth through homeownership on the suburban frontier.

Research that supports this theory focuses on the central role of the development and accessibility of the automobile in the growth of sprawl over the twentieth century (Glaeser and Kahn 2003). After all, there would be no outward housing development if there were no means of transport to and from those places. The percentage of workers driving to their jobs, for example, increased from 64 percent in 1960 to 84 percent in 1980 (Nechyba and Walsh 2004). Related explanations for the rise in sprawl focus on the suburbanization of employment, as businesses also take advantage of cheaper land and operating costs outside cities. Technological developments also make working from home much easier for some Americans, allowing them to dismiss transportation to employment as a concern (Nelson and Dueker 1990).

The Tiebout Model

While the monocentric city theory accounts for the relative roles of housing and commuting costs, certainly people take more than these costs into account when deciding where to live. The so-called Tiebout model emphasizes other factors significant to residential choices, particularly those that push Americans out of cities and pull them to the suburbs, such as crime rates and school quality. Suburbs are able to pull urban residents by limiting the provision of social goods to "desirable" groups—i.e. those that are perceived to be pulling their financial weight—through zoning and property taxes. Perceived or real social problems concentrated in cities, on the other hand, push mobile urban residents (Nechyba and Walsh 2004). But while the Tiebout sorting model generally explains residential choices, it does not necessarily explain why sprawl in particular is the dominant form of housing development in the U.S.

Public Policy

Politics and public policy, many scholars argue, better account for the rise in sprawl. In this view, sprawl is simply the spatial expression of unfettered capitalism, aided and abetted by government policies (Gonzalez 2009). Nelson and Dueker note that U.S. metropolitan policy

> favors new construction over rehabilitation or reuse of buildings, highways over public transit, converting open space to urban uses over leaving it alone, construction of single-family (owner occupied) over multiple-family (renter) housing, growing areas over depressed ones, and new locations over old ones.

> (Nelson and Dueker 1990)

Local governments use tax breaks and/or subsidized infrastructure to lure development to particular places, and federal tax breaks can work to encourage or discourage development of new land rather than redevelop underused land (Bagstad *et al.* 2007).

Other policies also contributed to sprawl. Paradoxically, one anti-sprawl zoning technique is to require large lots for rural housing development. Designed to prevent subdivisions, this technique backfired in that it simply encouraged very low-density development in rural and exurban places (Bruegmann 2005). In addition, the U.S. is unique in its highway/road trust funds from gas and other car-related taxes, relatively low fuel taxes, and reliance on local governments to regulate land use. Localities, in turn, have often imposed minimal regulation on housing and real estate development, a reflection of Americans' suspicion of government (Jackson 1985). The peculiar American policy of mortgage interest and property tax deductions also incentivizes suburban life (Jackson 1985). But perhaps most importantly, places that regulate housing development exhibit lower rates of sprawl, while those places that mandate low-density development have greater sprawl. And places that rely more on property taxes to fund schools and other services sprawl more than those with a more diverse tax base (Pendall 1999).

American Values: Racism and Anti-Urban and Anti-Immigrant Biases
Other accounts of the rise of sprawl focus on the role of American values and character as causes—particularly American racism and anti-urban and anti-immigrant biases. As Jackson famously noted: "Suburbia has become the quintessential physical achievement of the United States; it is perhaps more representative of its culture than big cars, tall buildings, or professional football" (Jackson 1985: 4). Jackson locates the causes of urban sprawl in the American suburban ideal, population growth, racial prejudice, and cheap housing. The American Dream is also intimately tied to the suburbs, exurbs, and rural places. A recent study confirmed that 77 percent of Americans prefer to live in a suburb, small town, or rural area, and rural and suburban residents rate their communities better than residents of small towns and cities (Taylor *et al.* 2011). American sentiments are rooted in Thomas Jefferson's ideal that the U.S. should be a nation of independent farmers—a staunchly anti-urban stance (Frumkin *et al.* 2004; Krall 2002). Suburbanization has always been intimately tied to racism (see Chapter 3); Americans continue to pursue the suburban and rural frontier to escape the density and perceived social problems of urban life.

A Mass Phenomenon
Other scholars argue that none of these attitudes is particularly American, but that what makes American sprawl unique is that it is a mass

phenomenon. Richardson and Gordon (2001) and Bruegmann (2005) argue that sprawl is simply the natural manifestation of human preferences. Bruegmann (2005), for example, argues that sprawl predates the automobile, is the trend in cities with large and small minority populations alike, and has taken place in regions all over the globe with very different tax and other public policies. Sprawl has been a feature of urban societies since the beginning of history. What makes contemporary American sprawl unique, he argues, is that it is a mass phenomenon. He argues: "Many more citizens have obtained the ability to exercise the choices that once were the sole prerogative of the wealthy and powerful" (Bruegmann 2005: 10). Other research that supports this explanation focuses on the role of rising income in U.S. society during the period of mass suburbanization. Margo (1992), for example, found that as much as half of the increase in suburbanization in the U.S. between 1950 and 1980 can be explained by rising incomes.

Impacts of Sprawl

The second major debate around housing development focuses on the impacts of sprawl. One the one hand, researchers find that sprawl has extensive fiscal, health-related, and especially environmental impacts. On the other, scholars argue that these negative impacts have been exaggerated and that sprawl has important benefits not to be ignored.

Critiques of Sprawl

Critics of housing sprawl argue that its financial costs are unnecessarily high and that it negatively impacts people's health, exacerbates metropolitan social inequalities, and has widespread negative environmental impacts, in part due to car dependence and extensive energy usage.

To start, the infrastructure necessary for housing costs more in sprawling, low-density communities than in higher-density developments. Water and sewer lines, schools, roads, and emergency services can cost twice as much in low-density communities as in high-density neighborhoods, and government expenses there are higher (Livingston *et al.* 2003).

Critics of sprawl also argue that it aggravates metropolitan social inequalities. As affluent and middle-class people continue to move to new housing on the metropolitan outskirts, they take much-needed tax revenue away from cities and older suburban communities. Tax-funded services like schools, waste collection, transit, and a host of other services within metropolitan areas are thus highly uneven. As people move out of central cities, they are increasingly populated by poorer residents who require more social services at the same time that their tax bases are eroded. Sprawl, then, intensifies the negative consequences of racial and economic segregation (Squires 2002; see also Chapter 3).

Furthermore, housing sprawl may have serious public health implications. Research suggests that the physical landscape of sprawling communities may impact the health of their residents because they are less walkable and accessible (Kelly-Schwartz *et al.* 2004). People who live in walkable, safe communities walk more and have lower BMIs than those who do not (Doyle *et al.* 2006; Lee *et al.* 2009). Indeed, compactness is associated with lower BMIs and lower rates of obesity, heart disease, high blood pressure, and diabetes, and lower rates of coronary heart disease among women (Ewing *et al.* 2014; Griffin *et al.* 2013; Kostova 2011). Sprawl is associated with significantly higher traffic and pedestrian fatality rates, likely because sprawl requires that Americans drive more miles at higher speeds (Ewing and Hamidi 2015). It is also associated with longer ambulance response times and a higher probability of delayed ambulance arrival (Trowbridge *et al.* 2009).

Finally, researchers find that housing sprawl impacts the environment in a host of ways. First, housing construction consumes great amounts of natural resources, such as oil, timber, copper, aluminium, iron, and other materials —a factor aggravated by Americans owning multiple homes (Peterson *et al.* 2013). Low-density housing construction, in particular, has more significant environmental consequences than high-density development (Mockrin *et al.* 2013).

Second, people who live in sprawling communities must rely on cars for transportation, which is responsible for the majority of the negative environmental impacts of sprawl (Cieslewicz 2002). Suburban households drive 31 percent more than their urban counterparts (Kahn 2000). Car-dependent housing development exacerbates the negative impact of vehicle emissions on air quality and the atmosphere. As Cieslewicz aptly notes:

> By dividing land into vast large-lot, single-family-home subdivisions connected to even larger shopping malls and business "parks" by wide highways and streets, we have made driving mandatory in virtually every new [housing] development in the last half of the 20th century.
>
> (Cieslewicz 2002: 26)

Globally, between 70 percent and 90 percent of total emissions of carbon monoxide—a greenhouse gas that contributes to global climate change—come from transportation (Rodrigue 2013). Urban areas in the U.S. are among the most sprawling in the world, and the U.S. is the most car-dependent nation in the world (Kenworthy and Laube 1999). As a result, the U.S. is among the highest emitters of carbon dioxide, both absolutely and per capita, in the world (Emission Database for Global Atmospheric Research 2016). Other harmful emissions from cars and trucks contribute to air pollution and related health problems such as asthma (Bullard *et al.* 2000). In 2014, traffic congestion caused Americans to travel an extra 6.9 billion hours and purchase an extra 3.1 billion gallons of fuel (Schrank *et al.* 2015). Approximately 200,000 early deaths occur in the U.S. each year due to combustion emissions, a leading cause of which is road transportation (Caiazzo *et al.* 2013).

As a result of car dependence, metropolitan areas in the U.S. with greater sprawl exhibit higher concentrations and emissions of air pollution and carbon dioxide after controlling for other factors (Bereitschaft and Debbage 2013; Stone 2008). As Ewing, Pendall, and Chen note:

> Even when controlling for income, household size, and other variables, people drive more, have to own more cars, breathe more polluted air, face greater risk of traffic fatalities, and walk and use transit less in places with more sprawling development patterns.
>
> (Ewing *et al.* 2002)

New housing developments in sprawling exurban and rural communities bring other unique environmental challenges. As Peterson, Peterson, and Liu note: "Sprawling development requires more per capita energy for transportation and infrastructure" (Peterson *et al.* 2013: 4). Furthermore, housing in sprawling developments leads to more residential energy use. Larger, detached houses—characteristic of new housing construction in exurbs and rural areas—use more energy for temperature control and lighting than the smaller attached or semi-attached houses characteristic of cities and some older suburbs (Ewing and Rong 2008; Peterson *et al.* 2013). Indeed, housing sprawl across the country inflates residential energy consumption and associated greenhouse gas emissions (Ewing and Rong 2008).

Furthermore, housing sprawl itself may contribute to the "urban heat island" effect, a well-known phenomenon of higher temperatures in urbanized places attributable to rapidly heating surfaces like buildings, asphalt, bare soil, and short grasses (Kim 1992). The urban heat island has typically been associated with very large, dense cities. In fact, low-density housing development—sprawl—constitutes more of a heat island than high-density, more compact housing development (Stone and Norman 2006). In fact, extreme heat events (i.e. heat waves) increased in sprawling metropolitan regions in the U.S. at twice the rate of those in more compact regions between 1956 and 2005 (Stone *et al.* 2010).

Sprawl also impacts water availability and quality. Low-density development uses significantly more water than high-density development, mostly because of higher water usage for landscaping. Sprawl also puts waterways in danger of toxic runoff from construction sites, lawn chemicals, and gasoline and oil residue from cars (Cieslewicz 2002; Livingston *et al.* 2003). Homeowners in exurban and rural areas further impact the environment by paving driveways and other areas, managing yards, having pets, combating "nuisance" wildlife, using more light, and a host of other behaviors (Mockrin *et al.* 2013).

Sprawling housing development also threatens biodiversity by disrupting habitats with housing and infrastructure construction (Swenson and Franklin 2000; Theobald *et al.* 1997). For example, more new housing construction was built adjacent to national forests than the national rate during the 1990s (Hammer *et al.* 2009). In the West and Southeast, in particular, 28.3 million and 9.2 million housing units were added between 1940 and 2000, respectively, many of them in the "wildlife-urban interface," where urbanized settlements meet wildnerness (Hammer *et al.* 2009).

As Mockrin *et al.* note: "Ecosystems are dynamic and complex, so that even small disturbances such as clearing a lot for construction of a home may initiate a cascade of changes in vegetation, with implications for wildlife populations and ecosystem functioning" (Mockrin *et al.* 2013: 402). Research shows that housing development limits the size of bird and mammalian species and their habitats (Frisen *et al.* 1995; Marzluff *et al.* 2001; Joly and Myers 2001). In the U.S., urbanization—the expansion of urban land uses, including commercial, industrial, and residential (Brown *et al.* 2005)—is primarily responsible for the population declines of more than half of all federally listed threatened and endangered species (Czech *et al.* 2000).

Housing sprawl also impinges on farmland. The nation loses about two acres of farmland every minute, every day, largely to development, and this impacts our food system (American Farmland Trust 2002; Brown *et al.* 2005). As Cieslewicz notes: "As farms are pushed from these more productive soils by the sprawling suburbs being spun out from cities, agriculture demands more chemical inputs to increase its production per acre" (Cieslewicz 2002: 27). Housing development in new (formerly rural) exurbs also limits land available for emerging sustainable energy efforts such as wind power and agricultural products (Peterson *et al.* 2013).

Rural sprawl, in particular—housing development in nonmetropolitan counties—brings unique and possibly more severe environmental challenges because it affects much larger areas than exurban/suburban sprawl and is typically in areas with "attractive recreational aesthetic amenities" such as the coasts of lakes and oceans and near forests (Radeloff *et al.* 2005). Between 1940 and 2000 rural sprawl made up about a third of new housing construction in the Midwestern U.S., for example, triggering a unique set of environmental problems (Radeloff *et al.* 2005).

Pro-Sprawl Arguments
On the other side of the debate are scholars who hold that the negative impacts of sprawl are exaggerated and that sprawl may be beneficial. Bruegmann (2008), for example, challenges the notion that the car dependence that sprawl involves harms the environment. Cars are more fuel efficient than

ever before, and use barely more energy per passenger mile traveled than the average bus. The real issue, he argues, is the fuel source. Thus, sprawl and car dependence are not an issue—but dependence on gas is.

Richardson and Gordon (2001) famously dispute a host of other claims about the negative impact of sprawl. First, they argue, sprawl has very little impact on farmland. Urbanized land accounts for less than 5 percent of the area of the U.S. Empirical evidence shows that if the entire U.S. population lived at the low density of one acre per four-person household, only 3 percent of the contiguous U.S. would be used (Fischel 1985). Moreover, while the amount of land used for agriculture is certainly declining, agricultural output has soared in recent decades. Second, while critics of sprawl argue that its infrastructure is too costly, they argue that older and more compact urban infrastructure is also costly. Third, they argue that continuous sprawl relieves traffic congestion by giving motorists more options and alleviates traffic pressures on central cities. And as industry and thus employment has also migrated to the urban fringe, many people enjoy shorter commutes (Gordon and Richardson 1997). Empirical evidence does suggest that sprawl is associated with shorter commute times (Crane and Chatman 2003).

In addition to disputing claims made about the negative impacts of sprawl, some scholars emphasize the potential benefits of sprawl, including "satisfying residential preferences, consumer sovereignty, access to good schools, relative safety from crime, access to countryside and recreational amenities, and a high degree of mobility" (Richardson and Gordon 2001). But perhaps the most significant benefit of sprawl is that exurban and rural housing in current housing markets is more affordable. Expanding the supply of single-family residences on the urban fringe functions to lower housing prices—which has also been shown to improve housing options for African Americans in particular (Kahn 2001). Critics of sprawl counter that rehabilitating and reusing urban housing stock could have the same function while limiting the negative impacts of sprawl, but sprawl supporters argue that Americans want larger houses in lower densities.

Should We Limit Sprawl?

Ultimately, most critics of sprawl call for more organized, centralized planning of land use in the U.S. to stave off its negative effects. They argue that the housing market is inefficient and that the costs of current trends in housing development—namely sprawl—are not borne by those who produce it. From an equity standpoint, the goods and services associated with sprawl are not distributed evenly. On the other hand, the majority of scholars that dispute claims about the negative impacts of sprawl call instead for the housing and real estate markets to operate with few restrictions. They assume that the current housing market is competitive and efficient, that regulations are not needed to place the costs of development on the producers of housing, and that public goods can be provided by the market (Chin 2002).

Many of the advocates for more restrictions on and planning of housing development are proponents of Smart Growth, a housing and economic development strategy that serves as an alternative to sprawl. Smart Growth advocates compact, mixed-used, transit-friendly development. Supported by a broad coalition of politicians, planners, developers, environmentalists, and others, Smart Growth developments offer a range of housing options, foster walkability and diverse transit options, preserve open space, foster distinctive communities, and "encourage community and stakeholder collaboration in development decisions" (Tregoning *et al.* 2002). The Smart Growth movement has grown considerably since its inception in the 1990s. Americans voted on more than 500 state or local ballot initiatives focused on planning and Smart Growth in the 2000 elections alone, with approval ratings over 70 percent (Tregoning *et al.* 2002). Other advocates for restricting sprawl call for gas and energy taxes to discourage driving and increase funding for mass transit to incentivize its use.

Critics of Smart Growth and other efforts to limit sprawl, such as gas and energy taxes and subsidies for mass transit, argue that these efforts undermine consumer preferences and can inhibit economic growth. If we decrease sprawl, we would put a wrench in our economic engine: incentivizing development of smaller living quarters in dense urban areas would lessen demand for land on the urban periphery, cars, electricity, gas, appliances, furniture, and home goods. Smart Growth and higher energy taxes to limit sprawl particularly threaten the car industry, as larger vehicles that use more gas are more profitable (Gonzalez 2009).

Furthermore, they point to the failure of governmental policies that encourage mass transit. Bruegmann (2008) notes that European governments have poured billions of dollars into mass transit to encourage its use while transit ridership has remained largely the same since World War II. (It should be noted, however, that European ridership far outweighs that of Americans.) He argues that incentivizing mass transit for a populace that prefers driving is doomed to failure, and that Smart Growth by itself would not result in increased mass transit ridership. In this vein, Gordon and Richardson (1997) note that public funding of mass transit far outweighs subsidies for highways and parking.

In sum, Bruegmann argues, Smart Growth proponents harken back to a golden age of urbanism that never existed, as all measures of quality of life have improved as cities have sprawled. Rather that attempting to limit sprawl, we should let the market respond to consumer demands for low-density, car-dependent living.

Housing Development and Natural Disasters: The Debates

In a separate but related vein, there are significant debates about the relation-ship between housing development, land use planning, and natural disasters. Housing sprawl continues relatively unabated in highly hazardous areas. A host of recent scholarship documents show natural disasters are at least partly social disasters in that societal characteristics help to determine their scope, impact, and our recovery from them (Gotham and Greenberg 2014; Hartman and Squires 2006). For example, Hurricane Katrina had a more severe impact on poor, African American residents of New Orleans as a result of longstand-ing racial and economic residential segregation that concentrated them in the low-lying Ninth Ward. And a history of building public housing on outlying, coastal land in New York City left the city's poorest residents at highest risk during Superstorm Sandy. Indeed, the poorest Americans are often relegated to the lowest-lying land, putting them at increased risk when natural disasters increasingly ensue. As housing development continues in areas at high risk for fires, floods, and storms, the question of who should bear the cost of the impacts when disasters inevitably ensue—and how.

Housing sprawl is the single greatest factor that challenges federal fire management policies (Dombeck *et al.* 2004). Moreover, the cost of rebuild-ing homes after fires, floods, and storms is often greater than aid provided by government and private insurance. Furthermore, restoring wetlands in coastal areas can mitigate the impact of storms. Given these facts, should we count on individual property owners to bear the costs of living in a high-risk area? Or should we limit the geographical areas available for housing to reduce the costs of disaster management? These questions ultimately touch on the fundamental American problem of reconciling the right to private property with responsibility to the public good.

On one hand, we expect people who build, purchase, and/or live in housing in places at high risk for natural disasters to limit their risk to the best of their ability (by not keeping fuel around in wildfire-prone areas, for example) and purchase insurance to cover any damage from fires, earth-quakes, floods, storms, and other natural disasters. On the other hand, we provide billions of dollars in public funds to victims of disasters and operate public insurance and mitigation programs. More than $15 billion dollars, for example, was allocated to fund the Federal Emergency Management Agency (FEMA) in 2014—constituting 25 percent of the Department of Homeland Security's budget (U.S. Department of Homeland Security 2016). At first glance this seems to be a practical approach that covers all bases. Upon further reflection, questions remain as to whether this is the wisest approach.

First, trusting that developers and homeowners will make the appropriate choices to minimize vulnerability to disaster is risky. A bulk of evidence shows that property owners in high-risk areas across the board do not "voluntarily adopt cost-effective loss reduction measures" for a host of reasons, including underestimating or ignoring the risk of living where they do, thinking in the short term, and budget constraints (Kunreuther 2006). Property owners are even less likely to adopt mitigation efforts if they are insured (Kunreuther and Kleffner 1992).

Second, purchasing insurance is not mandatory in high-risk communities, and even where it ostensibly is there are gaps in coverage. While mortgage lenders often require the purchase of additional insurance for fire, flood, wind, etc., people who purchase properties with cash or those who have paid their mortgages off are not everywhere required to have disaster-related insurance. Furthermore, as many stories in the wake of Hurricane Katrina reveal, not every disaster-prone area is required to have additional insurance, and among those that are, insurance often does not cover the cost of destroyed property. Localities tend to avoid mandating insurance because responsibility falls on them for oversight (Bagstad *et al.* 2007).

Third, insurance in disaster-prone areas is subsidized by the federal government in an inefficient and detrimental scheme. The National Flood Insurance Program subsidizes insurance premiums for property owners in coastal and other flood-prone areas. Like any other insurance program, NFIP was designed to be self-sufficient, but it is anything but. The program lost $450 million annually prior to 2005 (Gaul and Wood 2000). The $23 billion in Katrina-related claims far outpaced the $1.5 billion—increased to $20.7 billion in 2006—that the agency was authorized to borrow that year (Bagstad *et al.* 2007). In order to absorb the costs of increasingly common catastrophic seasons like the 2005 hurricane season, insurance premiums would need to increase substantially. A 1993 estimate showed that while insurance premiums ran about $800 per year in high-risk coastal communities, private insurers would need to charge $12,000 per year to maintain an actuarially sound program (Bagstad *et al.* 2007). The NFIP also pays multiple claims for the same properties when they are damaged in subsequent events without raising premiums, encouraging rebuilding in the most disaster-prone places. In fact, "repetitive loss properties account for about 2% of policyholders but almost 30% of all claims" (Bagstad *et al.* 2007). At the same time, the NFIP is not authorized to condemn disaster-prone properties or require they be moved; only local officials can do that. Without massive subsidies, private insurance would not be offered in disaster-prone areas. As Bagstad, Stapleton, and D'Agostino (2007) note: "The concept of pooling risk is not efficient when the only purchasers or a policy are those at great and predictable risk" (Bagstad *et al.* 2007: 288). The NFIP has encouraged risky development in disaster-prone places.

Ultimately our approach to building homes in high-risk areas is to allow it, except in cases where localities develop zoning or other mitigation schemes to prevent development in disaster-prone places. We expect property owners to weigh the risks responsibly, we subsidize their disaster insurance rates, and we provide additional disaster funds if needed. In this way our policy reflects the sentiment that protecting private property is in the public interest, even if the cost is extraordinarily high—perhaps higher than the prevention of development in high-risk areas.

Housing Development Policy

As the previous section has shown, there is considerable debate over whether we should limit sprawl because of its impacts and whether we should limit housing development in disaster-prone areas. But even among those who support limiting housing sprawl and/or regulating housing development to mitigate the impact of natural disasters, there is considerable debate about what is the appropriate approach. Researchers and practitioners have advanced a wide variety of policy proposals to limit housing development in particular places in recent eras.

American land use regulation and planning in general is decidedly decentralized: there is no national land use policy; it is up to states and localities to impose their own regulations. There is little or no coordinated effort on the part of the national government to regulate land use for housing, environmental protection, or any other purpose. In addition, in contrast to many European cities and localities, local governments in the U.S. simply regulate land use; they typically do not purchase land for public ownership with the exception of green spaces (Bengston *et al.* 2004; Bruegmann 2005).

Sprawl-Related Policies

Anti-sprawl policies typically come in the form of growth management strategies (including Smart Growth), regulation of housing development through zoning and other land use regulations, transportation and energy-related policies, and a small set of more radical options.

Growth Management

States and localities began to regulate land use in earnest in the 1960s and 1970s in a "quiet revolution" of what has come to be known as growth management (Gillham 2002; Bosselman and Callies 1971). Growth management can be defined as public policies that "guide the location, quality, and timing of development" in efforts to balance environmental protection with economic development (Porter 1997: vii). Concerns over other environmental impacts of suburbanization and sprawl arose during this time, particularly over shrinking open spaces and the encroachment of housing development onto wetlands, floodplains, and hillsides. As a result, Hawaii was the first state to pass a land use law in 1961 that designated urban, rural, agricultural, and conservation districts. New York, Massachusetts, Wisconsin, California, Minnesota, Florida, Vermont, and Maine adopted regulations that variously limited home construction in wetlands, forests, and along lakeshores, preserved open space, and attempted to deal with the contamination of drinking water (Rome 2001). Localities like Ramapo, NY (a suburb of New York City), Petaluma, CA (north of San Francisco), and Boulder, CO (outside Denver), adopted strict growth limits. Ramapo, for example, prohibited new residential development without accompanying public facilities in 1969 (Gillham 2002).

These regulations ranged greatly in scope, focus, and impact, but reflected a national trend toward regulating the environmental problems associated with housing development in outlying areas. By 1975, twenty-three states had some sort of land use regulations—regulations upheld by courts in a "quiet judicial revolution" that strengthened state efforts to shape development and land use patterns (Rome 2001).

But state and local land use regulation was generally inconsistent and uneven. This issue, coupled with federal trends toward environmental protection (President Nixon signed the National Environmental Policy Act in 1970), prompted a national conversation about possible federal land use regulations. Congress debated a bill between 1972 and 1975 that would provide federal funding to states willing to summarize the ecological characteristics of their land and propose appropriate land use regulations. While the bill had broad support from politicians and the Nixon administration, environmentalists criticized it because it was essentially voluntary, and conservatives feared it infringed upon individual property rights. Representatives from the business community feared that the bill would undermine the economics of the housing market and organized grassroots property-rights movements, with citizens flooding congressional representatives with appeals to oppose regulating land use. The opposition to the bill reflected a bias toward top-down land planning and the sentiment that "the trend toward public control over the use of private property threatened the American system of free enterprise and individual liberty" (Rome 2001), a theme that continues to haunt contemporary debates about land use regulation in the United States. Ultimately the bill went nowhere, despite support in the Senate; the House and Nixon administration withdrew support by 1974.

National land use regulation failed, but growth management continues in a piecemeal fashion, just as in the postwar period. A handful of states have adopted growth management programs, including California, Florida, Georgia, Hawaii, Maine, Maryland, New Jersey, Oregon, Rhode Island, Vermont, and Washington (Weitz 1999). Localities in these states are either mandated or strongly encouraged to regulate land use according to the state's plans and priorities (Anthony 2004). Local growth management plans usually balance infrastructure provision, environmental protection, and economic development. Hawaii, Florida, Maine, New Jersey, and Oregon are considered the most regulated states in terms of growth (Weitz 1999).

Perhaps the most debated growth management strategy is the urban growth boundary of Portland, Oregon—what Bruegmann calls the country's "longest-running, most extensive, best documented, and most controversial assault on sprawl" (Bruegmann 2005: 203). Oregon was among the first states to establish growth controls during the "quiet revolution" of the 1960s and 1970s. The three counties and various municipalities that make up the Portland metropolitan area cooperated to establish a line around the metropolitan area, outside which higher-density housing development could not be approved. The boundary is static but can be revised, and has been since its inception in 1979. The boundary had a limited impact in the 1980s, mostly because the population and economy were relatively static and the boundary encompassed a great deal of land (Bruegmann 2005).

Since then, the growth boundary has without a doubt prevented a great deal of housing development on rural land outside the boundary. Supporters note that the boundary has led to a thriving downtown, more transit-friendly development, more diverse housing stock, and smaller lots, and that it has helped to preserve farmland (Richardson and Gordon 2001). Critics, on the other hand, attribute Portland's "livability" to its small size, relatively homogeneous population, and natural amenities—not the growth boundary. Furthermore, they argue, the growth boundary has led to rising prices for housing due to a diminished supply—a factor likely to have the strongest impact on newcomers to the housing market, immigrants, and the poor (Richardson and Gordon 2001). Supporters of the growth boundary counter that rising housing prices are reflective of demand for the smart-growth lifestyle that Portland provides, and that new, high-density infill development will meet the demand. Critics note that this kind of infill development will anger current residents who may not want to change the character of their neighborhood, and that these kinds of "NIMBY" (not in my backyard) campaigns may be more successful among affluent neighborhoods—adding an important dimension of social inequity to the city. While supporters of the boundary laud its focus on public transit, critics note that only about 2 percent of trips in the region are on public transit (Bruegmann 2005).

Other growth management strategies include outright development moratoriums or quasi-moratoriums to allow communities to stave off severe problems with fast development, rate of growth controls that cap the number of building permits issued each year, and adequate public facility ordinances (APFOs) that require adequate public infrastructure, such as utilities and schools, in accordance with new development (Bengston et al. 2004).

Smart Growth and the New Urbanism
Another strategy that localities employ to counter sprawl is the previously mentioned "smart growth," strategy, closely related to the "new urbanist" movement. This approach uses zoning, incentives, and other strategies to encourage development of walkable communities with diverse housing stock, ample transit, and employment, commercial, and recreational activities in close proximity. In contrast to sprawling communities, in which long stretches of space are zoned for one purpose, such as housing, localities can zone areas for mixed use: homes can be built in commercial areas, for example. The City of Santa Barbara, CA, for example, allows residential use in most commercial zones. As a result, it is the fourth-most compact, connected city nationally and has the greatest land use mix of all small metropolitan areas in the U.S. (Hamidi *et al.* 2015).

Another popular technique is to create more flexible zoning, to allow "cluster developments" and planned unit developments—essentially new developments of housing with buildings for other uses—along with open spaces (Bruegmann 2005). Other zoning strategies designed to encourage compact development include increasing density limits and floors, reducing minimum lot sizes, and offering density bonuses to entice developers to pursue dense projects (Ewing and Rong 2008).

"New urbanist" communities can be found all over the U.S., in Atlanta, North Carolina, Oklahoma, Utah, Florida, Maryland, Washington, Missouri, Oregon, Colorado, Arizona, Texas, New Jersey, and Alabama. While demand for new urbanist living appears to be increasing (Myers and Gearin 2001), some scholars point to potential downsides of such developments.

First, new urbanist development can threaten other parts of the economy. As Gonzalez notes:

> Denser urban areas, with smaller living quarters, would lessen demand for land, automobiles, electricity, gasoline, appliances, and furniture. Particularly significant for the automobile industry, densely organized communities, coupled with increased fuel costs, could push consumers away from larger and more profitable vehicles (for example, light trucks), which are substantially less fuel efficient than smaller, less profitable vehicles.
>
> (Gonzalez 2009)

Certainly many environmentalists would argue that this is not a bad thing.

Second, homes in new urbanist communities are generally more expensive than to their counterparts in more traditional areas (Eppli and Tu 1999). One interpretation of this is that there is great demand for this type of living (Myers and Gearin 2001); another is that it excludes people with modest incomes (Richardson and Gordon 2001). Some scholars also note that new urbanist developments in low-income communities can displace the people already living there (Day 2003). This is a real challenge given the problems discussed in Chapters 2 and 3.

Regulating Development

Another anti-sprawl strategy regulates housing and related development directly through fees, incentives, and requirements of developers. Localities can employ development exactions—essentially fees paid by developers that help offset any negative impacts of the development and/or fund infrastructure needed to support it, such as water, sewage, parks, roads, and services (Been 2005; Brueckner 2000). Localities may also use development impact taxes as another way to have developers shoulder some of the burden of sprawling development, some of which may take into account the value of lost open space (Bengston *et al.* 2004; Brueckner 2000). In 2000, the most recent year for which data is available, 59 percent of cities (with populations of more than 25,000) and 39 percent of counties use development impact fees (U.S. Government Accountability Office 2000). Since the 1980s, the communities with the most housing development on the urban fringe (i.e. in exurbs and in rural places) are the heaviest users of development impact fees (Been 2005).

Localities may also require environmental impact statements from developers in an effort to bring to light any potential negative environmental impacts from new developments. The requirement has been characterized as "clumsy, expensive, time consuming, and easily manipulated by special interest groups" (Bruegmann 2005: 191), and in some cases it has caused such delay that developments are abandoned.

While development impact fees and environmental impact statements are used by the majority of localities in the U.S. to mitigate some of the negative impacts of sprawl, they may unintentionally work to increase the unaffordability of housing by restricting housing supply or because developers may pass those costs on to homebuyers. As Been argues: "Impact fees also can be abused—to either exclude low- and moderate-income residents or people of color from communities or exploit new homebuyers who have no vote in the community" (Been 2005: 168). Knowledge of the potential downside of development impact fees can be used to amend these policies, to ensure equity.

Transportation and Energy-Related Strategies

A final set of anti-sprawl policies focuses on transportation and energy. Perhaps the most visible strategy is the extension and/or improvement of public transit systems. Extensions are often designed to mitigate the car-related negative impacts of sprawl; improvements are often designed to attract residents to more compact neighborhoods. Currently all levels of U.S.

government spend more transportation funds on highways and roads than on public transit; the federal government spends 80 percent of transportation funds on highways and roads (Pew Charitable Trusts 2016). Increasing spending for public transportation extension, improvement, and maintenance could lead to more public transit use and increase demand for more compact housing near public transit. Indeed, people who live near public transit stations tend to use public transit more (Cervero 1993). Critics of funding and expanding public transit argue that Americans prefer private travel in cars, and no amount of investment will change that (Bruegmann 2005; Richardson and Gordon 2001). Another strategy is to impose road tolls that discourage commuting from far distances. In theory, as individuals weigh the relative cost of housing and transportation, they are more likely to live closer to their jobs (Brueckner 2000). A further strategy is to increase the gas tax to encourage more Americans to choose public transportation.

Other Anti-Sprawl Strategies
Other, more radical strategies may prevent or mitigate the negative impacts of sprawl. The most radical option is to abolish the mortgage interest and property tax deductions in an effort to stop subsidizing single-family homeownership; this is unlikely to be implemented (Richardson and Gordon 2001). A less radical option that would curtail the ways in which sprawl exacerbates metropolitan social inequalities would be for cities to annex suburbs and exurbs into consolidated regions with shared tax bases (Rusk 2003). When cities are able to annex new developments, they are more socially integrated and resources are distributed more equitably (Rusk 2003).

Disaster-Related Housing Policy

Just as there is substantial debate over whether and how to limit sprawl, researchers and policymakers debate how best to deal with the impact of natural disasters. These separate but related debates both touch on fundamental problems with American land use planning for housing.

There are two basic approaches to dealing with the impact of natural disasters: mitigation and response (Board on Natural Disasters 1999). Mitigation actions are those that attempt to minimize the impacts of natural disasters; response actions are those that immediately "reduce suffering and hasten recovery of the affected population and region" (Board on Natural Disasters 1999: 1944). Response strategies have typically dominated natural disaster policy in the U.S., although mitigation strategies are increasing. Still, most experts agree that "No single approach to bringing sustainable hazard mitigation into existence shows more promise at this time than increased use of sound and equitable land-use management" (Second National Assessment on Natural and Related Technological Hazards, cited in Mileti 1999). As

Burby *et al.* explain: "Land-use planning is the means for gathering and analyzing information about the suitability for development of land exposed to natural hazards, so that the limitations of hazard-prone areas are understood by citizens, potential investors, and government officials" (Burby *et al.* 2000: 99).

As noted in the previous section, American disaster policy consists of a combination of reliance on individuals to protect their properties, subsidizing disaster insurance, and providing extensive disaster aid. Researchers have noted that this is not a particularly wise approach: individuals do not necessarily minimize their disaster risks; purchasing insurance is not necessarily mandatory; the National Flood Insurance Program is inefficient at best; and providing extensive post-disaster aid is costly. Perhaps the biggest problem with federal hazard mitigation policy is that it does not include land use regulation for housing.

Burby (2006) argues that these problems stem from two fundamental issues with government disaster policy: the safe development paradox and the local government paradox. The safe development paradox is that in efforts to make hazardous areas safer, the federal government has actually encouraged housing development in hazardous areas. Subsidized insurance and disaster protection public works were intended to mitigate the costs of disaster; instead, they incentivized housing development in hazardous regions.

The local government paradox is that local governments do little to limit the vulnerability of residents to disasters, even as they bear the brunt of losses. As Mileti notes:

> Few local governments are willing to reduce natural hazards by managing development. It is not so much that they oppose land use measures (although some do), but rather that, like individuals, they tend to view natural hazards as a minor problem that can take a back seat to more pressing local concerns such as unemployment, crime, housing, and education. Also, the costs of mitigation are immediate while the benefits are uncertain, may not occur during the tenure of current elected officials, and are not visible (like roads or a new library).
>
> (Mileti 1999: 160)

The federal government's extensive disaster aid programs may also deter local governments from adopting natural disaster plans, as they know they can rely on that aid (Burby 2006). In New Orleans, for example, the city allowed housing development to sprawl into hazardous areas at the same time that it refused to pay for the cost of increased flood and hurricane protection (Burby 2006).

In the wake of these problems, researchers have suggested a number of small and large-scale housing policy changes to encourage more functional and extensive disaster prevention and recovery. In general, these policy proposals focus primarily on what state and local governments can do, partly as a result of the American tradition of decentralized government, but also because natural disaster risk and response is specific to particular regions.

Federal Policies

Federal disaster policy is largely limited to FEMA mitigation and response programs. Notably, federal policies have begun to stress the importance of mitigation in addition to response (Board on Natural Disasters 1999). FEMA currently operates a disaster mitigation program designed to reduce vulnerability to disasters before they occur. Individual localities can apply for federal funding that must be matched by state and/or local funds to engage in mitigation efforts after a disaster, such as strengthening or elevating structures, acquiring property in high-hazard areas for conversion to open space, and implementing vegetation management programs to reduce wildfire damage (Burby 2006; Federal Emergency Management Agency 2016b)). Recent analyses show cost–benefit ratio of mitigation strategies to be about 4:1, with the highest ratio for flood mitigation and lowest for earthquake mitigation (Rose *et al.* 2007). But federal policy tries only to provide incentives to states and localities to develop plans and mitigation strategies—it does not compel them to do so.

Federal policy could change. One change might be to shift NFIP coverage from individual properties to communities. Premiums would be determined by the degree of risk faced by the entire community, with premiums paid by local governments through tax revenue (either general tax revenue or higher taxes in higher-risk zones.) The federal government could withhold disaster relief to localities failing to adopt insurance, up to the amount that insurance would have covered. This change in NFIP policy would lead to 100 percent coverage of all high-risk properties and would likely lead some localities to restrict development in high-risk areas rather than bear the brunt of the insurance cost (Burby 2006).

State Policies

In lieu of federal hazard mitigation requirements, state governments can (and some have) adopted comprehensive land use plans by which localities must abide. In these schemes, any local land use decision must correspond to state plans and priorities. These plans often contain anti-sprawl elements as well. Comprehensive mitigation planning specifically includes determining the nature and location of potential natural hazards, identifying populations and properties that are vulnerable to these hazards, establishing "standards for acceptable levels of risk," and implementing mitigation strategies based on the costs and benefits of development in hazard-prone areas (Board on Natural Disasters 1999). Where states intervene and require that localities adopt comprehensive mitigation planning, losses from natural disasters are substantially lower (Burby 2006; Burby *et al.* 2006). At the same time, fewer than half of states require this kind of plan from local governments, and fewer than ten states require those localities to consider natural disasters (Burby 2006). In other words, these plans tend to be successful, but few states employ them.

Another policy possibility is to require local governments to "assume greater financial responsibility for the consequences of their urban development decision making" (Burby 2006: 172). Requiring localities to prepare plans that consider disaster risk and to take greater financial responsibility for that risk would force them to make more sound land use decisions. In weighing the benefits and costs of continued development versus disaster risk, for example, they may restrict housing development in hazardous areas altogether.

Local Policies

Disaster mitigation policy in the U.S. is extremely localized and somewhat haphazard, but some localities have been extraordinarily creative in planning for natural disasters. In designing comprehensive plans that take into account disaster risk, localities from North Carolina to Missouri to California weigh the costs and benefits of residential and commercial development against environmental impact and disaster risk. In some cases development is restricted to certain areas to preserve open space or because of high natural disaster risk; in others development may be approved but only under certain conditions, such as using hazard-resilient construction standards or requiring developers to pay for disaster protection. Plans can also include "building codes, acquisition of hazard areas with open space or environmental value, relocation of existing development at risk, infrastructure location and design standards, and public information programs that raise awareness of hazards" (Burby *et al.* 2000: 99).

Lee County, Florida, for example, charges residents of flood-prone areas for mitigation directly in an effort to disincentivize development in highly hazardous areas (Berke 1998). New York State, on the other hand, implemented the NY Rising Housing Recovery Program, which assists property owners impacted by Superstorm Sandy, Hurricane Irene, and Tropical Storm Lee. The program includes a wide range of recovery programs, including a relatively atypical buyout and acquisition program. Designed as a long-term mitigation strategy, the state will purchase badly damaged properties at market value (prior to damage) for conversion to wetlands, open space, and/ or stormwater management programs (Governor's Office of Storm Recovery 2016). The conversion of previously developed areas in coastal areas and floodplains at continued high risk for natural disasters is thought to save money and lives in the long run. Undeveloped wetlands can absorb the initial impact of storm surge and flooding, while property owners are compensated to live elsewhere at lower risk for disaster. Countless other localities across the U.S. have adopted similar buyout-conversion plans in floodplains and coastal areas.

Miami: A Case Study in Sprawl and Disaster Management

Mirroring trends all over the U.S., and particularly in the Sunbelt Southern and Western states, Miami, FL's population increased by nearly 85 percent in the 1940s and nearly 90 percent in the 1950s (Mohl 1982). The postwar suburban boom was unmatched in Miami, which by 1954 led the U.S. in new home construction, aided in part by an aggressive attempt to drain parts of the Everglades to make way for development (Burby *et al.* 2006; Mohl 1982). Tourism and building construction led Miami's economic boom, while state officials and private developers sought to tame the region's swamps and floodplains into land suitable for real estate. But Miami is unique in one major respect: over the past 135 years the region has experienced a hurricane approximately once every 2.7 years (Burby *et al.* 2006).

By 1965 Florida's state government began to address the massive risk of construction on Biscayne Bay and into the nearby Everglades with laws that strengthened local government's capacity to shape urban development and protect the surrounding environment. State laws followed in 1972, 1975, 1984, and 1985 that protected the Everglades from development and mandated local growth management plans. Multicounty regions and localities are required to design and implement both growth management and disaster prevention programs that align with state land use goals. These goals include limiting public subsidies for development in hazardous areas, directing residential development away from highly hazardous areas, limiting hurricane evacuation times, and designing post-disaster plans that reduce risk to human life and property (Burby *et al.* 2006).

Dade County, which houses the Miami metropolitan area, not only complied with new state regulations but also imposed an urban growth boundary in 1975, to prevent further development in the Everglades' wetlands and floodplains. This has contributed to high housing prices in the Miami metropolitan area, but has also decreased losses from regularly occurring hurricanes and floods (Burby *et al.* 2006). The State of Florida continues to lead the U.S. in hurricane risk, with Tampa-St Petersburg and Miami at highest risk (RealtyTrac 2015).

Terms

Exurban sprawl
Rural sprawl
Gentrification
Suburbanization
Infill development
Urbanization
Zoning
Growth management
Urban growth boundary
Smart Growth
Safe development paradox
Local government paradox
Land use planning

Discussion Questions

What are the dominant forms of housing development in the U.S.? Why?

Should we limit housing sprawl? Why or why not? If so, how?

What is the relationship between housing development and natural disasters?

How are sprawl and disaster-related land use regulations similar or different?

Should the American approach to land use regulation change? Why or why not?

Application

You are an urban planner employed by a moderately populated Midwestern county. A nearby city of about two million people has recently experienced a resurgence, and housing prices have become high enough that many people are choosing to buy land and build homes about an hour away, in formerly rural land with access to a well-maintained highway. The county has approved building in those areas thus far, but the population there has exploded, and there have been two catastrophic floods in those places in the past ten years. Your job is to decide whether and how to regulate housing development in the county, within a radius of one and a half hours from the major city. Design a comprehensive land use plan that reflects a careful consideration of how to balance housing affordability with the negative impacts of sprawl and the prospect of more flooding.

References

Alonso, William. 1964. *Location and Land Use.* Cambridge, MA: Harvard University Press.

American Farmland Trust. 2002. "Farming on the Edge: Sprawling Development Threatens America's Best Farmland." Washington, DC. Retrieved December 7, 2016. www.farmlandinfo.org/sites/default/files/Farming_on_the_Edge_2002_1.pdf.

Anthony, Jerry. 2004. "Do State Growth Management Regulations Reduce Sprawl?" *Urban Affairs Review* 39(3): 376–397.

Bagstad, Kenneth J., Stapleton, Kevin, and D'Agostino, John R. 2007. "Taxes, Subsidies, and Insurance as Drivers of United States Coastal Development." *Ecological Economics* 63: 285–298.

Been, Vicki. 2005. "Impact Fees and Housing Affordability." *Cityscape: A Journal of Policy Development and Research* 8(1): 139–185.

Bengston, David N., Fletcher, Jennifer O., and Nelson, Kristen C. 2004. "Public Policies for Managing Urban Growth and Protecting Open Space: Policy Instruments and Lessons Learned in the United States." *Landscape and Urban Planning* 69: 271–286.

Bereitschaft, Bradley and Debbage, Keith. 2013. "Urban Form, Air Pollution, and CO_2 Emissions in Large U.S. Metropolitan Areas." *The Professional Geographer* 65(4): 612–635.

Berke, Philip R. 1998. "Reducing Natural Hazard Risks Through State Growth Management." *Journal of the American Planning Association* 64(1): 76–87.

Board on Natural Disasters. 1999. "Mitigation Emerges as Major Strategy for Reducing Losses Caused by Natural Disasters." *Science* 284: 1943–1947.

Bosselman, Fred and Callies, David L. 1971. *The Quiet Revolution in Land Use Control.* Washington, DC: Council on Environmental Quality and Council of State Governments.

Boustan, Leah Platt and Shertzer, Allison. 2010. "Demography and Population Loss from Central Cities, 1950–2000." Los Angeles, CA: California Center for Population Research. Retrieved June 28, 2016. http://papers.ccpr.ucla.edu/papers/PWP-CCPR-2010-019/PWP-CCPR-2010-019.pdf.

Brown, Daniel G., Johnson, Kenneth M., Loveland, Thomas R., and Theobold, David M. 2005. "Rural Land-Use Trends in the Conterminous United States, 1950–2000." *Ecological Applications* 15(6): 1851–1863.

Brueckner, Jan K. 2000. "Urban Sprawl: Diagnosis and Remedies." *International Regional Science Review* 23(2): 160–171.

Bruegmann, Robert. 2005. *Sprawl: A Compact History.* Chicago, IL: University of Chicago Press.

Bruegmann, Robert. 2008. "Point: Sprawl and Accessibility." *Journal of Transport and Land Use* 1(1): 5–11.

Bullard, Robert D., Johnson, Glenn S., and Torres, Angel O. 2000. *Sprawl City: Race, Politics, and Planning in Atlanta.* Washington, DC: Island Press.

Burby, Raymond J. 2006. "Hurricane Katrina and the Paradoxes of Government Disaster Policy: Bringing About Wise Governmental Decisions for Hazardous Areas." *ANNALS of the American Academy of Political and Social Science* 604: 171–191.

Burby, Raymond J., Deyle, Robert E., Godschalk, David R., and Olshansky, Robert B. 2000. "Creating Hazard Resilient Communities Through Land-Use Planning." *Natural Hazards Review*, May: 99–106.

Burby, Raymond J., Nelson, Arthur C., and Sanchez, Thomas W. 2006. "The Problems of Containment and the Promise of Planning." In E. L. Birch and S. M. Wachter, eds, *Rebuilding Urban Places After Disaster: Lessons from Hurricane Katrina*, pp. 47–65. Philadelphia, PA: University of Pennsylvania Press.

Burchell, Robert W., Shad, Naveed A., Listokin, David, Phillips, Hilary, Downs, Anthony, Seskin, Samuel, Davis, Judy S., Moore, Terry, Helton, David, and Gall, Michelle. 1998. *The Costs of Sprawl—Revisited*. Washington, DC: National Academy Press.

Caiazzo, Fabio, Ashok, Akshay, Waitz, Ian A., Yim, Steve H. L., and Barrett, Steven R. H. 2013. "Air Pollution and Early Deaths in the United States. Part 1: Quantifying the Impact of Major Sectors in 2005." *Atmospheric Environment* 79: 198–208.

Calem, Paul S., Gillen, Kevin, and Wachter, Susan. 2004. "The Neighborhood Distribution of Subprime Mortgage Lending." *Journal of Real Estate Finance and Economics* 29(4): 393–410.

Cervero, Robert. 1993. "Surviving in the Suburbs: Transit's Untapped Frontier." *Access*, Spring: 29–34.

Chin, Nancy. 2002. "Unearthing the Roots of Urban Sprawl: A Critical Analysis of Form, Function and Methodology." UCL Centre for Advanced Spatial Analysis Working Papers Series, Paper 47-Mar 02. Retrieved December 7, 2016. www.bartlett.ucl.ac.uk/casa/pdf/paper47.pdf.

Cieslewicz, David J. 2002. "The Environmental Impacts of Sprawl." In Gregory D. Squires, ed., *Urban Sprawl: Causes, Consequences, and Policy Responses*, pp. 23–38. Washington, DC: The Urban Institute Press.

Crane, Randall and Chatman, Daniel G. 2003. "Traffic and Sprawl: Evidence from U.S. Commuting 1985–1997. *Planning and Markets* 6(1): 14–22.

Cutter, Susan L. and Emrich, Christopher. 2005. "Are Natural Hazards and Disaster Losses in the U.S. Increasing?" *EOS, Transactions, American Geophysical Union* 86(41): 381–396.

Czech, Brian, Krausman, Paul R., and Devers, Patrick K. 2000. "Economic Associations among Causes of Species Endangerment in the United States." *BioScience* 50: 593–601.

Day, Kristen. 2003. "New Urbanism and the Challenges of Designing for Diversity." *Journal of Planning Education and Research* 23: 83–95.

Dombeck, Michael P., Williams, Jack E., and Wood, Christopher A. 2004. "Wildfire Policy and Public Lands: Integrating Scientific Understanding with Social Concerns across Landscapes." *Conservation Biology* 18(4): 883–889.

Doyle, Scott, Kelly-Schwartz, Alexia C., Schlossberg, Marc, and Stockard, Jean. 2006. "Active Community Environments and Health: The Relationship of Walkable and Safe Communities to Individual Health." *Journal of the American Planning Association* 72(2): 19–31.

Dwyer, Rachel E. 2009. "The McMansionization of America? Income Stratification and the Standard of Living in Housing, 1960–2000." *Research in Social Stratification and Mobility* 27(4): 285–300.

Emanuel, Kerry. 2005. "Increasing Destructiveness of Tropical Cyclones over the Past 30 Years." *Nature* 436: 686–689.

Emission Database for Global Atmospheric Research (EDGAR). 2016. European Commission, Joint Research Center/PBL Netherlands Environmental Assessment Agency. Retrieved June 28, 2016. http://edgar.jrc.ec.europe.eu.

Eppli, Mark J. and Tu, Charles C. 1999. *Valuing The New Urbanism: The Impact of the New Urbanism On Prices of Single-Family Homes.* Washington, DC: The Urban Land Institute.

Ewing, Reid, and Hamidi, Sima. 2015. "Urban Sprawl as a Risk Factor in Motor Vehicle Occupant and Pedestrian Fatalities: Update and Refinement." *Transportation Research Record* 2513: 40–47.

Ewing, Reid and Rong, Fang. 2008. "The Impact of Urban Form on U.S. Residential Energy Use." *Housing Policy Debate* 19(1): 1–30.

Ewing, Reid, Pendall, Rolf, and Chen, Don. 2002. *Measuring Sprawl and Its Impact.* Washington, DC: Smart Growth America.

Ewing, Reid, Meakins, Gail, Hamidi, Shima, and Nelson, Arthur C. 2014. "Relationship Between Urban Sprawl and Physical Activity, Obesity, and Morbidity: Update and Refinement." *Health and Place* 26: 118–126.

Federal Emergency Management Agency. 2016a. "Disaster Declarations by Year: Hurricanes and Tropical Storms." Retrieved December 1, 2016. www.fema.gov/disasters/grid/year?field_disaster_type_term_tid_1=6840.

Federal Emergency Management Agency. 2016b. "Overview of Federal Disaster Assistance—Unit 3." Retrieved July 10, 2016. http://training.fema.gov/emiweb/downloads/is7unit_3.pdf.

Fischel, William A. 1985. *The Economics of Zoning Laws: A Property Rights Approach to American Land Use Controls.* Baltimore, MD: Johns Hopkins University Press.

Fischel, William A. 2003. "An Economic History of Zoning and a Cure for Its Exclusionary Effects." *Urban Studies* 41(2): 317–340.

Fischler, Raphael. 1998. "The Metropolitan Dimension of Early Zoning: Revisiting the 1916 New York City Ordinance." *Journal of the American Planning Association* 64(2): 170–188.

Frisen, Lyle E., Eagles, Paul F. J., and Mackay, R. J. 1995. "Effects of Residential Development on Forest Dwelling Neotropical Migrant Songbirds." *Conservation Biology* 9: 1408–1414.

Frumkin, Howard, Frank, Lawrence D., and Jackson, Richard. 2004. *Urban Sprawl and Public Health: Designing, Planning, and Building for Healthy Communities.* Washington, DC: Island Press.

Gallagher, Leigh. 2014. *The End of the Suburbs: Where the American Dream is Moving.* New York, NY: Penguin.

Gardner, Todd and Marlay, Matthew C. 2016. "Population Growth in the Exurbs Before and Since the Great Depression." Washington, DC: Urban Institute. Retrieved June 15, 2016. http://metrotrends.org/commentary/Exurban-Population-Growth.cfm.

Garreau, Joel. 1992. *Edge City: Life on the New Frontier.* New York, NY: Anchor Books.

Gaul, Gilbert M. and Wood, Anthony R. 2000. "A Flawed Program Facilitates Building in Hazardous Areas." *Philadelphia Inquirer*, March 7. Retrieved December 1, 2016. http://marine.rutgers.edu/cool/education/coast08.htm.

Gillham, Oliver. 2002. *The Limitless City: A Primer on the Urban Sprawl Debate.* Washington, DC: Island Press.

Glaeser, Edward and Kahn, Matthew. 2003. "Sprawl and Urban Growth." NBER Working Paper No. w9733.

Gonzalez, George A. 2009. *Urban Sprawl, Global Warming, and the Empire of Capital.* Albany, NY: State University of New York Press.

Gordon, Peter and Harry W. Richardson. 1997. "The Geography of Transportation and Land Use." In Randall G. Holcombe and Samuel R. Staley, eds, *Smarter Growth: Market Based Strategies for Land Use Planning in the 21st Century,* pp. 27–58. Westport: Greenwood Press.

Gotham, Kevin Fox and Greenberg, Miriam. 2014. *Crisis Cities: Disaster and Redevelopment in New York and New Orleans.* Oxford: Oxford University Press.

Governor's Office of Storm Recovery. 2016. Retrieved July 26, 2016. http://storm recovery.ny.gov/housing.

Griffin, Beth Ann, Eibner, Christine, Bird, Chloe E., Jewell, Adria, Margolis, Karen, Shih, Regina, Slaughter, Mary Ellen, Whitsel, Eric A., Allison, Matthew, and Scarce, Jose J. 2013. "The Relationship Between Urban Sprawl and Coronary Heart Disease in Women." *Health and Place* 20: 51–61.

Hamidi, Shima, Ewing, Reid, Preuss, Ilana, and Dodds, Alex. 2015. "Measuring Sprawl and Its Impacts: An Update." *Journal of Planning Education and Research* 35(1): 35–50.

Hammer, Roger B., Stewart, Susan I., and Radeloff, Volker C. 2009. "Demographic Trends, the Wildland-Urban Interface, and Wildfire Management." *Society and Natural Resources* 22: 777–782.

Harris, Richard, and Lewis, Robert. 2001. "The Geography of North American Cities and Suburbs, 1900–1950: A New Synthesis." *Journal of Urban History* 27: 262–284.

Hartman, Chester and Squires, Gregory D. 2006. *There is No Such Thing as a Natural Disaster: Race, Class, and Hurricane Katrina.* New York, NY: Routledge.

Jackson, Kenneth T. 1985. *Crabgrass Frontier: The Suburbanization of the United States.* New York, NY: Oxford University Press.

Johnson, Kenneth M. 1999. "The Rural Rebound." *Population Reference Bureau Reports on America* 1(3): 1–20.

Johnson, Kenneth M. and Beale, Calvin L. 1994. "The Recent Revival of Widespread Population Growth in Nonmetropolitan Areas of the United States." *Rural Sociology* 59: 655–667.

Johnson, Kenneth M., Nucci, Alfred, and Long, Larry. 2005. "Population Trends in Metropolitan and Nonmetropolitan America: Selective Deconcentration and the Rural Rebound." *Population Research and Policy Review* 24(5): 527–542.

Joly, Kyle and Myers, Wayne L. 2001. "Patterns of Mammalian Species Richness and Habitat Associations in Pennsylvania." *Biological Conservation* 99: 253–260.

Kahn, Matthew. 2000. "The Environmental Impact of Suburbanization." *Journal of Policy Analysis and Management* 19(4): 569–586.

Kahn, Matthew. 2001. "Does Sprawl Reduce the Black/White Housing Consumption Gap?" *Housing Policy Debate* 12(1): 77–86.

Kelly-Schwartz, Alexia C., Stockard, Jean, Doyle, Scott, and Schlossberg, Marc. 2004. "Is Sprawl Unhealthy? A Multilevel Analysis of the Relationship of Metropolitan Sprawl to the Health of Individuals." *Journal of Planning Education and Research* 24: 184–196.

Kenworthy, Jeffrey R. and Laube, Felix B. 1999. "Patterns of Automobile Dependence in Cities: An International Overview of Key Physical and Economic Dimensions with Some Implications for Urban Policy." *Transportation Research Part A* 33: 691–723.

Kim, H. H. 1991. "Urban Heat Island." *International Journal of Remote Sensing* 13(12): 2319–2336.

Kingsley, G. Thomas. 2009. "High Cost and Investor Mortgages: Neighborhood Patterns." Washington, DC: Urban Institute. Retrieved December 1, 2016. www.urban.org/research/publication/high- cost-and- investor-mortgages.

Kinney, Aaron. 2016. "Brisbane: Bay Area's Need for Housing Clashes with Small Town's Values." *Mercury News*, July 27. Retrieved August 1, 2016. www.mercury news.com/san-mateo-county/ci_30177242/brisbane-bay-areas-need-housing-clashes-small-towns.

Kostova, Deliana. 2011. "Can the Built Environment Reduce Obesity? The Impact of Residential Sprawl and Neighborhood Parks on Obesity and Physical Activity." *Eastern Economic Journal* 37(3): 390–402.

Krall, Lisi. 2002. "Thomas Jefferson's Agrarian Vision and the Changing Nature of Property." *Journal of Economic Issues* 36(1): 131–150.

Kunreuther, Howard. 2006. "Disaster Mitigation and Insurance: Learning from Katrina." *ANNALS of the American Academy of Political and Social Science* 604: 208–227.

Kunreuther, Howard and Kleffner, Anne. 1992. "Should Earthquake Mitigation Measures be Voluntary or Required?" *Journal of Regulatory Economics* 4: 321–333.

Lang, Robert E. and LeFurgy, Jennifer B. 2007. *Boomburbs: The Rise of America's Accidental Cities*. Washington, DC: Brookings Institution Press.

Lee, I-Min, Ewing, Reid, and Sesso, Howard D. 2009. "The Built Environment and Physical Activity Levels: The Harvard Alumni Health Study." *American Journal of Preventative Medicine* 37(4): 293–298.

Lees, Loretta, Slater, Tom, and Wyly, Elvin. 2010. *The Gentrification Reader*. New York, NY: Routledge.

Leinberger, Christopher B. and Lynch, Patrick. 2014. *Foot Traffic Ahead: Ranking Walkable Urbanism in America's Largest Metros*. Washington, DC: George Washington University School of Business. Retrieved December 1, 2016. www.smartgrowthamerica.org/documents/foot-traffic-ahead.pdf.

Livingston, Ann, Ridlington, Elizabeth, and Baker, Matt. 2003. *The Costs of Sprawl: Fiscal, Environmental, and Quality of Life Impacts of Low-Density Development in the Denver Region*. Denver, CO: Environment Colorado Research and Policy Center.

Lopez, Russell. 2014. "Urban Sprawl in the United States: 1970–2010." *Cities and the Environment* 7(1). Retrieved June 15, 2016. http://digitalcommons.lmu.edu/cate/vol. 7/iss1/7.

Lucy, William H. 2010. *Foreclosing the Dream: How America's Housing Crisis is Reshaping our Cities and Suburbs*. Chicago, IL: American Planning Association.

Madsen, Travis and Figdor, Emily. 2007. *When It Rains, It Pours: Global Warming and the Rising Frequency of Extreme Precipitation in the United States*. Boston, MA: Environment America Research & Policy Center. Retrieved June 27, 2016. www.environmentamerica.org/sites/environment/files/reports/When-It-Rains-It-Pours--US--WEB.pdf.

Margo, Robert. 1992. "Explaining the Postwar Suburbanization of Population in the United States: The Role of Income." *Journal of Urban Economics* 31(2): 301–310.

Marzluff, John, Bowman, Reed, and Donnelly, Roarke. 2001. *Avian Ecology and Conservation in an Urbanizing World.* Norwell, MA: Kluwer Academic Publishers.

McGranahan, David. A. 1999. "Natural Amenities Drive Population Change." Agricultural Economics Report No. 781. Washington, DC: USDA Economic Research Service.

Mileti, Dennis S. 1999. *Disasters by Design: A Reassessment of Natural Hazards in the United States.* Washington, DC: Joseph Henry Press.

Mills, Edwin S. 1967. "An Aggregative Model of Resource Allocation in a Metropolitan Area." *American Economic Review* 57: 197–210.

Mockrin, Miranda H., Stewart, Susan I., Radeloff, Volker C., Hammer, Roger B., and Johnson, Kenneth M. 2013. "Spatial and Temporal Residential Density Patterns from 1940 to 2000 in and around the Northern Forest of the Northeastern United States." *Population and Environment* 34: 400–419.

Mohl, Raymond A. 1982. "Changing Economic Patterns in the Miami Metropolitan Area, 1940–1980." *Tequesta* 42(198): 1–12.

Muth, Richard. 1969. *Cities and Housing.* Chicago, IL: University of Chicago Press.

Myers, Dowell and Gearin, Elizabeth. 2001. "Current Preferences and Future Demand for Denser Residential Environments." *Housing Policy Debate* 12(4): 633–659.

National Aeronautics and Space Administration. 2016a. "Global Climate Change: Vital Signs of the Planet—Climate Change: How Do We Know?" Retrieved June 27, 2016. http://climate.nasa.gov/evidence/.

National Aeronautics and Space Administration. 2016b. "Global Climate Change: Vital Signs of the Planet—Sea Level." Retrieved June 27, 2016. http://climate.nasa.gov/vital-signs/sea-level/.

Natoli, Salvatore. 1971. "Zoning and the Development of Urban Land Use Patterns." *Economic Geography* 47(2): 171–184.

Nechyba, Thomas J. and Walsh, Randall P. 2004. "Urban Sprawl." *Journal of Economic Perspectives* 18(4): 177–200.

Nelson, Arthur C. and Dueker, Kenneth J. 1990. "The Exurbanization of America and Its Planning Policy Implications." *Journal of Planning Education and Research* 9(2): 91–100.

Nicolaides, Becky. 2002. *My Blue Heaven: Life and Politics in the Working-Class Suburbs of Los Angeles 1920–1965.* Chicago, IL: University of Chicago Press.

Pendall, Rolf. 1999. "Do Land-Use Controls Cause Sprawl?" *Environment and Planning B: Planning and Design* 26(4): 555–571.

Percent Change in Housing Units, 2000–2010. Social Explorer, www.socialexplorer.com/054be672f0/view (based on data from 2010 and 2000 US Census; accessed December 7, 2016).

Peterson, M. Nils, Peterson, Tarla Rai, and Liu, Jianguo. 2013. *The Housing Bomb: Why Our Addiction to Houses is Destroying the Environment and Threatening Our Society.* Baltimore: Johns Hopkins University Press.

Pew Charitable Trusts. 2016. "Funding Challenges in Highway and Transit." Retrieved July 22, 2016. www.pewtrusts.org/en/research-and-analysis/analysis/2015/02/24/funding-challenges-in-highway-and-transit-a-federal-state-local-analysis.

Pielke, Roger A. and Landsea, Christopher W. 1998. "Normalized Hurricane Damages in the United States: 1925–95." *Weather and Forecasting* 13: 621–631.

Porter, Douglas R. 1997. *Managing Growth in America's Communities*. Washington, DC: Island Press.

Radeloff, Volker, Hammer, Roger B., and Stewart, Susan. 2005. "Rural and Suburban Sprawl in the U.S. Midwest from 1940 to 2000 and its Relation to Forest Fragmentation." *Conservation Biology* 19(3): 793–805.

RealtyTrac. 2015. "43% of U.S. Homes with an Estimated Market Value of $6.6 Trillion in Counties with High Natural Disaster Risk." Retrieved June 20, 2016. www.realtytrac.com/news/realtytrac-reports/realtytrac-2015-u-s-natural-disaster-housing-risk-report/.

Richardson, Harry W. and Gordon, Peter. 2001. "Compactness or Sprawl: America's Future vs. the Present." In M. Echenique and A. Saint, eds, *Cities for the New Millenium*, pp. 53–64. London: Spon Press.

Rodrigue, Jean-Paul. 2013. *The Geography of Transport Systems*. New York, NY: Routledge.

Rome, Adam. 2001. *The Bulldozer in the Countryside: Suburban Sprawl and the Rise of American Environmentalism*. Cambridge: Cambridge University Press.

Rose, Adam, Porter, Keith, Dash, Nicole, Bouabid, Jawhar, Huyck, Charles, Whitehead, John, Shaw, Douglass, Eguchi, Ronald, Taylor, Craig, McLane, Thomas, Tobin, L. Thomas, Ganderton, Philip T., Godschalk, David, Miremidjian, Anne S., Tierney, Kathleen, and Taylor West, Carol. 2007. "Benefit-Cost Analysis of FEMA Hazard Mitigation Grants." *National Hazards Review* 8: 97–111.

Rusk, David. 2003. *Cities without Suburbs*. Washington, DC: Woodrow Wilson Center Press.

Sander, William. 2004. "On the Demand for City Living." *Journal of Economic Geography* 5(3): 351–364.

Sander, William and Testa, William. 2013. "Parents' Education, School Age Children, and Household Location in American Cities." *Regional Science* 94(3): 573–595.

Schrank, David, Eisele, Bill, Lomax, Tim, and Bak, Jim. 2015. *2015 Urban Mobility Scorecard*. College Station: Texas A&M Transportation Institute and INRIX.

Short, John Rennie, Hanlon, Bernadette, and Vicino, Thomas J. 2007. "The Decline of Inner Suburbs: The New Suburban Gothic in the United States." *Geography Compass* 1(3): 641–656.

Squires, Gregory D. 2002. *Urban Sprawl: Causes, Consequences, and Policy Responses*. Washington, DC: The Urban Institute Press.

Stone, Brian. 2008. "Urban Sprawl and Air Quality in Large U.S. Cities." *Journal of Environmental Management* 86(4): 688–698.

Stone, Brian and Norman, John M. 2006. "Land Use Planning and Surface Heat Island Formation: A Parcel-Based Radiation Flux Approach." *Atmospheric Environment* 40: 3561–3573.

Stone, Brian, Hess, Jeremy J., and Frumkin, Howard. 2010. "Urban Form and Extreme Heat Events: Are Sprawling Cities More Vulnerable to Climate Change Than Compact Cities?" *Environmental Health Perspectives* 118(10): 1425–1428.

Swenson, Jennifer J. and Franklin, Janet. 2000. "The Effects of Future Urban Development on Habitat Fragmentation in the Santa Monica Mountains." *Landscape Ecology* 15: 713–730.

Taylor, Paul, Morin, Rich, Parker, Kim, Cohn, D'Vera, and Wang, Wendy. 2009. *For Nearly Half of America, Grass is Greener Somewhere Else*. Washington, DC: Pew Research Center. Retrieved June 23, 2016. www.pewsocialtrends.org/2009/01/29/for-nearly-half-of-america-grass-is-greener-somewhere-else-denver-tops-list-of-favorite-cities/.

Taylor, Paul, Parker, Kim, Kochhar, Rakesh, Wang, Wendy, Velasco, Gabriel, and Dockterma, Daniel. 2011. *Home Sweet Home. Still*. Washington, DC: Pew Research Center. Retrieved Decmber 6, 2016. www.pewsocialtrends.org/2011/04/12/home-sweet-home-still/.

Theobald, David M., Miller, James R., and Hobbes, N. Thompson. 1997. "Estimating the Cumulative Effects of Development on Wildlife Habitat." *Landscape and Urban Planning* 39: 25–36.

Tregoning, Harriet, Agyeman, Julian, and Shenot, Christine. 2002. "Sprawl, Smart Growth, and Sustainability." *Local Environment* 7(4): 341–347.

Trenberth, Kevin. 2005. "Uncertainty in Hurricanes and Global Warming." *Science* 308: 1753–1754.

Trowbridge, Matthew J., Gurka, Matthew J., and O'Connor, Robert E. 2009. "Urban Sprawl and Delayed Ambulance Arrival in the U.S." *American Journal of Preventive Medicine* 37(5): 428–432.

U.S. Census Bureau. 2013. *National Coastal Population Report: Population Trends from 1970 to 2020*. Washington, DC: U.S. Census Bureau. Retrieved June 27, 2016. http://oceanservice.noaa.gov/facts/coastal-population-report.pdf.

U.S. Census Bureau. 2016. "Median and Average Square Feet of Floor Area in New Single-Family Houses Completed by Location." Retrieved June 16, 2016. www.census.gov/const/C25Ann/sftotalmedavgsqft.pdf.

U.S. Department of Homeland Security. 2016. *Budget-in-Brief: Fiscal Year 2016*. Retrieved July 11, 2016. www.dhs.gov/sites/default/files/publications/FY_2016_DHS_Budget_in_Brief.pdf.

U.S. Government Accountability Office. 2000. Survey of Local Growth Issues. Retrieved July 22, 2016. www.gao.gov/special.pubs/lgi/sabq13g.html.

Walker, Richard, and Schafran, Alex. 2015. "The Strange Case of the Bay Area." *Environment and Planning A* 47: 10–29.

Weiss, Marc A. 1987. *The Rise of the Community Builders: The American Real Estate Industry and Urban Land Planning*. New York, NY: Columbia University Press.

Weitz, Jerry. 1999. "From Quiet Revolution to Smart Growth: State Growth Management Programs, 1960–1999." *Journal of Planning Literature* 14: 267–338.

Westerling, Anthony L., Hidalgo, Hugo G., Cayan, Daniel R., and Swetnam, Thomas W. 2006. "Warming and Earlier Spring Increase Western U.S. Forest Wildfire Activity." *Science* 313: 940–943.

Wiese, Andrew. 2004. *Places of Their Own: African American Suburbanization in the Twentieth Century*. Chicago, IL: University of Chicago Press.

Wilson, Steven G., Plane, David A., Mackun, Paul J., Fischetti, Thomas R., and Goworowska, Justyna. 2012. *Patterns of Metropolitan and Micropolitan Population Change: 2000 to 2010*. Washington, DC: U.S. Census Bureau.

CHAPTER 7

Conclusion

Housing is not just shelter. It is home, opportunity, and security. Indeed, homes are not just sources of personal joy and security. As this book has shown, our homes also in large part determine how we are embedded in our larger society. The cost of our homes determines how much of our income and wealth we are able to invest in ourselves and in the larger economy. The location of our homes, whether we own them and if so, how they are financed, impacts our health, our wealth, and our quality of life.

At the same time, our larger social positions largely determine the extent to which we have to confront the problems presented in this book. Certainly the poor and working class and people of color are more likely to face larger housing cost burdens, homelessness, and negative effects of housing segregation. But this book has also shown that we are all impacted by the problems presented here. As a society we paid to bail the financial industry out of the crisis that resulted from fraud in the mortgage industry. Many of us share the burden of housing costs. And certainly we all stand to experience the negative impacts of sprawl and the increasing incidences of natural disasters. Thus, we are all positioned to benefit from meaningful changes in the ways we house our population.

The Big Picture

Each of the chapters in this book delves into a distinct housing problem, but all of the problems are deeply intertwined. The fact that affordability, homelessness, segregation, homeownership and financing, and housing development are all so interconnected suggests that perhaps a few sets of carefully designed policies could solve multiple housing problems at once. Housing vouchers that subsidize rents for some of the lowest-income Americans, for example, are meant to both provide housing aid to the poor and to deconcentrate high-poverty neighborhoods to reduce racial and economic segregation.

But just as likely is the possibility that a well-meaning policy designed to solve one housing problem could exacerbate another. New Deal-era housing policies designed to make homeownership affordable for working Americans did just that, but they also greatly contributed to housing segregation and the veneration of homeownership in American society. Similarly, New York City's policy of giving homeless families priority for public housing and housing vouchers helped scores of homeless families off the streets, out of temporary shelters, and into permanent housing, but it concentrated very poor families in public housing—contributing to severe economic segregation. And while Smart Growth strategies of urban revitalization may be better for the environment than suburban housing sprawl, they can contribute to new forms of housing segregation and the higher housing prices that come with gentrification.

This book encourages us to think carefully about why housing problems endure and how we might truly alleviate them. If so many of the possible solutions cause more problems, what are we to do? Are lasting solutions even possible?

Solutions

Thinking Pragmatically

The answer, of course, is yes. There are at least two approaches. The first is to take a pragmatic approach, accepting that no policy is perfect while attempting to minimize any attendant negative impacts. For example, new urbanist developments, discussed in Chapter 6, are walkable communities with diverse housing stock and easy access to public transit, employment, and recreation that are designed as a more sustainable housing development alternative to sprawl. New urbanist homes are generally more expensive than other housing, and developments in low-income communities can displace current residents (Day 2003; Eppli and Tu 1999). A pragmatic approach might be to guarantee the right to return to a new urbanist development with a housing voucher for displaced families, or to subsidize developers to set aside a certain set of units for low- and middle-income families. To be sure, subsidies would need to increase dramatically and many more developments would need to be built to make a dent in the affordable housing market and to have a significant impact on housing development patterns.

Another pragmatic approach, this one focused on homelessness, might be to adopt the policy of giving priority to homeless families in public housing and for housing vouchers. Preventing the possibility that the very poor would be concentrated in public housing simply requires a dramatic increase in the number of low-income housing units available to the poor, either through vouchers or public housing. Increasing the low-income housing supply by building new public housing, as Singapore has done, or subsidizing its construction in the private market, would provide enough units for all low-income people, not just the very poor.

A final possible pragmatic approach might be to institute stricter regulation of the housing and real estate industries. One of the major criticisms of American housing policy is that we rely far too much on the private market to meet our housing needs. American taxpayers continuously bail out financial institutions that trade in housing as a commodity for profit while housing expenses for the average American rise. Until very recently, fair housing laws have gone basically unenforced, and the deregulation of the mortgage lending industry led to enough widespread fraud and inefficiency that it caused a global economic meltdown. A pragmatic approach might be to create a much more robust regulatory system to help protect the American public from the wild volatility of capital markets and help the housing and lending markets better serve ordinary Americans, protecting us from fraud and discrimination.

Thinking Radically

There are countless other pragmatic approaches to solving the interrelated housing problems presented in this text. But there are also more radical approaches that focus on the common root causes of multiple housing problems. The massive economic shift from a manufacturing-based economy to a service economy, for example, meant lower wages and higher housing prices for Americans in general, making it a key component in the rise of housing unaffordability and homelessness, and central to housing segregation. Similarly, the pre-eminence of local control over land use laws and zoning contributes to rising housing unaffordability, racial and economic segregation in housing, housing sprawl, and the negative impacts of natural disasters. Perhaps most importantly, the commodification of housing in America is at the root of all the problems discussed in this book.

Decommodifying Housing
The first radical approach to solving housing problems in the U.S. might focus on its status as a commodity. Every problem discussed in this book has at its root the commodification of housing in America. Housing is less affordable to the average American than it was in the past because relative

housing prices have increased, largely due to speculation in the housing market and the increasing popularity of housing as a financial investment. Meanwhile, the affordable housing market shrinks, because low-income housing is essentially unprofitable for private developers, and we refuse to build more public housing. Decreasing housing affordability has led to an uptick in homelessness in pricey markets, while the development and protection of valuable urban real estate has led to criminalizing the homeless. Indeed, our government pursued public housing as an affordable housing strategy only because it was linked to downtown real estate development, and we became concerned about the homeless as a class of people only when Skid Rows threatened to overtake valuable urban real estate. And localities often use zoning to both prohibit affordable housing and to enable suburban sprawl in efforts to boost property values, regardless of the negative impacts. Finally, and perhaps most clearly, housing's status as a commodity to be bought, sold, traded, and profited from created a massive global economic collapse.

Thus, one radical approach to solving many of the housing problems discussed in this book is to begin to decommodify housing in the U.S. There are at least two ways to begin to do this. The first is to incentivize social ownership of housing in housing cooperatives, community land trusts, and other forms, such that they constitute a significant portion of the housing market. Pooling ownership of housing allows cooperatives to keep costs down and retain affordability for generations. Low-income and limited-equity cooperatives offer some of the most high-quality and affordable housing in the U.S. and have the added advantage of helping households accrue wealth. Cooperative housing gaining a foothold in the overall housing market would make the availability of affordable housing less dependent on wild fluctuations in property values and lending markets, and it could keep private housing prices at more affordable levels. If enough cooperatives existed in a diverse set of high-quality neighborhoods, incentivizing social ownership would go a long way toward solving the affordability, segregation, and homeownership/home financing problems in the U.S.

Another approach to decommodifying the housing market is to reshape tax laws dramatically, so that there is little incentive to speculate in the housing market. U.S. tax policy fosters speculation in housing values: housing sales prices are exempt from capital gains taxes, encouraging speculative investment in real estate that can artificially inflate housing prices. Abolishing or limiting this exemption would remove one speculation incentive. In addition, abolishing the mortgage interest and property tax deductions in the tax code would force us to consider housing more of a social good than an opportunity for profit. In lieu of abolishing the tax deductions, they could be limited such that they do not continue to benefit high-income homeowners disproportionately. Proposals include capping the mortgage loan amount on which homeowners can deduct interest, offering a one-time-only credit for first-time homebuyers, and limiting deductions to primary residencies (McCabe 2016). Abolishing or reforming tax deductions for homeowners would also have the advantage of limiting subsidies for housing sprawl.

The goal of these more radical approaches to decommodify housing is to ensure housing security and availability, treating housing as a social good rather than an avenue for profit (Stone 2006).

Addressing the Bifurcated Economy
Another radical approach to solving America's housing problems is to address the problems caused by the shift from a manufacturing-based economy to a service economy, in which labor and wages are largely bifurcated. The flight of stable, highly paid manufacturing jobs and the rise of low-paying service-sector jobs have resulted in the reduction of real wages of American workers. The result has been less affordability for housing, a rise in homelessness, and a dramatic rise in the segregation of the poor/working-class communities. Supporting unions and unionization, raising the minimum wage, campaigning for living wages, and other strategies designed to close the gap between the nation's highest and lowest earners would help to make housing more affordable and less segregated.

The Problem of Local Control
A final radical approach to addressing housing issues in the U.S. would be a fundamental change in how land use is regulated. Local control over zoning further reduces affordability of housing and inhibits regulation that could decrease the negative environmental impacts of housing sprawl and the impact of natural disasters on Americans. Local control over zoning allows local officials to refuse to build their fair share of affordable housing and to avoid proactive participation in fair housing efforts. Restricting the construction of multifamily homes, for example, decreases the affordable housing supply and prevents families with modest incomes from accessing high-quality neighborhoods. Anti-density policies like this also exacerbate suburban sprawl. Other local zoning initiatives allow new housing construction in places at high risk for natural disasters, at great cost to the country as a whole. More centralized land use planning and tools for enforcement would ensure that all communities provide a fair share of affordable housing and engage in environmentally and socially responsible housing development.

Housing endures as a social problem precisely because it is a locus of struggles to form a consensus about the fundamental rights of residents, the role and function of American government, and the status of private property in American society. Each of the pragmatic and radical approaches to solving the problems of housing affordability, homelessness, segregation, home-ownership, and housing development attempts to reconcile the often contradictory social and economic goals of housing in America.

Strategies for Change

This book is unquestionably policy oriented, and as such says little about the rich tradition of social movements in the United States that have challenged our ongoing housing issues over the decades. Contemporary social movements are already at work trying to solve America's housing problems. The national Right to the City movement works to ensure equal access to housing and prevent displacement of low-income people from the nation's cities in the face of gentrification. Picture the Homeless, a New York City-based grass-roots organization of and for homeless people, fights for the right to housing for homeless people—including a campaign for more community land trusts. The California Reinvestment Coalition advocates for fair and equal access to sound financial services for California's low-income communities and communities of color. Meanwhile, countless grassroots environmental groups work for more dense, sustainable communities away from environmental hazards and protected from natural disasters.

These social movements have real power to influence policymakers, elect officials, and pressure them to solve the complex housing problems described in this book. Indeed, many of the social changes—in policy, in governing, in culture—required to solve America's most fundamental housing problems are already in motion.

The Imperative

Fundamental social changes are already underway in the U.S. By 2030, a full 20 percent of the American population will be sixty-five or older (Colby and Ortman 2015). The "baby boom" generation will need accessible, affordable housing that meets the needs of an aging population. By 2044, the U.S. will be a "majority-minority" society, even as racial and ethnic discrimination persist in the housing market (Colby and Ortman 2015). These demographic changes ensure that the housing problems described in this book will only become more detrimental if we do not act now to meet the evolving needs of our society. But while the challenges may seem insurmountable, the opportunity is greater. The multifaceted societal changes on the horizon open up the space to implement an unprecedented set of visionary housing policies that truly serve the needs of all Americans.

References

Colby, Sandra L. and Ortman, Jennifer M. 2015. "Projections of the Size and Composition of the U.S. Population: 2014 to 2060." *Population Estimates and Projections, Current Population Reports*. Washington, DC: U.S. Department of Commerce Economics and Statistics Administration.

Day, Kristen. 2003. "New Urbanism and the Challenges of Designing for Diversity." *Journal of Planning Education and Research* 23: 83–95.

Eppli, Mark J. and Tu, Charles C. 1999. "Valuing The New Urbanism: The Impact of the New Urbanism On Prices of Single-Family Homes." Washington, DC: The Urban Land Institute.

McCabe, Brian J. 2016. *No Place Like Home: Wealth, Community, and the Politics of Homeownerhsip*. Oxford: Oxford University Press.

Stone, Michael E. 2006. "Housing Affordability: One-Third of a Nation Shelter-Poor." In R. G. Bratt, M. E. Stone, and C. Hartman, eds, *A Right to Housing: Foundation for a New Social Agenda*, pp. 38–60. Philadelphia, PA: Temple University Press.

Index

Page numbers in *italics* denote tables, those in **bold** denote figures.

Taylor & Francis eBooks

Helping you to choose the right eBooks for your Library

Add Routledge titles to your library's digital collection today. Taylor and Francis ebooks contains over 50,000 titles in the Humanities, Social Sciences, Behavioural Sciences, Built Environment and Law.

Choose from a range of subject packages or create your own!

Benefits for you

>> Free MARC records
>> COUNTER-compliant usage statistics
>> Flexible purchase and pricing options
>> All titles DRM-free.

| REQUEST YOUR **FREE** INSTITUTIONAL TRIAL TODAY | **Free Trials Available** We offer free trials to qualifying academic, corporate and government customers. |

Benefits for your user

>> Off-site, anytime access via Athens or referring URL
>> Print or copy pages or chapters
>> Full content search
>> Bookmark, highlight and annotate text
>> Access to thousands of pages of quality research at the click of a button.

eCollections – Choose from over 30 subject eCollections, including:

Archaeology	Language Learning
Architecture	Law
Asian Studies	Literature
Business & Management	Media & Communication
Classical Studies	Middle East Studies
Construction	Music
Creative & Media Arts	Philosophy
Criminology & Criminal Justice	Planning
Economics	Politics
Education	Psychology & Mental Health
Energy	Religion
Engineering	Security
English Language & Linguistics	Social Work
Environment & Sustainability	Sociology
Geography	Sport
Health Studies	Theatre & Performance
History	Tourism, Hospitality & Events

For more information, pricing enquiries or to order a free trial, please contact your local sales team:
www.tandfebooks.com/page/sales

 Routledge Taylor & Francis Group | The home of Routledge books | **www.tandfebooks.com**